KU-112-888

First published 2017 by The Midland Railway Society
Copyright (C) John Earl, Steve Huson, The Midland Railway Society and the individual
copyright holders specifically named within the work. The moral rights of the authors have
been asserted.

ISBN 978-0-9955142-1-8

Typeset in Californian FB by Finnick Creative, Cheltenham

Printed by Wheatons Exeter Ltd, Exeter.

FOREWORD

This book is different; in my view delightfully different.
When John and Steve first suggested the idea of Midland
Retrospective I imagined that it would be similar to the
first book I ever had published, together with Peter Truman and
entitled Midland Railway Portrait, which rarely strayed beyond
the boundary fence in its coverage.

How wrong could I be?

In these pages the story of the Midland Railway is much
enhanced, not just by the excellent writing styles of the authors
but also in other ways. First of all, several of the subjects
covered have previously had little or no attention from earlier
writers and of those that have, they have not been looked at
from the same viewpoint or in as much detail. Secondly, by
paying attention to how the Midland fitted in to the social
and cultural environment as well as the current affairs of the
time, Messrs. Huson and Earl have enabled us to broaden our
understanding of how the system worked and was seen by
those who operated and travelled on it. Additionally, the chosen
layout is refreshingly different from that of most railway books
with marginal illustrations that reflect the nearby text in a way
that enhances the overall picture of each piece. Also the careful
selection of the illustrations matches the eclectic choice of
subjects and the thought that has gone into their presentation.
All in all, this is a fine work that will surely attract any Midland
Railway aficionado and I welcome its inclusion in the Midland
Railway Society's list of publications. It will, I am sure, enhance
the Society's standing as well as that of its authors, from whom
I hope to see more works in the future.

Dave Hunt
Chairman, Midland Railway Society

ACKNOWLEDGEMENTS

British Boxing Board of Control
Derby Local Studies Library
Derbyshire Records Office
Gloucester Record Office
Historic England/RCHAMS
John Alsop Collection
Magic Attic Archive, Swadlincote
National Tramway Museum, Crich, Derbyshire
National Railway Museum, York
Royal Institute of British Architects

Brian and Andrew Hillier
Chris Witts, www.severn tales .co.uk
David Collins, Heysham Heritage Association
Gary Peacock, General Manager Midland Hotel Bradford.
Donald Stewart, General Manager of the Hallmark Midland
Hotel, Derby
Richard Casserley
Rod Jewell
Joel Smith
www.sungreen. co.uk
Peter Huestis, National Gallery of Art, Washington
Laura Minh Hong, Roger-Viollet collections, Paris
Mark Dowd, Topfoto, London
Emily Dean at the Imperial War Museum
Sarah Gunn and Peter Palmer of the Western Front
Association
Lea Cristoph, Gera Nova Bruckmann Verlagshaus GmbH

Midland Railway Society Colleagues:
Dave Hunt, Ian Howard, Dave Harris, Tony Overton, Paul
Walpole, Robin Cullup and the late Peter Witts. Plus of
course, the amazing resources of the Midland Railway Study
Centre at the Silk Mill in Derby.

David Postle – Kidderminster Railway Museum
Folk-rock legend Michael Chapman for letting us borrow the
title of one of his songs.

And last but certainly not least, our wives, Steve`s wife Anne
(who usually drives) and John`s wife Patti for putting up
with our sudden desires to go and look at a sodden morass
filled with brambles and being expected to believe it was
once a railway.

Note: The authors have tried their best to find names of
authors and photographers for full acknowledgement, but in
some cases despite their best efforts have not been able to find
them. We apologise sincerely for any omissions.

CONTENTS

134. THE EXPERIENCED TRAVELLER

The Midland Railway's Hotels were famous for the high quality of their facilities. This chapter concentrates on the development of the company's lesser known hotels in Derby, Morecambe, Bradford and Heysham and the genius behind their success, William Towle (SH)

162. THE LAST RAILWAY PIONEER

William Marriott started building a railway on the Norfolk coast that eventually became an important part of the Midland empire. Here are some of the adventures of a life lived "on the edge" in more senses than one. (JE)

181. ANY MORE FARES PLEASE?

The Burton & Ashby Light Railways was a street tramway built by the Midland Railway to compete with its own passenger services in the area. This chapter uses a lot of previously unpublished material from the Midland Railway Study Centre. (SH)

MIDLAND RETROSPECTIVE - PREFACE

"Retrospective" is a word more often applied to the works of an artist than to the excavations, buildings and locomotives of a railway company. However, for both of us it is not too much of a stretch to see the works of the Midland Railway as a major artistic achievement, working not with paint and canvas but with time, space and landscape, and if that seems too grandiose, it is impossible to forget that all of it was achieved with nuts, bolts and very human labour. Although the Midland Railway only lasted from 1844 until 1923, in that short time it went from a geographically limited concern serving the Midlands to one of the greatest railways in the land. Not only did its engineers blast a way through the limestone of the Peak District to get to Manchester, they also tunnelled their way through Pennine grit on their way across the roof of England to Carlisle. As well as conveying mindboggling amounts of coal to London, they ran carriages for everyone, not just the rich, that were a byword for comfort and style, and developed a string of hotels many of which are still in use and still convey the grandeur and good taste that mark them out as indelibly Midland. In looking back we look at the personalities behind these achievements, and we feel it is a good time to reassess their contribution, particularly in the centenary years of the First World War, a testing time beyond any other for the early railway companies. It is important to remember that though these people can seem austere and remote, from another world almost, the fact that one of them was known personally to John`s father and grandfather means that it is a good time to look back when living memory can yet be called into play. For both of us, the Midland is still a living presence, and we hope that this book, which uses present day images as well as those from the past, will also remind you that if you keep your eyes open you will see the evidence of this company in a surprising number of places still. The Midland did not go away.

It is very important to remember also that there are still things to discover, despite the many books written already on the Midland. Steve is more than pleased to find that he has been able to put English Heritage and Historic England right on the accuracy of several of their listed building descriptions - and he is even more smug about getting them altered as a result! He has also taken on folklore in the Forest of Dean, something not for the fainthearted, especially

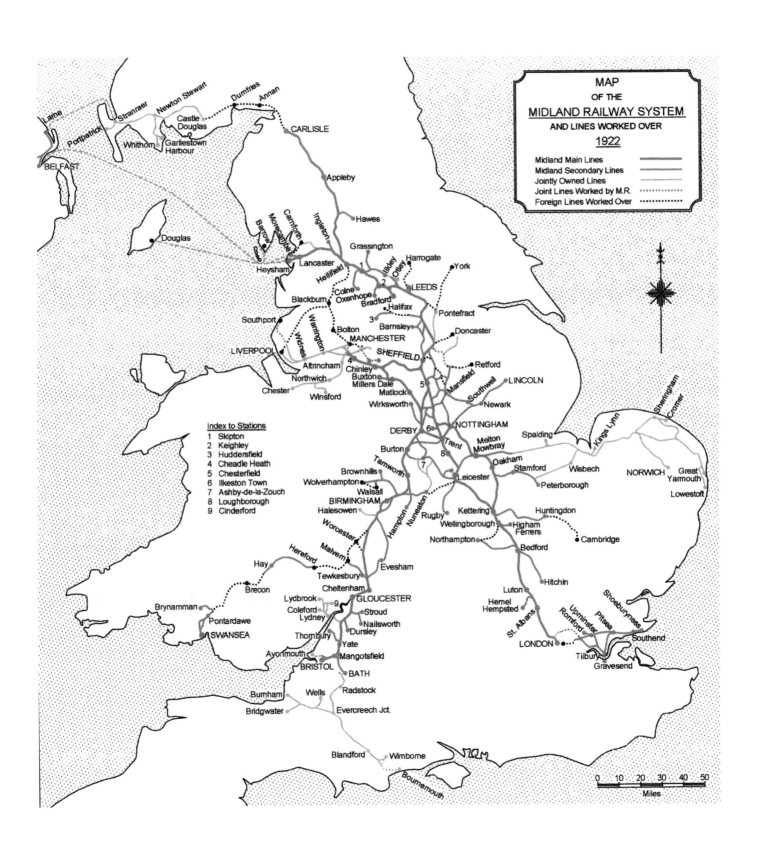

when the late Henry Cooper is involved. John has managed to follow the gestation of one of the most-altered locomotives in British Railway history from start to finish, a job not often tackled because most railway histories are looked at from the point of view of one particular company; and he is proud to have chased the only British locomotive prisoner of the First World War to behind enemy lines! For us it was important to follow a story through no matter where it led and the detective work has been enormous and very stimulating. We are very grateful to all those who have helped us in our quest, first and foremost Dave Harris of the Midland Railway Study Centre in Derby and his chief helper Tony Overton. The Study Centre is something the Midland Railway Society is extremely proud of, and if you have not visited its extensive archives then it is high time you did.

This book showcases some of its treasures not published before, and although we have been further afield, the Study Centre it was that usually set us on the trail.

Our collaboration must be unique. Although we only met for the first time in 2014, we have a common denominator in travelling through Ambergate on the same train, thousands of times, albeit in different years, on our way to and from school. If we had not spent our formative years trundling along these tracks, meeting the old railwaymen who talked to us about the job they loved and occasionally letting us ride with them in the guards van or sit by the fire in the porter`s room, we probably would not have ended up so imbued with the Midland`s influence. The fact that we then spent our weekends travelling up into the Peak, hanging over bridges or dangling off cliffs watching the Black Fives and 4Fs thundering down the valleys, only cemented in our minds that of all the old railways, the Midland was undoubtedly, in its own words, the Best Way.

We hope you will see this book as a springboard to make explorations of your own, and perhaps, along with the other heroes bringing the railways back, do your own bit to keep the Midland alive.

John Earl and Steve Huson, January 2017

AMBERGATE – THE GOLDEN TRIANGLE

Ambergate is an enigma, and it is one that has fascinated me since I began travelling through it every morning on my way to school in Belper in the sixties. It is a legend in its own way, being the first station mentioned in Flanders and Swann's elegy for the disappearing rail network, "The Slow Train", as well as being possibly the smallest village ever to have a major projected railway line named after it: the Ambergate, Nottingham, Boston and Eastern Junction Railway; its main claim to fame, however, is in having been one of only three completely triangular stations in Britain. Add to that the fact that it was engineered by the great George Stephenson, who further left his mark in an incline angling its way down from the heights above, and you have the ingredients for a unique study in railway history.

It was the first station we stopped at after Whatstandwell and I can well remember the difference you sensed as the valley opened up and the road and river ran far (it seemed) beneath it. The staff seemed to waft along the platforms in a blissful state of suspended animation, separated from the common rout by their elevation and three quarters of a mile of aerial platform. They looked down on the gabled roofs of the Hurt Arms and the traffic on the roads to and from Matlock and Derby and Ripley that met outside its front door.

Occasionally one of the porters would release a basketful of pigeons as the train pulled out. These exploded into the air in a flurry of feathers and wheeled round the entire triangle of the station before engaging on a flight path north, south or east. It emphasised the way you were wedged halfway up a landscape from which it was not easy to get out; but now that the engineers had shown the way, nature could follow.

After I moved up to Northumberland to work, Ambergate became the place to look out for on long journeys up and down the country. I eagerly awaited bursting out of Toadmoor tunnel and across the bridge into the wide valley of the Derwent from where the long ridge of the Chevin and the broad floodplain of the valley opened out before we rattled across the two bridges over the Derwent Riverside Park near the dominating shape of Strutt's cotton mill at Belper. I can never forget how once (and we were only late for school that once) we swayed and creaked on a steam train as we waited for a signal before the first of these bridges while the wind howled around us after a particularly strong gale the previous night.

▼ Illustration: Ambergate from the north. The incline is not the one from Crich, but a later one used in the construction of a reservoir. The Cromford canal runs across the middle foreground. MRSC 60021

Ambergate seemed to me like the pivot on which the railway
system turned, partly because soon after that you were
in Derby and the landscape changed to a more southerly
orientation, partly because trains (and there were a lot
of them) seemed to depart from there to anywhere in the
kingdom, and mostly because, although other places lay claim
to being the Centre of England, it seems more "middle-ish"
than anywhere I know, certainly in terms of the Midland
Railway. And yet it was a village, much smaller than Belper,
and small enough to field a football team in the same league as
the one I played for from the even smaller Whatstandwell.

These days the CrossCountry Voyager units hardly miss a
beat as they glide through Toadmoor tunnel on their way
between Chesterfield and Derby in 21 minutes, a testament
to the surveying skills of the Stephensons who engineered
this alignment at a date when engines could only pull their
loads at a fraction of the speed of a Voyager`s 125mph. But
Ambergate now is only a ghost of its former self, and sadly
you cannot stop on the mainline side of the famous triangle;

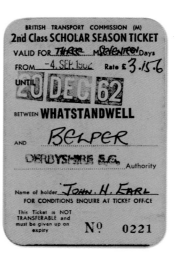

BRITISH TRANSPORT COMMISSION (M)
2nd Class SCHOLAR SEASON TICKET
VALID FOR *THREE MONTHS* Days
FROM -4. SEP.1962 Rate £ 3·15·6
UNTIL 20 DEC 62
BETWEEN **WHATSTANDWELL**
AND **BELPER**
DERBYSHIRE S.C. Authority
Name of holder JOHN. H. EARL
FOR CONDITIONS ENQUIRE AT TICKET OFFICE
This Ticket is NOT
TRANSFERABLE and
must be given up on
expiry N° 0221

▲ Bridge over the Derwent from the north, by Samuel Russell for the North Midland Railway's 1842 brochure. Steve Huson has calculated that the viewpoint is from the "Halfpenny Bridge", a toll bridge of 1792, but it is difficult to tell because of extensive tree growth since. A photograph of the entrance portal at the end of this article (surprisingly akin to the engraving), shows the rugged "picturesque style" percolating through to the details of design. MRSC 60018

the only bit that is left is a truncated single platform on the northerly alignment towards Matlock.

Nevertheless Ambergate is just about the perfect palimpsest, to use a useful coinage from archaeology, for the study of the many layers that went into the making of the Midland Railway.

To go back to the earliest layer, the engraving by Samuel Russell made for the brochure of the North Midland Railway in 1842 shows the bridge over the Derwent from the north. Longlands tunnel is to the right, and Toadmoor would be to the left if we could see it. The engraving is in the idealised style of the era, when railway companies seemed to vie with each other to recommend their transport system to the "Quality" above all, and brochures for early lines spent most of their pages pointing out which posh houses belonging to which section of the nobility you could see to most advantage from the railway.

The engraving is therefore in the "picturesque" style, perhaps to recommend the beauties of the area to those who might risk a ride on the train, or even to suggest in an early PR gesture that you were travelling in one of the extensive parklands of the aforementioned "Quality" in which the landscape was as likely as not to be moved about to please the artistic sensibility of the viewer just in case a manmade toll bridge, a cottage or even a natural feature such as a rock was in an aesthetically offensive position. By implication there was nothing that the railway company could not do to make your life better; the fine five-arched viaduct takes pride of place, as well it might, but then the railway engineers were well aware that they were in the business of moving the landscape about.

There is even a touch of the "Sublime" in the rock facing of Longlands tunnel on the right; it might be emphasised because an element of whatever is "horrid" or "frightening" in a landscape was thought to enhance your pleasure in viewing it. This refers to a theory of the philosopher David Hume in which he put landscape into three categories: the Sublime, the Beautiful (i.e. what gives pleasure to the eye without the element of Fear) and the Picturesque (broadly, a pleasing mixture of landscape elements). "You ain't seen nothing yet" comes to mind when we think of the Midland's determination to blast a way through the beauties of Monsal Dale and Miller`s Dale beyond, but the North Midland knew it was at the gateway to a fabled rocky landscape that was more than Sublime in places.

I have used the engravings to emphasise the long history of the railway, but also to show that there was not a lot there before it. There is no reference to Ambergate prior to 1818, but Toadmoor, through which the famous tunnel goes, is first recorded in 1397. By some sources the name comes from Derbyshire dialect "t`owd moor" ("The old moor"). Ambergate is described in White`s Derbyshire Directory of 1857 as: "a small hamlet on the Midland Railway...It consists principally of the Railway station with the offices and outbuildings attached thereto." The original Amber Gate was the toll booth seen in the illustration below built in 1818 for the Matlock and Nottingham toll roads; the North Midland Railway company annexed the name for their station, presumably because it sounded somewhat more elegant than "T`owd moor"; once again an example of an early instinct for public relations.

In 1876, Francis Hurt built the 'Hurt Arms' (on the left in the picture opposite) to replace the former 'Thatched House Tavern and Posting House' which the Midland Railway had converted into three cottages. When the North Midland to Chesterfield was the only rail route through Derbyshire, from 1840 to 1849, passengers were expected to alight at Ambergate and continue their journey by 'omnibus and posting conveyance' or on the Cromford canal to the tourist hotspots, sometimes thirty coaches in a day going towards Matlock Bath and Chatsworth, presumably through this toll gate. No wonder the railway companies wanted something more to their taste. And profit, because by 1838 Derbyshire had more than scenery to offer; the great gardener-showman Joseph Paxton was building his "Great Stove" at Chatsworth to house the latest exotics from around the world, and Chatsworth was becoming the Eden Project of its day; the difference was that the plants in its collection had never been seen in public before.

On the right of the tollgate picture is the Amber Viaduct of the Manchester, Buxton , Matlock and Midlands Junction Railway. The MBM&MJR line was envisioned as that rare

This view from the Amber river, seems ▲ more recognisable, if only because the triangular shaped field on the right is replicated in the postcard version from the John Allsop collection above, although the postcard is from a different angle above the station. Either way, the crest of woodland always known as "Top Hag" seems to be in much the same place. MRSC 65228, 60019

beast, a line that went across the country rather than north and south, and it was supposed eventually to make its way to the Wash via the exotic-sounding Ambergate, Nottingham, Boston and Eastern Junction Railway. Its Act was passed in 1846, two years after the Midland had been formed. The line opened from Ambergate as far as Rowsley in 1849 but got no further, having run out of money. The Manchester and Birmingham had been a staunch supporter of the line, wanting to find a way out east themselves, but when they merged with the London and North Western Railway that idea was no longer of pressing interest so the LNWR jointly agreed in 1852 with the Midland to lease the line for 19 years, the Midland to work it alongside the Cromford Canal.

By 1863 the route through the Peak, to Buxton initially, was finished. The Midland wanted to make sure that the gateway to the Peak line at Ambergate was fit for purpose, and the new south curve on to the main line was put into place for the through route ("The Direct Route" was a slogan the PR men at the Midland liked, emphasising the way their lines always went straight through terrain other companies might shun for its difficulty). The way was open to mass tourism in the

▼ The first Amber Gate, a tollgate. The toll gate posts can still be seen up Toadmoor Lane at the entrance to Devonshire street and adjacent to the fish and chip shop.
Photo Picture the Past

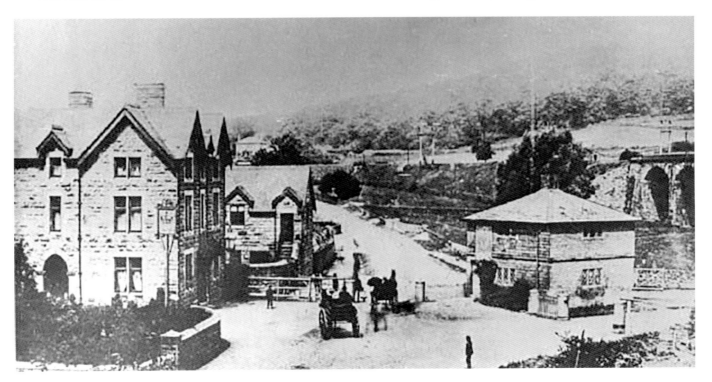

Derbyshire Dales and eventually (in 1867) a main line route to Manchester that vied with many in terms of speed, and certainly excelled in terms of scenery, was inaugurated.

The change in direction of traffic meant that the original North Midland station building had to be moved in 1863 to the triangle at the new South Junction. An ornate building in the Jacobean style by Francis Thompson, it was criticised at the time for perhaps being more suitable for a country estate than a functional railway station. However, this was no doubt again a good PR move to attract passengers. If they were going for a grand day out their mood would be lifted by starting from a grandiose building. By contrast (to jump forward to the unimaginable present), nothing would make for a more depressing start than the glorified bus shelters that have replaced this and other early buildings. The Francis Thompson building was in use until 1876 when a south to east curve was made avoiding the Toadmoor Tunnel, and the famous triangular platforms came into being. It then became a

Compound No.1063 negotiates the ▲ South Curve in 1932 on a Derby-Manchester slow train. "The Midland Railway always set itself to compete with the LNWR for the traffic between London and Manchester. This was no easy task, for whereas the North Western route via Crewe was so well engineered that the gradients were almost negligible, the Midland line was hilly from St. Pancras and mountainous...beyond. Yet the Midland achieved its object. If its trains were not as quick as the North Western's to the minute, it provided a generally comparable service, and its route has always been preferred by some travellers." Jack Simmons, 1961

This superb photograph by E.R. Morten shows a somewhat more relaxed attitude to things than might be the case today. Most passengers seem to be off platform 1, and a porter is taking in the view!

plans store, and lasted until the early 70's until it was knocked down. Luckily there is still one original building in place; the old goods shed, still in its original spot by the old NMR, and now used by a contractor. The original alignment of the MBM&MJR (via what was eventually the North Curve) was put in so that a direct connection could be made with the ANB&EJR, which, of course, never happened. It came into its own when coal trains started running to Manchester via the Pye Bridge Line from the Erewash Valley which came in at Crich Junction in 1875.

It seems the MBM&MJR trains used the back of the eastern end of the original NMR down platform while the line was effectively just a branch line to Rowsley between 1849 and 1863. Trains from Matlock ran into a headshunt alongside the NMR line and then set back into the station. The loco would then uncouple and be turned, coaled and watered and then returned to the west end of the bay via a special line that terminated at a turntable which allowed the loco to attach what originally had been the rear of the train. On departure the train would propel back into the headshunt and then head for Matlock and Rowsley with the loco leading. It was not an ideal arrangement, but was adequate whilst MBM remained a local branch line. Initially, temporary accommodation was provided at the second station before it was decided to build a new "V-shaped" structure which incorporated many materials reclaimed from the redundant Francis Thompson building. The new station although somewhat less ornate than the original, still retained a degree of the Thompson style.

The elaborate portico at the front did not survive the move, but the shot of the South Junction shows the grandeur still surviving; it was always something I looked out for when we travelled past on the morning train. I have always wondered how this new station was accessed by the road carriages of the time, since the road up to Toadmoor behind was at a very sharp angle, typically for this area, and it must have been quite a job for the coachman to bring the horses round in such a tight curve.

Moving north east from the station towards Chesterfield, the line crosses the road from Ripley and the river Amber (twice) before coming up against the next obstacle, the Cromford canal, which had been there since 1794. Traffic on

this canal, which stretched its northern arm into Arkwright`s Mill at Cromford and was therefore very profitable, was a regular 300,000 tons per annum, and in 1841 was bringing in £12,086. The Cromford and High Peak Railway made this an effective through route with considerable trade to Manchester. The North Midland installed an aqueduct to further complicate the writhing knot of junctions and crossovers which was starting to characterise the valley.

Ambergate South Junction, ▼
showing the triangular
building in use until the
main station was built in
1876. It was demolished in the
1970s by BR. MRSC 67296

Russell's view of the aqueduct at Bullbridge in 1842 (below) shows the railway in a kind of bucolic harmony with the canal and the road, the labourers digging up the track in a leisurely way while a train approaches from the north. However, the reality was that the railway provided some serious opposition to the canal, and by 1850 the latter's profits were only £7,588. This led to the canal being sold to the MBM&MJR for £103,500. Trade immediately began to decline, falling to less than 76,000 tons by 1888, by which time it had been taken over by the Midland Railway. The whole canal was closed in 1944 after notable breaches of the Butterley tunnel had rendered it less than efficient.

There was no doubt that the Midland Railway contributed to the canal's demise by omission, since they repeatedly failed to mend the breaches in the tunnel. A major collapse in 1889 had taken until 1893 to repair, and after an even

The Cromford Canal aqueduct at Bullbridge. To put it in, the North Midland railway first floated a pre-formed section down the canal, then sank it in the appropriate position before removing the earth underneath. MRSC 60017

bigger collapse in 1900 the tunnel never reopened and the Midland tried unsuccessfully to cease navigation. Ironically they still had to supply water to the forges of the Butterley Company despite the fact that it was that company's mining activities that had caused the collapse in the first place. Benjamin Outram's Butterley Company was a major player in the area. In 1793 the "Butterley Gangroad" was made from quarries at Crich to carry lime down to kilns built by the company at Amber Wharf. It was converted into a narrow gauge railway in 1840 and lasted until 1933. Only this year, 2015, the importance of this site for early technology was recognised when the Fritchley Tunnel on the line, believed to be the world's oldest railway tunnel, was given protected status. Early wagons were moved by horsepower, but it was latterly worked by steam. One of the earliest experimental steam engines worked this line for a short time around 1814. Seen now as "famously mad", it was described by its inventor William Brunton as resembling a man pushing a weight forward, having two steam-powered legs which propelled it forward. Unlikely as it seems, it did work well, to the extent that another was made for the Newbottle Colliery on Tyneside. Unfortunately for the design, this second engine blew up, due not to an inherent flaw in the design, but because the driver

This part of the railway line was called ▼ Crich Junction, an appellation that puzzled me until recently, because the section is nowhere near Crich, a village about three miles and three hundred feet higher. However, there is a connection with Crich village because in 1840 when George Stephenson built the North Midland he discovered coal seams in tunnels near Chesterfield and decided to use the coal in burning lime from the old Roman quarries under Crich Stand. He brought the lime down on a narrow gauge railway, burnt it in twenty huge kilns that dominated the valley until quite recently. Is this the only narrow gauge line that gave its name to a mainline junction? There are a number of Midland railway trucks visible in this shot, and two engines. The stacks of wood were presumably to prime the kilns. Collection Rod Jewell.

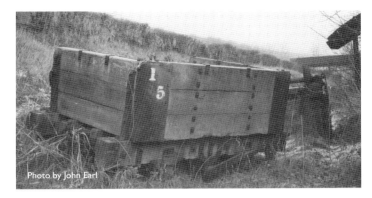

Photo by John Earl

Photo by Picture the Past

overloaded the boiler. The tragic loss of a dozen or more people saw the end of the experiment, but it was reported to have worked with a load up a gradient of 1 in 36 throughout the winter of 1814; important when the issue of adhesion was a live one.

In 1965 I took a walk into Ambergate down the steep incline (the line running diagonally from top) that led to the lime kilns, and found these narrow gauge trucks lying abandoned. The line closed in 1957 but they were still there eight years later , a strange "ghost ship" moment. This incline was self-acting and called "The Steep", running for 550 yards at a slope of 1 in 5 from Top Hag wood. The second image shows the bottom of the incline and wagons when they were much younger, in the late Victorian period.

On the same day in 1965, I walked to the east end of the lime kilns and took a photo of goods trains from the Pye Bridge line waiting for access to the main; unfortunately I could not get up closer, but the photo does show what was a typical sight for the time, freight trains stacked up and waiting to cross over the main to the right to go on to Rowsley or left for Derby.

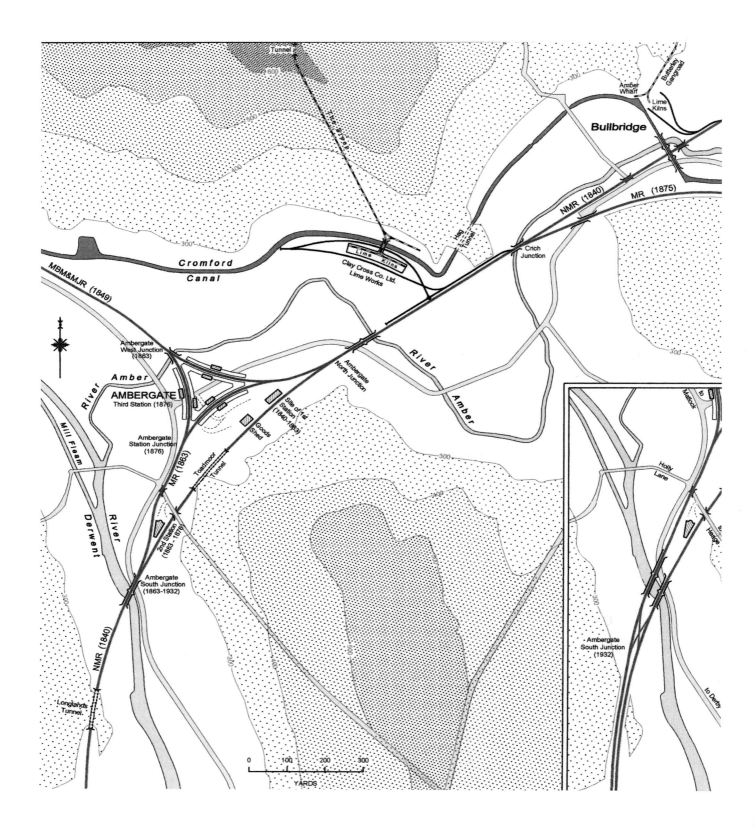

Tunnel

600

Butterley
Gangroad

500

Amber
Wharf

300

Lime
Kilns

Bullbridge

NMR (1840)   MR (1875)

Hag Tunnel

Crich
Junction

Lime Kilns

Clay Cross Co. Ltd.
Lime Works

MBM&MJR (1849)

Cromford
Canal

River   Amber

300

Ambergate
West Junction
(1863)

Ambergate
North Junction

AMBERGATE
Third Station (1876)

Amber

River

River   Amber

to
Matlock

Site of 1st
Station
(1840-1863)

Goods
Shed

Ambergate
Station Junction
(1876)

MR (1863)

Toadmoor
Tunnel

Mill Fleam

300

Holly
Lane

River

Derwent

2nd Station
(1863-1876)

500

Ambergate
South Junction
(1863-1932)

300

300

Ambergate
South Junction
(1932)

NMR (1840)

300

to Derby

Longlands
Tunnel.

0   100   200   300

YARDS

- 22 -

Finally, I walked on to the old Cromford canal aqueduct depicted in Russell's engraving, built in 1840, and took a picture looking south-west; the opposite direction to the artist's viewpoint. The car park spoils the rural idyll unfortunately, although the trees on the right disappearing into the mist by the river could at a stretch be older versions of the ones in the engraving. The line of trees does mark the river which went under the canal here through a culvert, though probably a wider one than the artist depicts. In the middle distance you can see the abutments of a road bridge. On either side are the large revetment walls that keep the track to its straight line over the embankment and away from the road on the left and river on the right, a major piece of engineering that stretches a long way. The straightness of the track echoes the straight track in the original, and again demonstrates what a good running line it was for expresses both then and now. Photos by the author.

Freights through Ambergate; in the left hand photo by Frank Ashley in 1956, 3F No.43650 trundles through Platform 6, while 4F No. 44202 approaches on Platform 5. Right, in LMS days 4F No.3308 pilots Beyer Garratt No.4997. The location is Johnson's sidings. Some seventy-odd freights went through Ambergate every day. Photo W.L.Good

A fine view of platforms 2 and 3 from the south in 1910, with a train in the south to east platform loading up. In the right distance, the lime kilns are going full blast, while the girder structure carrying the north curve can be clearly seen behind the station building. It was a station built for the kind of staffing levels you see here. In BR days there was only one porter on the station who was overstretched at times, as is evidenced by his reply to a question about non-attendance to a train on Platform 1: "I was out attending to the Bradford train, parcels and pigeon traffic being unloaded, this train delayed by four minutes as a result. Then attending the clerks' train on Platform 2, priority given to that train on account of the platform curve. When that train was despatched, the train on Platform 1 had gone." MRSC 65227

▲ At the far end of Platform 3 in 1941, No.43624 pauses with the 9.28 to Mansfield. When the Stanier 3 cylinder 2-6-4T 25XX locos took over working the London, Tilbury and Southend passenger services in LMS days, the original 4-4-2Ts became redundant and some were sent to Mansfield to replace the ageing MR 0-4-4Ts on local services. There were regular Mansfield – Ambergate services via Pye Bridge and Butterley. It seems that three of the LT&S tanks survived at Mansfield until 1956. Both photos H.C. Casserley

On a snowy Christmas Day in 1925, LMS 2P No.747 ▲ sets out for Derby past Ambergate South signal box. In 1936 the LMS staff magazine said this: "The South Junction box... is the only one to be affected by all movements between Derby and both the Sheffield and Manchester lines... consequently it handles the largest number of trains – 1,186 in a typical working week of the winter service..."The signalman's skill and knowledge was at a premium.

Picturesque grotto or tunnel? In 1928-1932 a new girder bridge was put in over the river Derwent and the track was quadrupled to accommodate the increasing traffic. At the same time the tunnel at Longlands built by the North Midland was opened out into a cutting and a new South Junction signal box sited there. The rough-hewn classical style of the original entrance refers us back to the engravings. RSC 67763 ▶

◀ The size of the task and the effort involved is shown here; it takes us back to the landscape shifting on the grand scale with which the North Midland started, albeit with steam navvies rather than real ones. The full effect is seen overleaf from Longlands with 424 and 531 double-heading over the bridges. Although in LMS days, this is very reminiscent of the Midland with the long rake of largely clerestory coaches. Postcard by F.Moore, 1920s

8483

As we know, Beeching ruthlessly amputated the Midland`s magnificent line to Manchester north of Matlock, so since 1968 trains have no longer disturbed the tranquillity of Monsal Dale, Miller`s Dale or the delightful Water-cum- Jolly. Maybe the gods, who according to John Ruskin, once inhabited the Wye Valley until the Midland Railway "blasted away its rocks and heaped thousands of tons of shale into its stream so that every fool in Buxton could be in Bakewell in half an hour", have returned and are revelling in the peace and quiet. On the other hand, I can imagine them harbouring some sneaky regard for the mortals who made those crimson lake engines run along their high rock galleries...perhaps they are not altogether averse to their return and are waiting for the sound of a Midland whistle to echo among the rocks again...

There are signs that once again, the efforts of ordinary individuals putting right what governments should never have allowed to happen may yet see trains running north of Rowsley; Peak Rail has plans to extend that way. But whatever happens in the future, Midland memories are long, and the golden years of the extraordinary elevated triangle of Ambergate will be among the last to fade.

Below: in the afternoon light, No.332 enters ▼
Ambergate in 1911. MRSC 60022

CROSSING
THE SEVERN

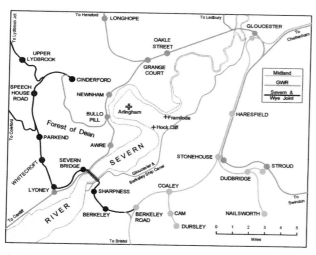

▲ Sketch map of south west Gloucestershire showing the River Severn and the main pregrouping lines and the non railway locations mentioned in the text. The freight only lines serving the docks at Lydney, Sharpness and Gloucester plus the mineral lines and some stations in the Forest of Dean have been omitted for reasons of clarity.

◄ Isambard Kingdom Brunel FRS (1806 – 1859) the Engineer of the South Wales Direct Railway

In the early 19th century several schemes for crossing the tidal River Severn downstream of Gloucester were put forward. Some involved constructing a bridge across the river; others proposed the alternative approach of boring a tunnel. Most ideas were destined to be stillborn, but as early as 1812, work actually began on boring a tunnel from the western bank, between Newnham and Bullo Pill, eastwards towards Arlingham. At this point, the river is comparatively narrow. The purpose of the tunnel was to provide an eastward extension to the recently opened Bullo Pill Railway – a 4'-0" gauge plateway which carried coal from the mines of the Dean Forest to the Severn for onward shipment. However, after a promising start and getting about half way to the opposite side (about 240 yards), disaster struck. On Friday 13th November 1812, the workings suddenly flooded. Fortunately, all the miners escaped safely, but the tunnel was deemed to be a lost cause and the project was abandoned. Had it been successful, it would have been the world's first underwater tunnel.

This seems to have tempered the appetite for any future projects until Isambard Kingdom Brunel appeared on the scene in 1844. It was part of his proposed South Wales Direct Railway and the concept was spectacularly Brunelian as can be seen in the sketch map on the left, a few miles down stream from Gloucester, the River Severn describes a long horseshoe bend. As the crow flies the distance between the ends of the horseshoe at Framilode and Hock Cliff is about 1¼ miles; by water, it is about eight miles.

Brunel proposed that his new broad gauge line would head in a westerly direction from Stroud towards the village of Arlingham, in the middle of the horseshoe, where there would be a junction. One line would head north towards Hereford, the other in a south westerly direction towards Awre and thence on to Newport, Cardiff and Swansea. Both lines would cross the river on separate, low headroom timber viaducts, each about half a mile in length.

By this time, the majority of larger shipping that plied the Severn opted to leave the river at Sharpness and use the Gloucester & Berkeley Ship Canal which had opened in 1827. This provided a much easier, safer and shorter route northwards to Gloucester.

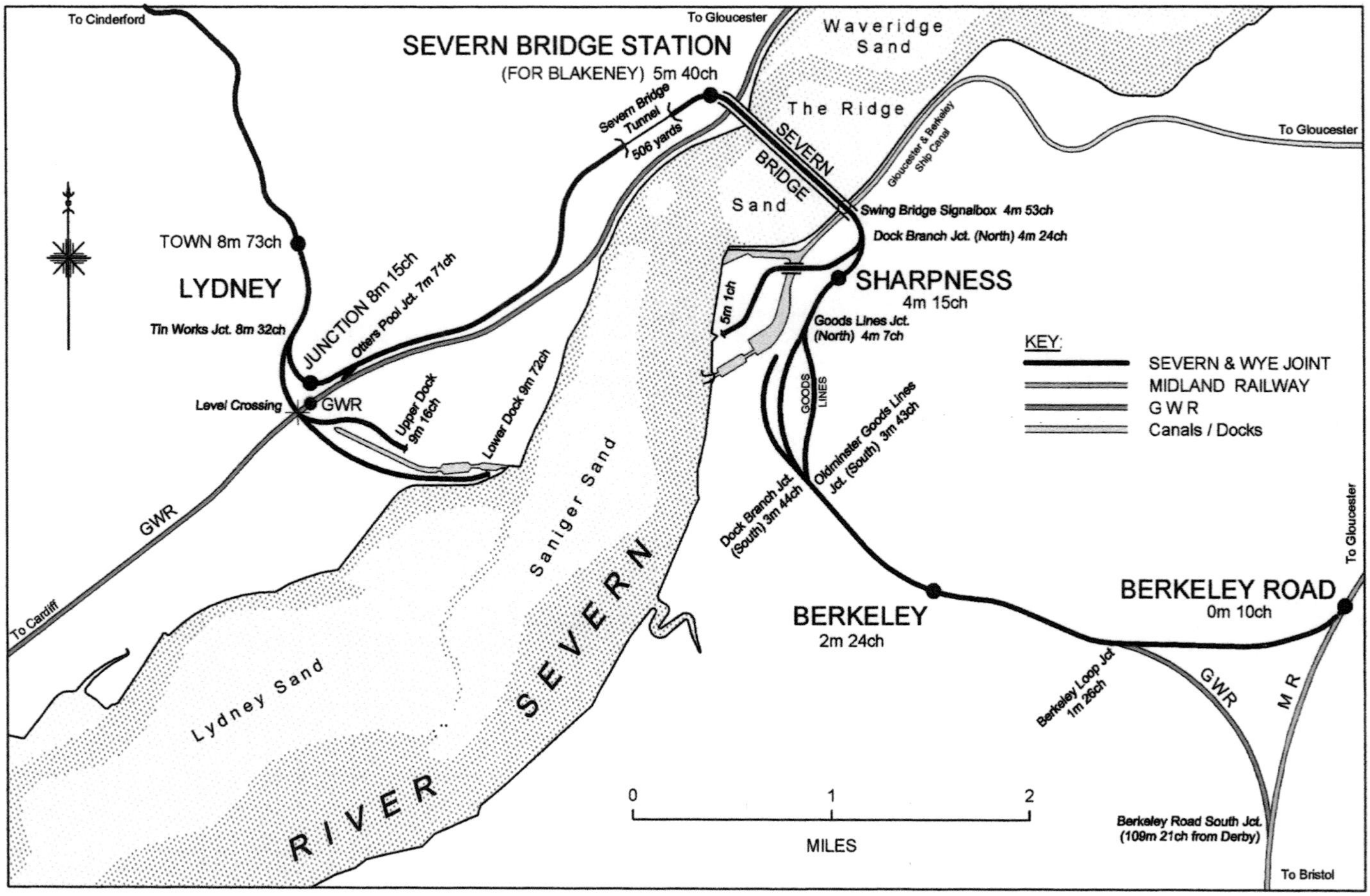

To Cinderford
To Gloucester
SEVERN BRIDGE STATION
(FOR BLAKENEY) 5m 40ch
Waveridge Sand
The Ridge
Severn Bridge Tunnel 506 yards
SEVERN BRIDGE
Sand
Gloucester & Berkeley Ship Canal
To Gloucester
Swing Bridge Signalbox 4m 53ch
Dock Branch Jct. (North) 4m 24ch
TOWN 8m 73ch
LYDNEY
Tin Works Jct. 8m 32ch
JUNCTION 8m 15ch
Otters Pool Jct. 7m 71ch
SHARPNESS
4m 15ch
5m 1ch
Goods Lines Jct. (North) 4m 7ch
KEY:
SEVERN & WYE JOINT
MIDLAND RAILWAY
GWR
Canals / Docks
Level Crossing
GWR
Upper Dock 9m 16ch
Lower Dock 9m 72ch
GOODS LINES
Oldminster Goods Lines Jct. (South) 3m 43ch
Saniger Sand
Dock Branch Jct. (South) 3m 44ch
To Gloucester
GWR
To Cardiff
SEVERN
BERKELEY
2m 24ch
BERKELEY ROAD
0m 10ch
Lydney Sand
Berkeley Loop Jct 1m 26ch
GWR
MR
RIVER
0
1
2
MILES
Berkeley Road South Jct. (109m 21ch from Derby)
To Bristol

A map of Severn Railway Bridge and its environs which is based on the 1917 Midland Distance Diagram Sheet 51A. Note: due to the transient nature of sandbanks, those shown above may differ in size and shape from those shown on later maps. ▲

Some vessels however continued to risk the vagaries of the Severn tides and the treacherous sandbanks, rather than pay tolls on the canal. Brunel's two proposed low headroom viaducts near Arlingham would effectively stop any boat with a mast height of over 20 feet navigating to or from Gloucester. To avoid any opposition to his scheme from the owners of such boats that still used this part of the river, Brunel proposed to build a new, short canal between Framilode and Hock Cliff.

The Achilles heel of the scheme was that Brunel's new railway avoided Gloucester; a fact which infuriated the citizens of the county town. Their response was swift and decisive. Below Gloucester, the Severn was the responsibility of the Admiralty, who were petitioned by the great and good of the city that irrespective of Brunel's new canal, the proposed low headroom viaducts would be detrimental to navigation on the river. The Lords of the Admiralty agreed and in the face of such powerful opposition, the Bill was thrown out. Later schemes for his South Wales Direct, which involved a single bridge with greater headroom, and the alternative 1½ mile long tunnel between Arlingham and Awre, also came to nothing. Although Brunel had failed, other engineers dreamed of success in building a Severn crossing and by 1871, no less than six proposals were in circulation. Two would come to fruition. One was the Great Western Railway's Severn Tunnel and what later became known as the Severn & Wye & Severn Bridge Railway. During its passage through Parliament and its subsequent approval, the scheme was known as the Severn Bridge Railway Bill No. 2, (Sharpness). It received the Royal Assent on 18th July 1872.

Amongst the Bill's influential supporters were James Allport, General Manager of the Midland Railway and his Chairman, W. P. Price, the latter also acting in his capacity as the MP for Gloucester. The Midland, of course, could see that its support for the bridge would be a means of gaining a foothold in the mineral rich Forest of Dean and accordingly, in return for running powers over the bridge, subscribed £50,000 to the project.

The Severn Bridge Railway Bill No. 2, (Sharpness) as approved by Parliament, authorised not only the 1,404 yard long bridge but the connecting lines on either side. From junctions with both the Severn & Wye Railway and the GWR's South Wales line at Lydney, the new line which included a tunnel (506 yards in length) climbed at 1 in 133 in a generally north easterly direction to a summit in the centre of the tunnel. Soon after reaching the open air again the line turned through almost 90 degrees to cross the river on a falling gradient of 1 in 134 towards the docks at Sharpness. The river crossing began with a gracefully curved 12 arch masonry viaduct which carried the new line above the South Wales line to the water's edge. From here it marched boldly across the river on a series of 21 fixed bowstring girder spans with a final bowstring span which acted as swing bridge over the Gloucester & Berkeley Ship Canal. The girders spanning the river navigation channel had a headroom of 70 feet above high water level. After crossing the canal terra-firma was reached again after a short two arch stone bridge. A short distance beyond this a branch diverged to serve Sharpness docks whilst the main

▼ A classic postcard view of the Severn Railway Bridge from the Sharpness side with, on the right, the swing bridge spanning the Gloucester & Berkeley Ship Canal. The canal, later renamed the Gloucester & Sharpness Ship Canal, is just visible along the bottom of the photograph. With an optimistic eye to increasing traffic in the future, the swing bridge was built to carry double track, although in the event, the single line proved to be more than sufficient. The signalmen allocated to the Swing Bridge signalbox not only had to be competent signallers, they were required 'multi task' and look after the boilers and the steam engines that rotated the bridge when a bridge driver was not on duty. Similarly, the bridge driver had to be a competent signaller and operate the instruments and signals when a signalman was not on duty. There were a series of special bell codes to communicate with the boxes on 'dry land' on both sides of the bridge. More importantly from the safety point of view, the tablet machines in these boxes were also interlocked with the bridge. Thus, if the swing bridge was not locked in the closed position, a single line tablet could not be withdrawn. Conversely, after a tablet had been withdrawn, the levers that operated the locking mechanism swing bridge could not be released. Photo: MRSC 23637

line continued to terminate in an end-on junction with the Midland Railway's branch line from Berkeley Road. The Bill for the latter was approved in the same Parliamentary session.Raising the capital proved to be the most difficult job which was not helped by the GWR playing prima donna. Although the GW were committed to spending £1 million on constructing the Severn Tunnel, they could see advantages in supporting the bridge and, like the Midland, had obtained running powers across the bridge in return for a £50,000 investment. However, the last thing that GWR management wanted was the MR expanding into the Forest of Dean and refused to contribute their £50k until the Midland had been stripped of its running powers. This, of course, was rejected outright by the MR and after a lot of squabbling, the matter was eventually referred to arbitration, who found in favour of the Midland. The petulant GWR promptly 'spat the dummy' and walked away to concentrate on their tunnel.

Bearing in mind the bridge had received Royal Assent in July 1872, the financial mountain that bridge company chairman, William Lucy, and his fellow directors had to climb can perhaps be judged by the delay of all but a few days short of three years before they felt confident enough to begin. This was marked by the laying of a 2 ton foundation stone by Lucy on the north bank at Purton on 3rd July 1875. By then however the main contractors for the bridge had been appointed. Hamilton's Windsor Iron Works Company of Garston (Liverpool) and London won the contract to fabricate and erect the bridge structure for the sum of £190,000. Vickers & Cooke of London were awarded the contract to construct the viaduct on the north bank, and the masonry works on the Sharpness side. This included the supporting tower for the swing bridge, the riverside pier (no. 1) and the two arch bridge on the land side. The Vickers & Cooke contract which was worth £90k also included the construction of the 506 yard tunnel, the other bridges and the stations.

Unlike several other long river bridges where the spans had been constructed on pontoons at the river's edge and then floated into position, the capricious Severn tides prevented Hamilton's from using this method. Spring tides at Sharpness can cause the river to rise and fall by up to 34 feet in just over two hours and run at 8 or 10 knots. This situation is often exacerbated by strong south westerly gales that blow up the Severn Estuary. Hamilton's solution to the problem was to fabricate and assemble each of the bowstring spans in their Windsor Iron Works at Garston. These were then dismantled and sent as a numbered kit of parts to Sharpness where the company had established a yard alongside the canal. The spans were then re-erected on site in their final positions from stagings below. To speed up the process, the components were temporarily bolted together; the bolts being later removed and replaced by rivets once the span was securely in position. The circular cast iron columns that supported the bridge were cast in four feet long sections at Hamilton's Windsor Foundry on Merseyside from where they were shipped to Sharpness. The outside diameters of the columns varied from six to ten feet. Depending on the position, the sections below the high water line were nine and ten feet in diameter, those above being six and seven feet in diameter.

▲ The main contractor for the bridge structure, Hamilton's Windsor Iron Works of Liverpool established a site alongside the Ship Canal at Sharpness where the cast and wrought iron components produced in their Merseyside factory and shipped to site by sea could be unloaded and stored. This is a view of Sharpness New Docks looking south on 25th July 1877 with the low level swing bridge on the centre right. Photo: MRSC/KRM 63258

The engineers had decided to work their way across the river from the Sharpness side. Their logic in this was that the river on this side was fairly shallow due to the sand bank known as The Ridge. Here, they reasoned, they would gain valuable experience both in piling and building the piers, and constructing the thirteen short 134 ft bowstring spans in-situ before venturing towards the deep water navigation channel that required the two 312 ft spans close to the opposite bank at Purton. Between the short and long spans there were 5 intermediate spans of 174 feet.

After the short approach viaduct, the first structure was a circular stone tower on the narrow strip of land between the canal and the river. This carried the 200 ft span swing bridge and the large cabin which controlled the signals and housed the boilers and the steam engine that moved the bridge.

With the experience gained, once the piers had reached their required height, the final few 134 foot span sections, each weighing 107 tons, were erected at a rate of one a week! Erecting the two main 312 feet long spans, 70 feet above high water in the deep navigation channel was a different story. Not only did the temporary stagings have to be strong enough to support the weight of the 534 tons of ironwork in each span, they had to be able to withstand the even greater horizontal forces imposed by the wind and the Severn tides. To complete the bridge, Hamilton's moved their operational base across the river to Purton in preference to trundling everything across the bridge from Sharpness. Erection of the first main span commenced in September 1878 but it was not until the following February that it was completed. There must have been some heart stopping moments for the engineers during that period and it would not have been much fun for the erectors working on such an exposed site during the dark winter months. A failure of the staging before the span had sufficient structural integrity to support itself would have been a complete disaster. The second main span was completed in August, thanks to the installation of an early form of floodlighting which allowed work to continue through the night.

The following series of photographs of the bridge under construction are copies of some of the 58 original photographs contained in an album held by the Gloucester Archives reference B417/23554.

▲ On the north bank of the river at Purton a curved 12 arch masonry viaduct was necessary to get from terra firma onto the bridge. Here on 19th September 1877 some of the piers are seen rising from their foundations. The contractors for this part of the work were Vickers & Cook of London but were later replaced by Griffith Griffiths of Lydney. Photo MRSC/KRM 62359

▲ The designer and Chief Engineer of the Severn Railway Bridge was George William Keeling who was certainly not shy about being photographed and appears in several images of the bridge under construction. Here he is seen on 8th May 1877 standing in one of the 10 ft diameter cast iron tubes that will make up some of the underwater sections of the bridge piers 19, 20 and 21. Photo MRSC/KRM 62373

▲ Here, on the right, one of the four foot long cast iron tubes that formed the bridge piers is being hoisted into position ready for sinking into the river bed. This is Pier 14. The group of men seen on the left on top of the temporary staging are working the air pump supplying the divers bolting the sections together. In the background a piling engine mounted on a Severn trow is busy driving the piles for Pier 15. Photo MRSC/KRM 62376

▲ 'Victoria' a Severn trow which was registered at Chepstow is seen here on 17th August 1876 delivering barrels of concrete for infilling Pier no. 15 which is fitted with an air-bell. Photo: MRSC/KRM 62367

▲ The temporary staging to support two of the 132 feet span bowstring girders, (Spans 2, 3 and 4) Each span was manufactured and erected in the Windsor Iron Works foundry on Merseyside before being dismantled and dispatched, as a kit of parts, to Sharpness where they were re-assembled, in situ, above the river. Bolts were used as temporary fixings as speed was of the essence until each span became self supporting. The gang of riveters followed on behind to make a stronger and more permanent fixing. The photo is dated 20th March 1876. Photo: MRSC/KRM 62372

▲ The first of the 132 foot long bowstring girder spans (no.2) nearing completion on 26th April 1876. With the experience gained, the final few 13 similar spans, each weighing 107 tons, were erected in a week! MRSC/KRM 62369

▲ Bridge designer and Chief Engineer, George Keeling is seen here again on far the right of this photograph taken on 16th June 1876 in Span no 2 with the riveting gang at work. Span no.3 can be seen beyond. MRSC/KRM 62363

▲ A view looking across the Severn on 16th November 1876 with the Gloucester and Sharpness Canal in the foreground. On the bank of the canal the civil engineering contractors Vickers & Cook have begun work on the circular masonry tower that will support the 200 foot span swing bridge over the canal. The erection of the fixed spans continues in the background.

▲ This photograph taken on 8th May 1877 shows the work in progress on the bridge and the circular support tower for the swing bridge over the canal. On the left can be seen a portable engine driving a crushing machine for producing the lime mortar for use by the masons. The canal towpath with a rather ineffective looking handrail can be seen running along the bottom of the photograph. Beyond and to the left of the tower the stonework for Pier 1 is rising from the river. Numerous pairs of cast iron piers have been completed and are carrying Spans 2 (nearest to the camera) to at least Span 9. Span no.1 could not be erected until Pier 1 had been finished.
MRSC/KRM 62356

▲ A group of V.I.Ps. photographed in Hamilton's Windsor Iron Works yard in Garston (Liverpool) on 10th September 1877 in front of the first assembled 312 foot bowstring girder that would span the navigation channel. Erection of the 534 ton structure on site began in the September of the following year and took until February 1879 before it was completed. George Keeling, is seen 7th from the left. Photo: MRSC/KRM 62357

Almost there! This rather dramatic contemporary engraving showing the first 312 foot span completed and work well under way with the final span. The temporary wooden staging not only had to support the weight of the girder, it also had to withstand the force of the Severn tides and the gales that blew along the river.

In spite of the steady progress being made by Hamilton's Windsor Iron Works, all was not well with the other contractor, Vickers & Cooke. They had fallen so far behind that after several warnings their contract was terminated and awarded to a local man, Griffith Griffiths of Lydney.

In the background there were other problems too. The building of the bridge coincided with a series of strikes and a general downturn in demand for coal and other minerals mined in the Forest of Dean. The consequential loss of revenue resulted in the Severn & Wye Railway & Canal Company (to give it its full title) experiencing severe financial difficulties. Merger talks between the S&WR and the Severn Bridge Railway culminated in the amalgamation being approved by Parliament in July 1878. When the bridge opened the new undertaking would be known as the Severn & Wye and Severn Bridge Railway Co.

The choice of Griffith Griffiths to complete the unfinished civil work on both sides of the river was inspired. Being locals, he and his men certainly had a vested interest in getting the associated works completed as quickly as possible so that the bridge could be opened for traffic. On the Sharpness side, freight trains had begun running along the Midland branch from Berkeley Road in October 1875 (only three months after Lucy had laid the foundation stone for the bridge at Purton). Passenger services on the new branch to a temporary station in Sharpness followed on 1st August 1876.

Once the final span of the bridge was in place, work continued apace and on Wednesday 3rd September 1879 the first passenger train from Lydney to Sharpness rumbled over the bridge. Essentially, it was a private "jolly" for the bridge's directors, contractors, engineers and a few other local dignitaries. The official inspection by Colonel Frederick Henry Rich R.E. on behalf of the Board of Trade was not carried out until the first week of October 1879. This included thorough static and dynamic load testing involving eight locomotives. The maximum deflection of the main spans was recorded as being 1½ inches. To the uninitiated this probably might seem excessive, but it is structurally fairly insignificant when compared to the 312 feet length of the main spans.

The official opening of the bridge took place on Friday 17th October 1879. The first train with several hundred invited guests on board left Gloucester and ran over the Midland lines to Sharpness, through the new permanent station (which had also opened that day) and across the bridge to Lydney. After a brief stop, the special returned to Sharpness. In the interim period 21 detonators had been placed on the track, one on each span, so on the return journey the equivalent of a royal salute echoed across the Severn. The special then crossed the river for a third time, but this time it only ran as far as Purton where most of the guests alighted. Led by William Lucy, the VIPs walked out onto the first 312 foot span where Lucy ceremonially tightened the last bolt and amidst three cheers, declared the bridge open. The walkers then continued across the bridge to Sharpness where a huge marquee had been erected to accommodate them for the usual junketing that marked the opening of new railways in Victorian Britain. The sumptuous lunch was followed by the inevitable and interminable speeches and toasts, starting of course with the health of Her Gracious Majesty and the Royal Family right through to the proverbial "Old Uncle Tom Cobley and all." One of the unscheduled toasts, proposed by Lucy himself, was to the health of "the non-subscribing companies" a tongue-in-cheek reference to the GWR who were represented at the junket by their chairman, Sir Daniel Gooch. Gooch replied politely and diplomatically, unaware that as he was speaking, the construction of GWR's alternative route via the tunnel under the river had received a severe setback when the workings were inundated as a result of his navvies puncturing the "Great Spring."

The encounter with the "Great Spring" in the GWR Severn Tunnel was to have a major impact on the project, because it was not until 1886 that the first train ran through the tunnel. It had taken 14 years to build. For the new Severn & Wye & Severn Railway Bridge Company, the GWR's tunnel setbacks in theory were good news. But the bridge soon had problems of its own in the wake of the Tay Bridge Disaster in Scotland on the night of 28th December 1879. That night as a violent storm raged along the Firth of Tay, part of the bridge collapsed whilst a passenger train was crossing. Every one of the 75 souls on board the train perished in the icy waters of the Tay.

SEVERN & WYE & SEVERN BRIDGE RAILWAY COMPANY.

REPORTS

AND

ACCOUNTS

TO 31st DECEMBER, 1882.

NOTICE IS HEREBY GIVEN, that the SEVENTH HALF-YEARLY GENERAL MEETING of the Proprietors of this Company will be held at the Royal Hotel, College Green, Bristol, on Friday, the 23rd day of February, at a Quarter past Two o'clock in the Afternoon, for the transaction of general business and for the election of Four Directors and One Auditor, in place of those retiring by rotation.

NOTICE IS HEREBY FURTHER GIVEN, that the Registers of Transfers of Shares will be closed from the 9th day of February until after the Meeting.

W. C. LUCY, Chairman.

G. R. RICHARDS, Secretary.

Lydney, January 8th, 1883.

NOTICE.—*Proprietors are requested to give early intimation to the Secretary, at the Company's Offices at Lydney, of any change of Residence. The Address now registered is that to which this Report is sent.*

CHANCE AND BLAND, PRINTERS, GLOUCESTER.

The public were understandably concerned about the safety of the Severn Bridge, but at the subsequent Court of Enquiry into the disaster it was revealed that the Tay Bridge had been poorly designed, poorly constructed and poorly maintained. In the design, little account had been taken of wind pressure on the structure, in spite of the strong gales that blew regularly along the Firth of Tay. In the construction, it was discovered that many of the safety-critical iron components were defective and should never have been used. Some castings which had blow holes (air bubbles) in them and should have been scrapped immediately were used after the visible holes were deliberately hidden by filling them with 'Beaumont's Egg' a mixture of beeswax, graphite and iron filings. Fortunately, the quality control standards employed by Hamilton's Windsor Ironworks were considerably more exacting. Equally, George Keeling, the Severn Bridge engineer had taken full account of the fearsome winds and tidal currents in his design for the bridge. After this brief hiccup, the public's confidence in the Severn Railway Bridge soon returned.

But gradually it became clear that the bridge was falling a long way short of its promoters' aspirations. Although the bridge reduced the distance by rail from Cardiff to Bristol by 40 miles, the GWR, once again lived up to its epithet, the Great Way Round, by continuing to go via Gloucester and use its running powers over the MR line from there to Bristol rather than pay tolls for using the bridge. On the positive side, in the early days, seven up and seven down local passenger trains used the bridge, but the hoped for mineral traffic from the Forest of Dean was not as great as expected. In fact the closing years of the 19th century were very unhappy ones throughout the Forest. Further downturns of demand for its coal and minerals, deterioration in labour relations and strikes caused further decreases in traffic. Inevitably the Severn & Wye and Severn Bridge Railway Co. began to find itself in serious financial trouble.

SEVERN AND WYE AND SEVERN BRIDGE RAILWAY.
FOREST OF DEAN.

Excursions, Pleasure Parties, &c., to Severn Bridge, Speech House, Lydbrook (Symonds Yat), &c.

During the Summer Months Excursion Tickets at low fares are issued on certain Week Days (see Bills) from Midland Stations at Cheltenham, Gloucester, Bristol, and Bath to Severn Bridge, Speech House, and Lydbrook.

Cheap Return Tickets will be issued to Pleasure Parties on any day for not less than Six First Class or Ten Third Class Passengers.

An attractive Guide to the Forest of Dean has been published by Mr. JOHN BELLOWS, Gloucester, and may be had of all Booksellers.

Special arrangements at Cheap Fares can be made for Schools, Benefit Societies, Working Men's Clubs or Manufacturers' Annual Trips, &c.

Near the Severn Bridge Station there is Hotel accommodation and Tea Gardens overlooking the River and the Severn Bridge.

The Speech House (within a few minutes' walk of the Station) is situated on a hill in the centre of the ancient forest, and is a most attractive place for pleasure parties.

Every accommodation can be provided by the Hotel in the Speech House, or for Picnics in the open forest, and there are Cricket, Quoit, Archery, and Lawn Tennis Grounds. Telegraphic communications to Speech House, address *viâ* Lydney.

Lydbrook is beautifully situated on the River Wye amidst charming scenery.

Symonds Yat and Goodrich Castle are within easy walking distance from the Lydbrook Junction Station, and tickets to that Station are available to return from Coleford Station, or *vice versâ*.

GEO. WILLIAM KEELING,
Engineer and General Manager.

During 1883 matters went from bad to worse resulting in the company being placed under the protection of the Court of Chancery. To a degree this meant business as usual because the Court appointed the Board as managers with the general manager and the company secretary as the receivers. For the chairman William Lucy, who had fought so long and so hard to build the bridge, this must have been a deep personal tragedy. Only four years previously he had experienced the heady euphoria when the bridge had opened. But to Lucy's lasting credit, his fighting spirit was undiminished. In fairness, much of the Severn & Wye and Severn Bridge Railway's problems were completely beyond Lucy's control. He was powerless to halt the lack of demand for the Forest's minerals or even begin to repair the appalling labour relations problems.

Although the company could hardly be accused of being wildly extravagant in the past, Lucy now had to ensure that every penny earned by the company was spent wisely on essential items such as maintaining the bridge and keeping the permanent way and structures in good order. However, following some major financial restructuring, the company was able to leave Chancery in 1885. The ensuing years proved to be very much a roller-coaster ride. During the very few and very brief occasions that demand for the Forest's minerals improved, the railway's finances consequently improved. The very modest profits which resulted from these brief upturns not only allowed improvements to be made at various places on the system, but also a modest dividend was paid on the preference shares.

But by 1893 the company were in serious financial difficulties again, this time seemingly worse than before, but again it was due entirely to external forces rather than any mismanagement. Once again the company found itself in Chancery. But by now, the board was growing increasingly battle weary and few shareholders would have been surprised when early in 1894 Lucy announced the terms that it proposed to seek Parliamentary authority to sell the Severn & Wye and Severn Bridge Railway Company to the Midland Railway and Great Western Railway. Although numerous objections were lodged against the sale, the Bill was approved and received Royal Assent in August 1894. The Severn & Wye Joint Railway was born. The deal included the Midland's branch from Berkeley Road to Sharpness.

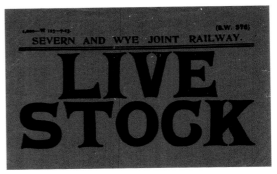

MRSC 18865

MRSC 18666

MRSC 18667

▼ This charming photograph of two young ladies enjoying the summer sunshine in the late 1940s was taken on the north bank of the river with the bridge in the background and the huge grain silo at Sharpness just visible in the distance beyond.

Only a few years previously, during WW2, some devil-may-care civilian pilots from the Air Transport Auxiliary (including at least one female pilot) chose to fly the aircraft they were ferrying to the airfield at Whitchurch (near Bristol) underneath the main spans of the bridge. This was very questionable behaviour with even a highly manoeuvrable machine such as a Spitfire with a wingspan of 36'-10'' and for a while the authorities seemed to turn a blind eye. However, the Air Ministry took fright when it came to their notice that a much larger and somewhat less manoeuvrable Wellington Bomber (wingspan 86'-2'') had also droned under the bridge. A detachment of RAF police were promptly despatched to the bridge specifically to record the identification markings of any aircraft repeating the stunt. After a few courts-martial of the culprits, the word quickly spread on the grapevine and the bridge was never 'buzzed' again!
Photograph: Gilbert Griffiths by courtesy of www.sungreen.co.uk

Under joint ownership the Severn & Wye could more easily weather the industrial ups and downs of the Forest. The most obvious change was that after ignoring it for so long GWR trains began rumbling through the girders. That apart, the bridge settled down to a relatively uneventful life. The Midland assumed responsibility for maintaining the permanent way, works, signals and gas fittings and carrying out new works on the line between Berkeley Road and Coleford Junction. This, of course, included the Severn Bridge. The MR also maintained the telegraphs and the weighing machines over the whole S&W. The GWR looked after the remainder of the joint line and had the responsibility for maintaining "all Water Appliances for locomotive purposes" Day to day operation of the S&W was in the hands of the Joint Traffic Inspector based at Lydney Town who reported to both the MR District Controller at Gloucester and the GW Divisional Superintendent at Gloucester.

The Severn Railway Bridge from the down platform of Severn Bridge Station taken by the late Henry Casserley on 5th July 1947. Like its Scottish cousin across the Forth, the bridge needed to be painted at regular intervals and four of the five intermediate (174 ft length) spans have recently received attention. Photo: H.C.Casserley by courtesy of R.M.Casserley

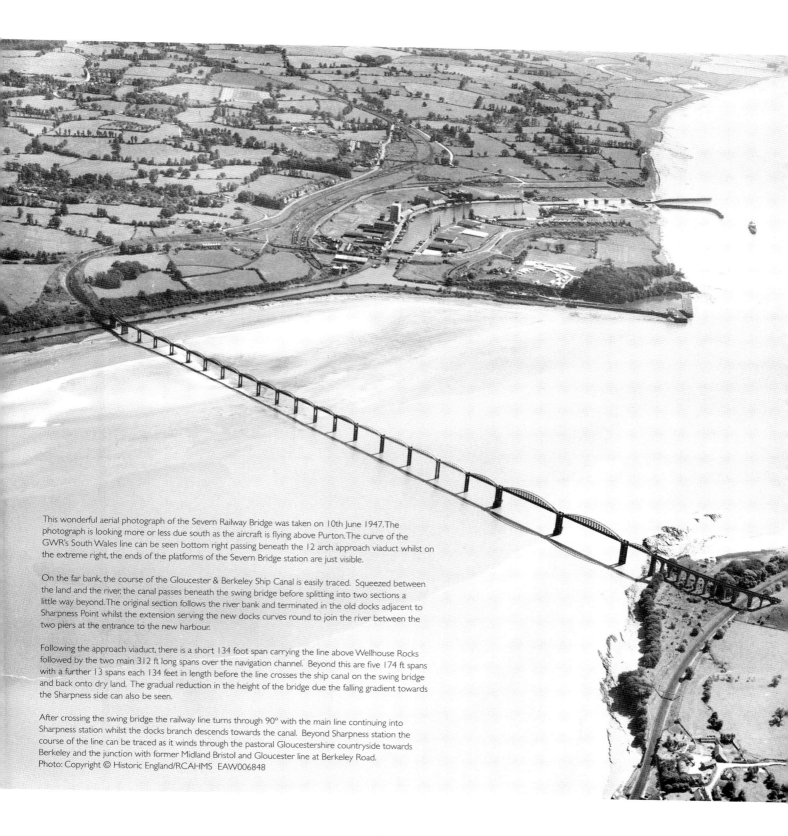

This wonderful aerial photograph of the Severn Railway Bridge was taken on 10th June 1947. The photograph is looking more or less due south as the aircraft is flying above Purton. The curve of the GWR's South Wales line can be seen bottom right passing beneath the 12 arch approach viaduct whilst on the extreme right, the ends of the platforms of the Severn Bridge station are just visible.

On the far bank, the course of the Gloucester & Berkeley Ship Canal is easily traced. Squeezed between the land and the river, the canal passes beneath the swing bridge before splitting into two sections a little way beyond. The original section follows the river bank and terminated in the old docks adjacent to Sharpness Point whilst the extension serving the new docks curves round to join the river between the two piers at the entrance to the new harbour.

Following the approach viaduct, there is a short 134 foot span carrying the line above Wellhouse Rocks followed by the two main 312 ft long spans over the navigation channel. Beyond this are five 174 ft spans with a further 13 spans each 134 feet in length before the line crosses the ship canal on the swing bridge and back onto dry land. The gradual reduction in the height of the bridge due the falling gradient towards the Sharpness side can also be seen.

After crossing the swing bridge the railway line turns through 90° with the main line continuing into Sharpness station whilst the docks branch descends towards the canal. Beyond Sharpness station the course of the line can be traced as it winds through the pastoral Gloucestershire countryside towards Berkeley and the junction with former Midland Bristol and Gloucester line at Berkeley Road.
Photo: Copyright © Historic England/RCAHMS EAW006848

Only the very lightest of the Midland, LMS and GWR's locomotives were allowed on the bridge. Double heading was strictly forbidden and in the event of a locomotive failing on the bridge, the rules required that there must be at least four wagons between the disabled locomotive and the rescuing loco to act as barrier vehicles. Speed across the bridge was limited to 15 miles per hour which equated to at least three minutes to cross from one side to the other..

On several occasions during the post grouping period the GWR asked the LMS to consider raising the weight limit for locomotives using the bridge, especially when the bridge was used as a diversionary route when the Severn Tunnel was closed. The frequency of these closures was increasing as the tunnel grew older. On each occasion the request was refused. However, following nationalisation and regional boundary changes, the operation of the bridge and its maintenance became the responsibility of the Western Region. The WR Civil Engineer was more sympathetic to the idea of raising the weight limit on the bridge, but before deciding he called on the resources of the BR Research Department in Derby for advice.

The result was that during the summer of 1956 the boffins from Derby installed strain gauges on the parts of the structure that they predicted would be subjected to the greatest loading when a train was crossing so that the long term effects of easing the weight restriction could be assessed. This included the likelihood of fatigue failure, the knowledge and understanding of which had improved considerably since Colonel Rich had inspected the bridge on behalf of the Board of Trade in 1879. The size of locomotives had increased considerably in the intervening period too.

No. 1639, a 16XX Class 0-6-0 pannier tank, ▲ rumbles across the bridge on 19th October 1956 with a down Class K freight. The loco, one of ten of the class allocated to Lydney for working the Severn & Wye lines, was built by BR at Swindon in 1951 to a design whose origins could be traced back to 1874. Having a very light axle loading of just under 14 tons, the class were ideal for working the Forest of Dean branches and across the Severn Bridge. To get this shot, the photographer, Brian Hillier, says that he was standing in the gap between spans so that he was well clear of the loco and the train, but he had to remember not to take another step backwards as there nothing to stop him falling 70 feet into the river below – and life jackets were not provided!
Photograph by courtesy of Brian Hillier

When he inspected the bridge in 1879, Col. Rich had used eight locomotives coupled together to provide the live test load. This time two GWR 4-6-0 Castle Class locomotives, each weighing in at over 120 tons, were used to provide the dynamic load. The Drivers and Firemen of the two locos, 5018 St. Mawes Castle and 5042 Winchester Castle must have been more than a little apprehensive about taking two locomotives onto a bridge that normally carried only a single locomotive of considerably less than half the weight of one of their Castles!

Interestingly, the maximum deflection of the main 312 foot span when the two Castles were crossing was 1½ inches, (approx 1/2500 of the span), the same as recorded by Col. Rich in 1879. Back in Derby, a careful analysis of the test results concluded that the diagonal bracings were subjected to the greatest stress but due to the over design of the structure the occasional failure of one of these would not cause an immediate and catastrophic failure of the span. This over design is known as structural redundancy and although it increases the initial cost, it equally provides increased margins of safety.

Provided that regular and thorough inspections were carried out, it was decided that Castle class locomotives could be allowed to work across the bridge occasionally without causing too much harm. However, it was recommended that to extend the long term life of the bridge as a whole, the diagonal bracings should all be replaced by ones of a more substantial design.

The contract for the work (worth £95,000) was awarded to the Fairfield Bridge & Shipbuilding Company who were based nearby in Chepstow. Work was to be carried out at night with Fairfield's given full possession of the bridge after the last up train (a freight) had crossed at around 10.00pm. The erectors set up their base at Severn Bridge station and began working from the Purton Side.

By the end of September 1960 the first short span and the two long spans across the navigation channel had had their new bracings fitted. Fairfield's then moved on to work on the five intermediate length (174 feet) spans.

THE NIGHT THE RIVER SEVERN CAUGHT FIRE...

In the early evening of Tuesday the 25th October 1960 the navigation lights of over a dozen small coastal vessels could be seen taking advantage of the incoming tide and sailing fairly close together in convoy up the River Severn heading towards either Lydney or Sharpness. Amongst those in the flotilla were two fuel barges the m.v. Wastdale H carrying 351 tons of petroleum spirit from Avonmouth to Worcester and a sister ship, the m.v. Arkendale H. The latter, which was also bound for Worcester, was carrying 296 tons of Britoleum light fuel oil which it had loaded earlier in the day at Swansea. Both barges, which were owned by John Harker Ltd of Knottingley and carrying a crew of four, were heading initially for Sharpness from where they would continue their onward journey to Gloucester by canal. From there they would complete the voyage to their final destination along the Severn.

The voyage was uneventful until around 9.30 pm when the flotilla ran into a bank of thick fog that straddled the river in the vicinity of the Berkeley Nuclear Power Station which was then still under construction. This was a fairly common phenomenon and as the vessels were not equipped with radar, the crews were well versed in listening for the fog horn on Sharpness Pier to guide them safely home. There was also a well rehearsed manoeuvre for boats to enter Sharpness harbour against the strong Severn tides. This involved overshooting the harbour entrance before turning and heading back under full power against the tide.

The Arkendale H, which was under the command of 35 year old George Thompson, was in the process of turning ready to enter the harbour when the tug Addie, bound for Lydney, suddenly appeared out of the fog in front of the Arkendale's bow. The Addie which was towing three lighters carrying timber had been part of the flotilla that had left Avonmouth earlier that evening. To avoid ramming the Addie and its tow, skipper Thompson put the Arkendale in full astern. His prompt action allowed the tug and its and its lighters to cross his path safely, but rather more seriously the Arkendale had lost all its forward momentum which, even under full power, it was unable to regain and the vessel began to be carried out of control by the tidal currents.

It can be seen from the map earlier in the chapter and aerial photograph of the river that between the bridge and the piers

▼ The MV Arkendale H.
Photo by courtesy Chris Witts

at the entrance to Sharpness docks, the land on that side projects out into the river to what is known as Sharpness Point. The narrowing of the river not only increases the speed of the incoming tide but alters its direction. The resulting back eddy creates the treacherous currents that had caught the Arkendale H.

In the meantime, the Wastdale H was also having problems. Its skipper, 42 year old James Dew had only been in charge of the vessel for three days whilst his regular command was in dry-dock. He had decided to play safe and find the river bank and wait until the weather conditions improved, but on hearing the Sharpness fog horn he changed his mind and decided to try to make it into the harbour. However, when Dew eventually caught sight of land he realised that he was too far north, near the entrance to the old harbour at Sharpness Point. As Dew turned to head south with the Wastdale H, he got caught in the same vicious current that the Arkendale H was already fighting a loosing battle against.

As he fought against the tide to head south with the Wastdale H, the already out of control Arkendale H suddenly appeared out of the fog. The vicious tidal currents were carrying the two barges inexorably towards each other and the vessels collided. As the two skippers fought desperately to separate their boats from the current that now held them together, the same current was sweeping the barges sideways upstream towards the Severn Railway bridge. The skippers' efforts to regain control were in vain. Some six minutes later, at about 10.30 pm, the port bow of the Wastdale H collided with bridge pier number 17.

The force of the impact was tremendous. Not only did it turn the vessel over onto its side, the pair of concrete filled iron columns that made up pier 17 toppled into the river followed by the two 174 foot span girders that it had supported. The girders fell onto the Arkendale H which after the collision had ridden up on top of the Wastdale H. Inevitably, the contents of both barges began to empty into the river and a spark, probably generated by the falling structure, ignited the highly flammable petrol vapour. In turn, this ignited the fuel oil leaking from the Arkendale H. Before long the fire had spread across almost the whole width of the river, creating so much heat that the fog cleared locally. Under such circumstances it is remarkable that anyone on the two barges survived the inferno, but James Dew, skipper of the Wastdale H and George Thompson, skipper of Arkendale H, together with the latter's engineer, Jack Cooper, somehow did manage to escape. Sadly their five shipmates were not so lucky.

By the end of the night the blazing barges, locked together by rails that had fallen from the bridge, drifted upstream until they grounded on The Ridge sandbank about a half a mile beyond the bridge.

Of course, the disaster could have been many, many times worse. One shudders at the thought of what the death toll would have been if a passenger train had been crossing at the time the bridge fell – shades of the terrible Tay Bridge disaster of 1879.

The final resting place of the Arkendale H, seen here on the left whilst its cargo of fuel oil was still ablaze. Alongside is the Wastdale H lying on its side. The rusting hulks of both vessels can be still be seen on The Ridge sandbank at low tide. Photograph: Chris Witts Collection.

A stark and rather sad portrait of the broken bridge taken on 13th May 1961 during the period that BR were still considering replacing the missing spans. Unfortunately, it was not to be...
Photo: H.C.Casserley, courtesy of R.M.Casserley.

But one curious story which seems to have become enshrined in Forest of Dean folk law is that the late, great, British heavyweight boxing champion, Henry Cooper, was responsible for saving several more from a watery grave that night. The story goes that the Fairfield's men working on strengthening the bridge should have been working on the spans that fell into the river. However, they had decided to make a late start and forgo a later break to remain at Severn Bridge station in order to listen to a radio commentary of a fight between Cooper and a German boxer, Karl Müller.

The facts however tell a somewhat different story. No less an authority than the British Boxing Board of Control have confirmed that "Our 'Enry" was not scheduled to fight anywhere that night, neither do they have any record of a heavyweight boxer by the name of Karl Müller being active around that time! On the factual side, the Fairfield men all certainly escaped unscathed from the disaster and between 9.15 pm and 10.30 pm that night the BBC's Light Programme did broadcast a live boxing commentary. This was a not a heavyweight bout but a title fight for the vacant World Bantamweight Championship at the Empire Pool, Wembley between the French boxer Alphonse Halimi and Freddie Gilroy from Belfast. For the record, the Frenchman won on points.

The bridge had become something that the inhabitants of Lydney and Sharpness and the surrounding districts took for granted. Few, if any, of even the oldest residents could not have remembered what life had been like before it opened. Before trains began rumbling across the bridge, the journey by road or rail between the two towns, via Gloucester, was around 40 miles. The alternative, albeit much shorter option, by ferry across the swirling, unpredictable waters of the Severn was definitely not for the faint hearted. The bridge changed all that. From Sharpness, the distance by rail to Lydney Junction was a mere 4 miles; to Lydney Town 4¾ miles with journey times of around 12 and 15 minutes respectively, which included the stop at Severn Bridge station. Many children from Sharpness attended schools across the river in Lydney; equally, many of the adult residents of both towns had found employment in businesses on the opposite side of the water to their homes.

For the British Transport Commission (the forerunner of the British Railways Board), the bridge disaster was a conundrum. In financial terms the bridge probably ran at a loss (British Railways' annual loss in 1960 was £42 million) so it was a liability rather than an asset. However, the bridge's value as a social amenity was enormous, a fact that a publicly owned and funded body simply could not ignore. In addition to rail traffic the bridge also carried a 12 inch diameter gas main (which served the Forest side) and GPO telephone cables.

By November 1960, the Western Region's Civil Engineer had formulated a scheme whereby the missing pier 17 would be replaced by a new concrete pier and pier 16, which had been damaged and knocked out of alignment by the disaster, would be repaired. This would allow the missing spans to be replaced by a single, welded, mild steel span supported in the centre by the new concrete pier 17.

But the slings and arrows of outrageous misfortune were still aimed at the crippled bridge, ready to inflict even more pain on the wounded structure.

On Friday 17th February 1961, less than four months after the disaster, another loaded fuel barge, the BP Explorer collided with the bridge. The vessel which was owned by Shell-Mex and B.P. Ltd., but being operated by John Harker Ltd., had earlier run aground and capsized in the Count's Channel, seven or eight miles downstream of the bridge with the loss of all five members of the crew. The upturned vessel had then been carried upstream by the rising tide and had safely passed under the bridge. However, before the capsized barge could be secured, the receding tide carried it back downstream but this time it collided with pier 20, causing damage estimated at nearly £13,000.

By then the first contract to begin repairing the bridge had been placed. This involved building a supporting trestle adjacent to pier 16 to reduce the load on the pier whilst remedial work was being carried out. In order to do this the contractors had hired the twin floating crane Tweedledum and Tweedledee but this did not arrive on site until after the BP Explorer incident.

But exactly seven weeks after the BP tanker had hit the bridge, the crane sent to begin the bridge repairs also made a significant contribution to its ultimate downfall.

On Friday 14th April 1961, the force of the incoming Severn tide put too much strain on its mooring ropes and Tweedledum and Tweedledee broke free and drifted upstream towards Awre on the tide. As it happened in daylight, the alarm was quickly raised and a boat soon set off from Sharpness in hot pursuit to capture the renegade crane. In scenes reminiscent of a Victorian melodrama, after several unsuccessful attempts to gain control of the crane, the propeller of the rescue vessel became fouled by a rope and those on board could then only watch helplessly as their quarry was carried back downstream towards the bridge on the ebb tide. Once again, pier 20 bore the brunt of the collision but this time, the crane's jib also hit the structure before the terrible twins ran aground near Lydney.

Although the "official line" was that the bridge would be still be repaired, doubts about the viability of doing so must have been growing at the British Transport Commission headquarters in London. The final straw probably came when it was discovered that John Harker's marine insurance liability was limited to a mere £5000. In spite of Harker's being jointly sued for damages in the High Court by the BTC, the Fairfield Bridge & Shipbuilding Co., the South Western Gas Board and the Postmaster General, the latter two received no compensation at all. Fairfield's were awarded a derisory sum of just over £100 but the BTC did get the full £5000. However when compared to the cost of repairing the bridge, this was an even more derisory amount than Fairfield's.

The BTC's days however were numbered. Unable to stem the haemorrhaging of public money by the railways, the Conservative Government decided that from 1st January 1963, the BTC would be abolished and replaced by a new British Railways Board. This would not be headed by a railwayman, but by an outsider. The first Chairman, seconded from ICI, was an economist, Dr. Richard Beeching. The rest is history ...

It is interesting to speculate about what the Severn Railway Bridge's fate, had it still have been functional, would have been under the Beeching regime. Passenger services on the S&W through the Forest from Lydney Town to Lydbrook Junction and the branches to CInderford and Coleford had been withdrawn as early as 1929. The only passenger services to survive the cull were those between Lydney Town to Berkeley Road. The fall of the bridge saw the immediate withdrawal of trains between Lydney Town and Severn Bridge station, but passenger services continued between Sharpness and Berkeley Road until November 1964. Most of the line was then retained for freight traffic generated by the new Berkeley nuclear power station.

With an estimated price tag of £300,000 to repair the bridge, it was becoming clear that those in authority were getting cold feet about authorising the repairs. By 1962 rumours that the bridge was to be abandoned began to circulate locally, but these were denied by BR who said that no firm decision had then been reached. Whether the BR spokesman was speaking with his tongue firmly in his cheek will probably never be known, but by the following year, BR was actively negotiating with the Central Electricity Generating Board for them to take over the bridge to carry high voltage cables across the river. However, after a promising start, the CEGB lost interest in the idea.

After the disaster in 1960, as well as repairing the bridge, the option of demolishing it was also seriously considered. Initially being discounted because of the costs involved, by 1965 it was rapidly becoming the only option open to BR. Indeed, in the summer of 1965, BR invited a group of high ranking British Army demolition experts to visit the bridge to assess the possibility of removing it as a military exercise. Led by a Brigadier, accompanied by an impressive entourage of lesser ranking 'top brass' officers, the group seemed initially interested, but once again, the interest soon waned and another door closed.

With nowhere else to go other than to grasp the nettle, BR invited no less than twenty four contractors to tender for the demolition of the bridge. Significantly, the majority, when the full scope of the work became apparent, followed the British Army's lead and retreated poste haste! The specification called for the bridge structure to be completely dismantled and the support columns and foundations be removed to the level of the river bed. The stone approach viaduct on the Purton side was also to be demolished in its entirety and the rubble removed from the site.

The contract was eventually awarded to Nordman Construction who were not even on the original list, but whose quotation was the lowest. Nordman, who had only been in business for six years, certainly put a lot of time and thought into planning the bridge's removal before announcing that work would start during the summer of 1967. After some preliminary work had been carried out, the massive German owned floating crane, Magnus II, was hired to quickly remove the structure. With its fly jib reaching to a height of 150 feet high and possessing a lifting capacity of 400 tons, Magnus II was certainly the right tool for the job. Highly manoeuvrable (it could rotate about its own centre line), it was at the cutting edge of floating crane technology. To counter balance the load on its hook and keep it stable, the crane was capable of quickly pumping thousands of gallons of water into its ballast tanks. It arrived on site after a week long voyage, under tow, from Hamburg on 22nd August 1967 and began work two days later by removing the remaining two 174 feet long spans on the Sharpness side. For anyone interested, a detailed account of the work carried out by Magnus II can be found in Ron Huxley's excellent book "The Rise and Fall of the Severn Railway Bridge 1872 – 1970" (ISBN 978-1-84868-033-3).

In spite of the effort that Nordman had put into planning the operation and the very promising start they had made with the floating crane, progress was soon reduced to a snail's pace, primarily because the company had only managed to recruit about ten percent of the specialist labour force of 60 or so, that it anticipated it would need. By the spring of 1968, BR were growing rather impatient at the delays, but these delays were also seriously affecting Nordman's financial situation. The terms of their contract with BR did not allow for any interim payments to be made. Thus, until the work was fully completed to BR's satisfaction, Nordman were responsible for financing the project themselves, but this was against a background of increasing difficulties in obtaining extended credit. To add to their woes, Nordman were in dispute with the owners of Magnus II, which resulted in a High Court claim and counter claim over the definition of "a day" in respect of hire charges. It seems Nordman had assumed that "a day" meant 24 hours, whereas the Magnus's owners considered it to be only a working day.

Although BR eventually relented and made an interim payment of £50,000 to Nordman, the company went into receivership in November 1968 and were subsequently liquidated. To cut this long and very sad part of the story short, BR decided to finish the job themselves using specialist subcontractors. The final act, the demolition of the masonry Pier 1, using high explosives, took place on 13th May 1970. Today, the only tangible remains of this once important and significant example of Victorian railway engineering are the circular stone tower on the canal towpath, that once carried the swing bridge and the short approach viaduct on the opposite side of the canal. (OS ref ST678034). Also, well over 50 years after the disaster, the remains of the hulks of the Arkendale H and the Wastdale H can still be seen in the distance at low tide from the canal towpath.

OPERATING
OVER
THE SEVERN
BRIDGE

From the beginning of the railway age, it was recognised that the basic tenet for the for the safe operation of a single line section was that only ONE train be allowed in that section at a given time. In the early days this was achieved by means of having a single metal or wooden staff which was given to the driver and carried through the section on the locomotive. Different single line sections had different shaped staffs (ie) round, square or hexagonal and for additional security staffs were painted different colours. An extension to this was the staff and ticket system. If a second train was to follow the first one through the section, the driver of the first train was shown the staff, but then given a ticket which then became his authority to travel through the section. The staff was then carried by the driver of the second train. However, the system was found to be rather restrictive and more importantly, not entirely foolproof, so engineers began looking at more flexible and safer alternatives. First on the scene was a system devised by Edward Tyer, an English signal and telegraph engineer whose first 'electric train tablet' instrument was patented in March 1878. The alternative Webb Thompson 'electric train staff' system soon followed which was adopted by some railways but the Midland, along with numerous others, opted to use Tyer's system.

Not content to rest on his laurels, Edward Tyer produced a number of refinements to his original design to improve reliability and flexibility. By the time he died on Christmas Day 1912, Edward Tyer had the satisfaction of knowing that his electric tablet machines had an impeccable 100% safety record.

In simple terms, every single line section that used the system had a Tyer's tablet machine installed at each end. The machines, which were electrically interlocked, both contained a number of 'tablets' which in reality were identical metal or fibre discs. Although there were variations, the majority of tablets were $4^3/_8$ inches in diameter by $^3/_8$ of an inch thick. A train was not permitted to enter a single line section without the driver being in possession of a tablet for that section and obeying all the associated signals. Communication between the machines was by means of plungers which caused a bell to strike in the other signalbox.

The interlocking was such that once a tablet had been withdrawn from one of the machines, it was impossible to

▲ A sketch of a Tyer's Electric Train Tablet based on a photograph of one of the actual Severn Bridge to Sharpness tablets in the Dean Forest Railway's Museum at Norchard. Each tablet was identical except for its identification number, in this case, 25. As mentioned in the text the tablets were 43/8 inches in diameter and 3/8 of an inch thick. The example on display at Norchard is metal.

withdraw another tablet from either machine until the first tablet had been replaced. Early versions of Tyer's machines were "non restoring" meaning that a withdrawn tablet could only be placed in the machine at the opposite end of the section. Later versions were more flexible allowing a tablet to be replaced in either machine. On the face of each tablet was inscribed the names of the ends of the section that it related to – for example "SEVERN BRIDGE – SHARPNESS." Although all the tablets for a particular section were identical, their shape was unique to prevent them being inserted into the wrong machine at the end of the section. This was achieved by means of different sized and shaped cut-outs, both in the centre and around the periphery of the tablet, as per the sketch opposite.

After being withdrawn from a machine, the tablet was placed in a thick leather pouch attached to a metal hoop, the hoop making it easier for the pouch to be caught by the footplate crew (usually the fireman) and/or signalman when a train was moving. One face of the pouch was cut away to form a window, so that the driver could read the inscription on the tablet and verify immediately that he had been given the correct one. Thus, being in possession of a tablet for a section and observing the relevant signals was not only the driver's authority to enter that section, it was his guarantee that his was the only train in the section. (Note - although I have used the past tense, the Tyer's system is still in use on a number of Britain's Heritage Railways today).

The Tyer's system, although rigid in terms of safety, was flexible in terms of operation. Each pair of machines contained a total of 30 tablets which could allow a procession of several trains through the section in the same direction. This was useful on special occasions, such as sporting events, race meetings or agricultural shows when there would be a heavy traffic flow in one direction in the morning and the corresponding return workings in the opposite direction, later in the day.

When the Severn Bridge opened in 1879, Tyer's machines were still very much in their infancy so the single line section across the bridge between the signal box at Sharpness Station (4m 15ch from Berkeley Road Junction) to the signal box at Severn Bridge Station (5m 42ch) was worked by the traditional staff and ticket system. This, as remarked earlier, was not entirely foolproof even on normal single lines. However, the Severn Bridge was not an ordinary single line section, because part of the bridge structure included the swing bridge that spanned the Gloucester & Berkeley Ship Canal. Thus, whenever the swing bridge was open for boats on the canal, there was a 200 foot long gap in the railway track.

In August 1889 the train staff and ticket system was replaced by a pair of Tyer's No.2 machines which were installed in the Sharpness Station and Severn Bridge Station signalboxes. These incorporated modified interlocking arrangements that ensured that the swing bridge operation did not compromise the safety of trains crossing the Severn Bridge.

Tyer's No.2 machines were the so called "non restoring" type where once a tablet had been withdrawn it could only be replaced in the machine at the opposite end of the section. In order to minimise problems in connection with this, strict instructions were issued to the effect that all station work had to be complete and the train was waiting to depart before a tablet was obtained.

The Canal Swing Bridge Signalbox, to give it its official title, was located 4 miles 52 chains from Berkeley Road Junction and was mounted across the top of the bridge structure so that trains could pass beneath. The name signalbox is perhaps a little misleading because it only controlled three signals – and one of those was for shipping on the canal! The main purpose of the building was to house the boilers, the engines and the controls that rotated the bridge, plus of course, the vital interlocking with the tablet machines at each end of the section.

The Swing Bridge box lever frame had seven levers. No.1 was the electric lock, No.2 locked and unlocked the bridge, No.3 was spare, No.4 operated the Up Home signal, No.5 the Down Home signal, No.6 was another spare and No.7 operated the canal signal.

According to the Severn & Wye Joint Railway's General Appendix dated 1st May 1906, when the railway was closed, the bridge was left open to allow boats on the canal to pass unhindered. During periods when the railway was open, the

Although this photograph was taken far away from the Severn Bridge, in an MR signalbox in Derbyshire, it is included to illustrate a typical Tyer's Electric Train Tablet Machine. Starting right at the top, is the bell box, the open coil of wire on the front which when struck vibrates and resembles the sound of a bell. Below this the round topped, glass fronted, timber box contains indicators which show if a tablet is IN or OUT and for which direction. In centre of the panel below the window is the plunger which operates the bell in the signalbox at the opposite end of the section and provided the main means communication between the two signalmen. Surrounding the plunger is a knob (known as the commutator) which is rotated through 90° to lock or unlock the slide in the bottom section of the machine. In the photograph, a tablet has been withdrawn and can be seen on the left, ready to be placed in one of the leather pouches seen hanging on the right.

The bottom section of the machine is a heavy cast iron box which contains the tablets, which are issued or returned via the metal slide or drawer. The large aperture in the drawer is designed so that only the correct shaped tablet can be inserted. When a tablet is returned it is stacked by pulling the restoring lever seen on the left hand side. The quantity of tablets in the stack can be seen through the glass panel above the drawer. Photo by courtesy of the National Railway Museum DY13984

▲ This view of the swing bridge which carried the railway across the Gloucester & Berkeley Canal was taken in October 1956. Note the railway type semaphore signal the top of which is visible to the right of the signal box. The arm of this was lowered to indicate to approaching boats that the bridge was about to open so there was no need to reduce speed. The circular stone support tower and the approach viaduct, (just visible in the shadow on the right of the photograph), are now the only tangible remains of the Severn Railway Bridge. (OS ref ST678034). Photograph by courtesy of Brian Hillier.

bridge was normally closed to canal traffic, but unless a train was due, the bridge was unlocked, ready to be swung open immediately. The fact that the bridge was unlocked, broke the electrical circuit between the tablet machines in both the Sharpness and Severn Bridge Station signal boxes, making it impossible to withdraw a tablet from either machine.

Vessels on the canal that needed the bridge to be opened were required to give an audible warning (three blasts on their horn or whistle) when about a quarter of a mile from the bridge. However, the signalmen were also required to keep a sharp lookout for the approach of any tall sailing vessels that were unable to give any such clear audible warning. If the bridge could be opened, the signal was lowered to indicate that there was no need for the boat to slow down. If the signal remained horizontal, it meant that a rail movement across the bridge was imminent and the approaching vessel would have to wait. After dark, the signal displayed the usual red or green aspects when it was across the canal. When the bridge was fully open, white navigation lights would be visible on both ends of the structure.

The Canal Swing Bridge signal box was normally staffed by two men, a signalman and an engine driver. In reality, the latter was the busier of the two for in addition to operating the bridge, he was responsible for keeping the two engines clean and in good order and looking after the two boilers which were used on a fortnight about basis. After a boiler had completed its two weeks in service, the engine driver was responsible for washing it out and cleaning the tubes and firebars, ready for its next turn of duty. The signalman was also tasked with helping with cleaning the engines and with the coaling. In the event of either man finding himself on duty alone, he had to be competent to perform the missing man's duties.

When the signalman at Sharpness or Severn Bridge became aware that an engine or train that required to cross the bridge was approaching his box, he first had to telephone his opposite number to ascertain if he was in a position to accept the engine or train. Let us assume, as an example, that it is a down train from Berkeley Road approaching Sharpness station. After talking to the Severn Bridge man on the telephone to confirm that the latter was able to accept the train, Sharpness would send "Call Attention" (a single beat on the tapper bell) to the Swing Bridge Box. When this was acknowledged, Sharpness would continue by sending the appropriate "Is Line Clear for ... ?" bell code to the Swing Bridge. If the bridge was open to allow a vessel to pass along the canal, the Swing Bridge man would immediately send "Obstruction Danger" (six consecutive beats) back to Sharpness. If the bridge was closed, but unlocked, the Swing Bridge man would respond by repeating the "Is Line Clear for" code back to Sharpness. Having done this, the Swing Bridge man would reverse (pull) Lever 2 followed by Lever 1. Pulling Lever 2 locked the bridge; Lever 1 locked lever 2 and operated a switch which closed the electrical circuit between the tablet machines in the Sharpness and Severn Bridge boxes which would then allow Sharpness to obtain a tablet. The withdrawal of a tablet in turn locked Lever 1 in the reverse position. The Swing Bridge man also cleared his Down Home signal which was located in the approach cutting on the Sharpness side.

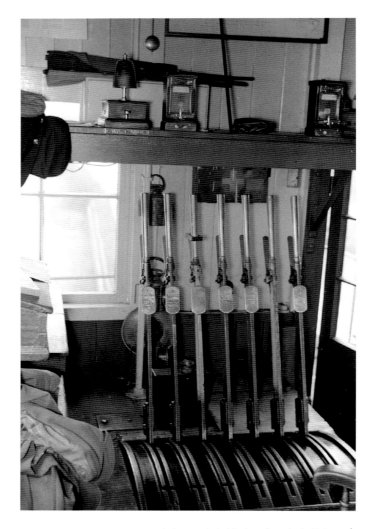

A close up shot of the lever frame in the Swing Bridge Signal Box in October 1956. The levers, which were numbered from left to right, are 1 – Electric Switch, 2 – Bridge Bolted/Unbolted, 3 – Spare, 4 – Up Home Signal, 5 – Down Home Signal, 6 – Spare, 7 – Canal Signal. On the shelf above the levers can be seen, on the left, the tapper bell to communicate with Severn Bridge Signal Box. The instruments centre and right are bridge locking indicators. Note the other essential items of signalling equipment on the back wall – a set of flags (red, yellow and green) and oil lamps for signalling at night. With Levers 1 and 2 in this (the normal) position, the tablet machines in Sharpness and Severn Bridge Station Signal Boxes were both locked so that the bridge could be swung if required. Both lever 2 and lever 1 had to be reversed (pulled) before a train could be allowed into the section
Photograph by courtesy of Brian Hillier

▲ The Swing Bridge Signal Box photographed from the first fixed span of the bridge looking towards Sharpness. Note the restricted clearance type Up Home Signal with its inboard spectacle plate fixed to the bridge structure. Note also the 12 inch diameter pipe on the left that supplied gas to parts of the Forest of Dean. Photograph by courtesy of Brian Hillier

▼ The Swing Bridge signalmen's "view from the office" looking across the Severn towards Purton, The swing bridge was designed to accommodate two tracks, but in the event, even the single line was under used. Photograph by courtesy of Brian Hillier.

The use of the "Obstruction Danger" bell code was unusual. Under normal circumstances hearing "six bells" would produce a heart stopping moment for the signalman at the receiving end. At best it could be simply a warning that a cow had strayed onto the line; at worst that a major disaster had occurred in the section. That said, it could be argued that a 200 foot gap in the track could be classed as an obstruction!

Other special bell codes used between the three boxes were as follows:

Train arrived, ready to unlock bridge	2 pause 1
Train arrived, but another one waiting	3 pause 2
Release Bridge Lock	2 consecutively
Bridge unlocked	2 pause 2
Lock Bridge for testing	4 pause 4 pause 4 pause 4

The first two are fairly self explanatory. After inserting the tablet in his machine he sent either a two-one or a three-two to Swing Bridge and Sharpness. Two pause one was the standard bell code for "Train out of Section" but had an additional meaning here. Having received the two-one from Severn Bridge box, the Swing Bridge man would give two beats on his tapper bell to both Severn Bridge and Sharpness requesting the Bridge Lock to be released. To achieve this required both the Sharpness and Severn Bridge signalmen to press and hold their tablet machine bell plungers and their tapper keys until receiving the two-two from the Swing Bridge after the man there had normalised Levers 1 and 2. Certainly it was a little complicated, but requiring the cooperation of all three signalmen to release the bridge lock made accidental unlocking virtually impossible.

Later versions of Tyer's machines were termed 'restoring' as they allowed the tablet to be returned to either machine. Additionally, many were interlocked with their corresponding starting signal for additional safety. However, in the case of the Tyer's No.2 machines used on the Severn Bridge, the starting signals were released by the opposite signalbox (ie) the Sharpness Down Starter was released by the Severn Bridge box and vice versa. This required additional bell codes which were given on the tablet machines bells, not the tapper bells:

Release Starting Signal	3 pause 4
Starting Signal Lowered	4 pause 3

This was yet another safeguard because unless Swing Bridge Lever 1 was locked in the reverse position the electrical circuit between the two machine would be open and the bells would be inoperative. The Severn & Wye Appendix to the Working Timetables dated 1932 quotes the same bell codes as above, (plus a few additional ones) but unfortunately it does not specify which type of Tyer's machines were then in use.

In 1956, by which time the S&W had become the sole responsibility of BR's Western Region, the former MR branch from Berkeley Road to Sharpness was singled as part of an economy drive to reduce costs. The same programme also included the closure of Sharpness Station signalbox on 27th October 1957 when responsibility for control of the Severn Bridge on this side of the river was transferred to Sharpness South. Key token working over the Berkeley Road to Sharpness section was extended over the Severn Bridge replacing 68 years of faithful service by the Tyer's system.

As mentioned earlier, in addition to the lever frame and signalling indicators, the Swing Bridge signalbox contained the two boilers and the two, two-cylinder steam engines that rotated the bridge.

The engines which worked at a pressure of 60 lbs per square inch had 8 inch diameter bores by 16¼ inch stroke. The bridge rotated on a series of closely spaced heavy duty iron rollers which ran around the top of the stone tower. The drive shafts from the engines were extended to the outside of the box where separate gearboxes operated both the locking and rotating mechanisms.

Another view of the interior of the Swing Bridge Signalbox with part of the lever frame, seen earlier, just visible on the right of the right hand photograph. In the foreground can be seen part of the two steam engines (one in use, one spare) that rotated the bridge. On the left of the staging in front of the engines can be seen the controls for operating the bridge and the signalmen's high back, Windsor chair. When sitting in the chair with the bridge in the closed position, the signalman looked out across the river but was able to keep watch for vessels approaching along the canal through the windows on either side. Over the years the signalmen appear to have made several attempts to upholster the chair to make it more comfortable. Note the strategically placed Tilley Lamp above the chair for reading after dark.
Photograph by courtesy of Brian Hillier

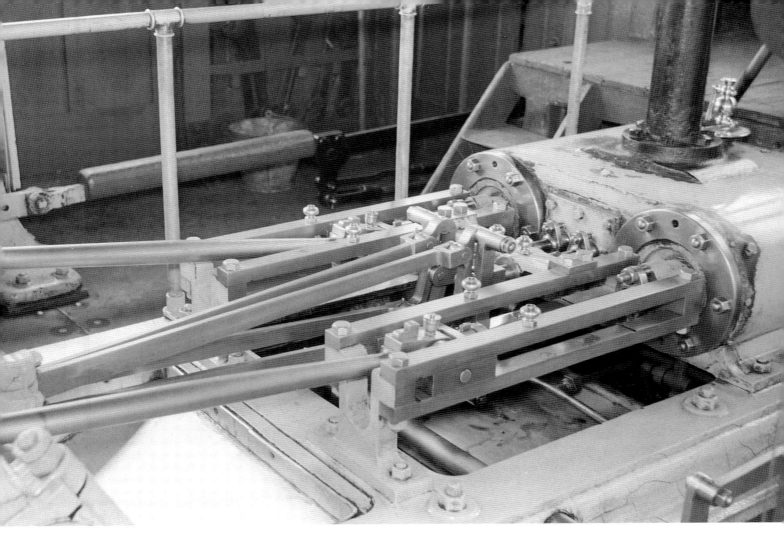

A close up shot of one of the pair of two-cylinder steam engines that powered the rotation of the bridge. The engines worked at a pressure of 60 psi and the cylinders were 8 inches bore by 16¼ stroke. Photograph by courtesy of Brian Hillier.

Mention has already been made that the Swing Bridge signalbox controlled two signals, an Up Home and a Down Home. The former was mounted on the fixed span of the bridge immediately before the swing bridge. The down home was located in the cutting approaching the bridge. For the obvious reasons, neither signal could be connected directly by wire to the Swing Bridge box in the normal way, but an ingenious, but never the less simple system was used to operate both signals as illustrated in Brian Hillier's photograph of the Down Home signal mechanism above. Here it is shown with the signal On (ie) in the Stop position. To clear the signal, the signalman reversed lever 5 in the signal box which is connected by wire to the top of the weighted lever on the left. This causes the lever to rotate a few degrees anticlockwise and in doing so moved the round slider bar connected to the bottom of the lever to the right.

This left hand slider bridges the gap between the bridge and terra firma and made contact with the right hand slider bar, the end of which has been belled out slightly to give a better contact. Further movement of the left hand slider caused the right hand lever to rotate. The wire connected to the top of the right hand lever then operated the signal. Note the fulcrum of the right hand lever is offset to compensate for the lost motion of the left slider bridging the gap. Effectively this was the final safety feature. If the bridge was only slightly out of alignment, the bridge home signals could not be cleared.

The author gratefully acknowledges the special help and advice provided by his Midland Railway Society colleagues, Dave Harris and Tony Overton and members of the Signalling Record Society, in the preparation of this final section of the chapter.

The operating mechanism ▲ for the Swing Bridge Down Home Signal is shown here with the signal On (ie) in the Stop position. A detailed explanation of its operation is given in the text. Photograph by courtesy of Brian Hillier.

THE PRINCESS
THAT DID
GO TO
THE BALL

Under a tarpaulin at Leicester station to hide its shame stood a once-proud single driver main line locomotive which was now used solely for supplying steam to pumping engines.

It was banished here in 1884 by a circular forbidding the use of any single drivers on the Midland owing to the many delays caused by wheelslip. The engine might have stayed in this ignominious position but for Robert Weatherburn, the District Locomotive Superintendent at Leicester, who "could not pass by the laid-up engine without the strong desire to make use of it."

He removed the tarpaulin and strengthened the springs by an extra plate. The sand-boxes were brought nearer to the wheels and the pipes trained as closely as possible to the tyres to ensure that the sand was delivered to the rail and not blown away. The alterations were completed the day before Leicester Fair and Weatherburn changed the engines of one train at Leicester, putting the single on to work south to London.

It was enough of a success for him to keep it working over the next few months, and he had almost forgotten the Circular until he was summoned to Derby by Samuel Waite Johnson, the Locomotive Superintendent of the Midland Railway. He was left in no doubt as to the importance of circular instructions, but Johnson also proved interested in axle loadings and the adjustments Weatherburn had made to achieve successful running, stopping and starting with this apparent misfit.

Although Johnson became the most famous of Midland designers, he was a pragmatist rather than a revolutionary who was inclined to wait until all the elements of a successful piece of motive power had fallen into place before manufacturing it. He was also adaptive enough to applaud initiatives such as Weatherburn`s and to make use of his new ideas, one of which was the use of a leading bogie. He would probably have been aware too of the Weatherburn`s family`s long association with the Midland Railway – his father had assisted George and Robert Stephenson on the footplate of the engine Comet when the Leicester and Swannington

Caption: World Fair at the palais de l'optique, "The 1900 big telescope", poster by Georges Leroux (1857-1957). Paris, musée Carnavalet.   Credit: © Musée Carnavalet / Roger-Viollet / TopFoto

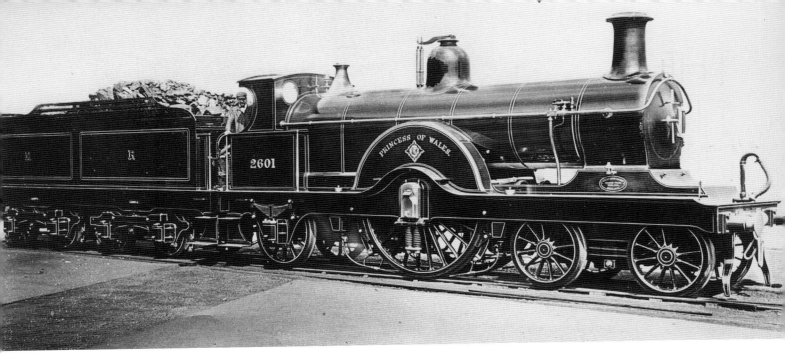

Railway was opened on July 17th 1832, and any association with that father of all pragmatic engineers was bound to stand him in good stead.

If Johnson needed more encouragement to re-engage with the single wheelers it came in the form of compressed air sanding developed by the works manager at Derby, Francis Holt, and trialled successfully on the Settle to Carlisle in 1886. After objections from Westinghouse that the use of "their" compressed air would compromise brake efficiency, Holt went on to pioneer the use of steam sanding.

Other things fell into place. The Great Northern was famous for its single driver engines, the Stirling Singles, and Johnson knew that they ran well with their flywheel motion and good fuel economy on the fluent Northern main line; he was more surprised when he removed the coupling rods on some of his 4-4-0 coupled engines and fitted them with the new sanding gear. In trials they did as well as the coupled engines on the level, and strangely showed up better on the gradients.

The stage was set for the big comeback. No.25 was the first to be built in June 1887, and a further 95 were built by Derby Works in the next 14 years. The revolution was complete and the "Spinners" were back in business. But how did the Princess get to the Ball?

Princess of Wales at ▼
Nottingham Station,
east end.

THE GIGANTIC IRON WATERLILY

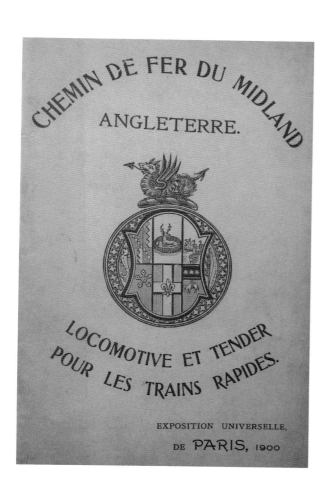

The Paris Exposition of 1900 was different; on that the authorities agree. For one thing, it was the springboard for Art Nouveau. For another, it was the first when art seemed predominant, instead of merely being a sideshow or embellishment to the works of the real superstars of the age, the engineers.

The Midland Railway was a keen participant, so much so that a brochure was produced in French, which remains in the collection of the Midland Railway Society in Derby. There cannot have been too many times when the Derby workforce saw themselves referred to as "Le Chemin de Fer Du Midland", but no doubt they took it in their stride, particularly when they saw that further on in the booklet their own "Chemin De Fer" seemed to dominate the railway map of La Grande Bretagne.

They were not alone in their admiration, for F. Barbier and R. Godferneaux in

"Les Locomotives à L`Exposition decembre 1900" said that the British locomotives exhibited were : "of a superb appearance and of a highly finished construction truly worthy of British engineers and that the extreme care in its execution and the harmony of its shape made "The Princess of Wales" the most remarkable engine at the exposition."

The Princess, Express Locomotive No.2601 of the Midland Railway, had arrived, and her Grand Prix was proudly displayed from then on. Her main rivals from Britain had been the LNWR`s La France and the Great Eastern`s Claud Hamilton, no mean competition.

It was not the first time that the Midland had conquered on the world stage. Another single, No.1853, had won a gold medal at the Paris International Exhibition of 1889, and one of Mr. Clayton`s fine Third Class coaches (with facilities rivalling most First Class carriages of the time) won a Grand Prix at the same event. So what sort of a victory was this? Historically, to win a prize in 1889, the exhibition which unveiled the Eiffel Tower to the world, was landmark enough. However, many of the countries that still had crowned heads at this point felt uneasy enough about this celebration of the centenary of the French Revolution for them to be either lukewarm about their contributions or to stay away. By contrast, the Exposition of 1900 had a full house, as everyone wanted to be there to mark the centennial. Germany, despite having its nose put out having lost the race to put the exhibition on in this important year, sportingly contributed handsomely in both buildings and exhibits. Britain`s contribution seemed very low-key in contrast, a Lutyens-designed manor house that echoed the influence of the Arts and Crafts movement in Britain at the time but did not seem to be in the forward-looking spirit of the majority. There was some diplomatic coolness between Britain and France at the time since there had been considerable French condemnation of the Boer War, so perhaps at least the quiet excellence of Mr. Johnson`s locomotive at this pivotal year in history stood as a reminder of what the exhibitions were really about – to celebrate and educate. In Prince Albert`s words, they were to show a

"true text and a living picture of the point of development at which the whole of mankind has arrived".

The French were the first to hold industrial exhibitions, and these stretched back to 1797 in the middle of the Napoleonic wars. In 1799 the Jacquard loom was displayed, an invention that certainly changed the course of the cloth industry. However, protectionism and perhaps lack of confidence (M.Buffet, the French Minister of Agriculture and Commerce, had suggested that the 1849 exhibition should be international in scope but the call was rejected) meant that the British Exhibition of 1851 was the first truly international one. There were no doubt some who felt nervous about passing on industrial secrets to the rest of the world, but the spirit of free trade, always a principle in this country, meant that in the words of commentators of the time: "Through it all one senses the tremendous thirst for knowledge, faith in life and almost religious fervour which was displayed by the exhibition and the visitors themselves." Prince Albert spoke with evangelical zeal of the differences between nations vanishing in the face of new invention, of the potential for the unity of mankind. And if there was anxiety beforehand about how British products would show up against the rest of the world`s, the evidence is that they need not have worried.

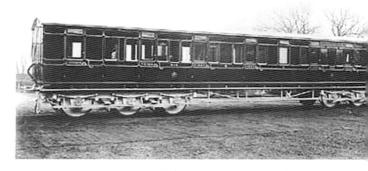

Clayton`s prizewinning ▲
coach, 1889

G.E.R. Claud Hamilton. ▼

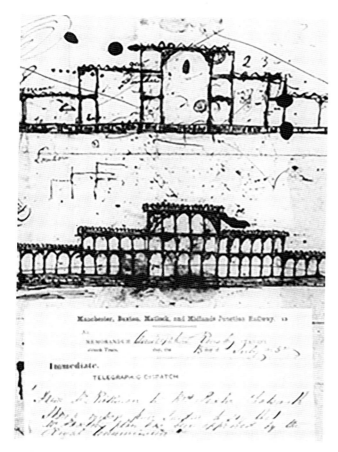

Joseph Paxton's original sketch for the Crystal Palace, doodled on blotting paper during a meeting of the Midland Railway Directors in Derby. This was June 1850 – by the next year it had to be up and running. He had help on the structural calculations from William Barlow, the Midland's chief Civil Engineer.

Indeed, the chief Wonder of the World at the 1851 exhibition was the astonishing Crystal Palace, a major reason for the many thousands of visitors from all over the world descending on London. And for those of us who are devotees of the Midland Railway, this also is a source of pride since it was devised by the self-effacing genius Joseph Paxton, gardener to the Duke of Devonshire at Chatsworth and Director of the Midland Railway. He is not now a household name, largely because his most obvious legacy, the Crystal Palace, burnt down in 1937 and was not rebuilt; nevertheless this was a leap forward in structural invention the like of which had not been seen before.

The building's three tiers contained 33,000 iron columns, 2,224 girders and 600,000 cubic feet of timber. At 49 x 12 inches, the panes were the largest sheet glass ever made; over 900,000 square feet of it were produced, to be held in place by over 205 miles of sash bars. There was nearly one million square feet of floor space; it was six times the size of St. Paul's Cathedral, which had taken 35 years to erect, whereas there was less than eight months to raise this monolith. And the inspiration for the whole design was the leaf of a waterlily, the massive Victoria Regia, discovered in 1837 in Guyana.

A building on such a grand scale, put up at so fast a rate – people were bound to ask, would it stay up? It did, of course, because Paxton had designed other huge glasshouses at Chatsworth, the most recent to house a fine specimen of Victoria Regia, the first to flower in this country. With some leaves over four feet across it was a sensation, and a picture of Annie Paxton, Joseph's daughter, standing on the leaf, brought the visitors flocking.

The secret to the strength of the plant was the deep veins that crisscrossed the underside of the leaf, and Paxton adapted this organic strength in his buildings. John Allwood says in "The Great Exhibitions": "The Crystal Palace was a break away from current thinking if only because it was so functional. In fact, to the Victorians it was not an architectural form at all – it was pure engineering." One might add, it was also breathtaking. This melding of form and function was a metaphor for the Exhibition for which it was an ideal. In Prince Albert's terms:

"Science discovers these laws of power, motion and transformation; industry applies them to the raw matter, which the earth yields us in abundance, but which becomes valuable only by knowledge. Art teaches us the immutable laws of beauty and symmetry, and gives to our productions forms in accordance to them."

The problem to the Victorians, in Britain especially, was that Art came a very poor second to engineering, and in the worst manifestations of the clash between the two, ornamentation appeared on many products with very little sense of why it was there or what historical period it was supposed to reflect. In fact, quite often patternmakers worked from books reflecting any and every period. There was a sense that form and function should exist in some kind of harmony, but the end result did not often echo the good intentions of the designers. The Crystal Palace was a vital landmark in design, partly because Art did not get in the way; it was artless.

If Midland ingenuity had done it once, it could do it again, and I believe that Johnson's fluid lines in his designs for steam engines represent such a milestone in aesthetic development partly because of this artlessness. The Spinners had to do a job, and that they did well.

Here is J.B. Radford on the class:

"As a whole the class gave excellent results, being among the most economical ever turned out from the Derby Works, consuming between 20 and 21lb of the local coal per mile with their usual average load of 115 tons. The drivers were thrilled with them and they were great favourites, becoming nicknamed "Spinners" on account of the odd spasm of slipping which they suffered from when starting with heavy trains; yet once in motion they swept along with seemingly effortless ease, there being of course no visible moving parts of the motion, just the large whirling wheels."

The language chosen in this description suggests that part of their elegance and grace arose from their functionality. In a telling phrase, Hamilton Ellis, who knew them in their heyday, says that they seemed to "pour themselves" along the line towards you. But this was not the whole story, and Johnson has been described as an "artist" many times; perhaps the finest there has ever been in engineering. So how did he achieve this status?

"Good grief! She stands on a leaf!" Victoria Regia supports little Annie Paxton at Chatsworth in 1840.

The Princess was scrapped in 1929, but luckily one Spinner survived; No.673, preserved at the NRM.

No. 673 was last seen on the tracks in 1983, at Butterley in Derbyshire. Steve Huson`s shots capture the grace that perhaps only showed itself in the open.

THE TRANSFORMATION

It seems fair to say that for the earliest railway engineers, aesthetic considerations were not a priority. William Hedley's "Puffing Billy" looked like a barrel on wheels, yet it worked in local collieries for 50 years, as did his "Wylam Dilly". They did not have to look like anything other than they were: workhorses to do a job.

In 1844 William Kirtley, the first Locomotive Superintendent of the Midland Railway, inherited a motley collection of engines from the three constituent companies which constituted the new conglomerate, and his first priority was to keep them on the road and working efficiently enough to keep his new empire supplied. His main concern was for a degree of standardisation since the engines came from different makers and the parts were not standard – in ten years he had achieved this and he was on the way, with other innovations like his introduction of the brick arch in the firebox for more efficient use of heat, to building one of the most effective fleets of engines in the country. He was responsible for the design of three principle types of engine to replace the varied collection he inherited: for express passenger trains he built a large number of 2-2-2 engines based on the "Jenny Lind" type, and a still more celebrated series of 2-4-0 engines. For goods traffic he designed a very strong and sturdy "six-coupled" type, double framed and immensely capable of hard work, as befitted a railway whose mineral and freight traffic was always very heavy. How good his engines were is attested by the fact that the last of his 2-4-0 express engines was only withdrawn in 1948, while the last of the goods engines, now preserved at Butterley, worked on British Railways until 1951. He was capable of mechanical innovation, like the Stephensons, and in 1859 he was the first locomotive engineer to use the firebox brick arch, thus making it possible to burn coal efficiently while not creating so much smoke that you have to use the more expensive coke.

Despite all of these achievements, and they were major ones, it is generally agreed that efficiency was his overriding preoccupation and aesthetic considerations came fairly low down in his system of priorities; perhaps rightly so for a pioneer who above all had to keep the trains running. Another consideration was that Matthew Kirtley was an ex-driver who had learnt his trade with Timothy Hackworth

▼ Kirtley Freight engine No. 2614 at Blackwell, date unknown. MRSC No.60191

Modified Kirtley No.35 ▲

▼ Midland Railway 2-2-2 locomotive number 1010 "Jenny Lind" built at Derby in May 1856. Photographed at Whitacre

and "prettiness", and it is obviously a stage further on in aesthetic terms from the rugged but rather ungainly-looking engines of the early years, but we are not yet at the stage of the sweeping lines and organic harmony of Johnson's most famous designs. However, it is important to note that he is adapting from Kirtley's design here, not designing in his own right. He joined the Midland as its Locomotive Superintendent on 2nd July 1873, having served in a similar position on the Great Eastern, and he spent several years adapting and reworking the Kirtley regulars. For some, these are as good as anything he did, and there are those who point to his early apprenticeship in the works of E.B.Wilson which originated the "Jenny Lind" type of engine; the nickname of these engines which came from a beautiful Music Hall star of the time tells its own story. However, the adjectives "pretty" and "neat" usually come to the fore when there is a discussion on the aesthetics of these earlier engines, 1840 to 1870. "Elegance", "symmetry" and "harmony" are the words more often applied to Johnson's superlative originals of the later nineteenth century, and these are the ones which swept the board at the Great Exhibitions.

In the Midland Railway Society we are indebted to the work of Jack Braithwaite who brought the subject of locomotive aesthetics to the fore again, and his writings are recommended for a fuller discussion. Beauty being very much in the eye of the beholder, the arguments will range long and loud depending on company loyalties and personal preference; there are many for whom the chunky shunter cannot be bettered for its simplicity of look and purpose. However, when the subject of aesthetics does come up, the name of Samuel Johnson is not far behind, and for many the litmus test of his quality lies either in his 4-4-0 engines, the prototypes for which were developed first just before he left the Great Eastern, or the elegant lines of the Singles. It is safe to say that such historical preoccupations did not really have much bearing on the judging committee of the Paris Exposition of 1900 – they were there to judge what came before them in the full glare of the electric light that was the presiding genius of the world spectacle, and they obviously liked what they saw. The various foreign enginemen who gathered around the Midland stand did not disagree. Their "open-mouthed admiration" of the "exquisite finish of the workmanship" was remarked on in the American press.

on the Stockton and Darlington, who in his turn had started his career with Hedley in Wylam. Again, the first priority of all the early pioneers was to get a service up and running; aesthetic considerations may have occurred later, say when Hackworth was trying to sell the first trains to Russia, but I think it is fair to say they were not of first importance. So Kirtley's freight engines, such as the one illustrated at Blackwell near Birmingham, was rugged but not a thing of loveliness; any aesthetic touches seem to be add-ons, ornamentation rather than integral to the whole design. By contrast Johnson's modification of another Kirtley design, the 2-2-2 express No.35 shown here, already shows a preoccupation with the symmetry and neat simplicity that were to be a hallmark of his designs. Not that he was working in a vacuum; this early Single, the "Jenny Lind" style of engine, had already achieved accolades for its symmetry

THE
FAIRY
ELECTRICITY

"It was then that a strange, crackling, condensed laughter resounded, the laughter of the Fairy Electricity. She triumphed at the Exhibition; she was born of the heavens, like true kings. The public laughed at the words: Danger of Death"written on the pylons; it knew that Electricity cured everything, even the neuroses fashionable at the time. It was Progress, the poetry of both rich and poor; it bestowed light in abundance; it was the great Signal...At night, projectors swept across the Champ de Mars and the Chateau d`Eau sparkled with cyclamen colours; it was a tumbling mass of greens, orchid-coloured flashes, flaming lilies, orchestrations of liquid fire, a riot of volts and amperes. The Seine was violet, dove-coloured, blood-red. Electricity was accumulated, condensed, put in jars, stretched along wires, rolled round coils, and then discharged into the water, over the fountains, over the roofs and into the trees. It was the scourge, the religion, of 1900." - Paul Morand.

Every fairytale needs a Fairy Godmother, and at the Exposition, Electricity fitted the bill. It was not new in 1900, but the Exposition celebrated its power to transform lives on a scale not imagined before. This was the first time electricity was used throughout an exhibition. This magical lady`s looking glass throws back her reflection over a hundred years later: Youtube will show you the massive Palace of Electricity, and some of the visitors that flocked to see it. You can also see some of the massive and extraordinary buildings that flanked the banks of the Seine, such as the Porte Binet, whose construction had partly benefited from the development of new, lighter materials such as aluminium, invented in 1754 and still a precious metal in Chicago 1893, so much so that the largest instance of its use was in an elaborate teaset.

The other great engineering masterpiece (apart from the Eiffel Tower of course, which was new in 1889) was Cotamin`s Palais de Machines, in which the Princess was on show. Drawing on Joseph Paxton`s Crystal Palace and the work of another Midland designer, William Barlow, who had produced the largest roof span to date (240 ft) with his St. Pancras station, the French engineers had excelled themselves with a 375 foot central aisle using Barlow`s pioneering techniques of tie beams in the ground and a gigantic pin at the centre of each arch, ensuring that any internal structural movement would be taken up and dispersed. Their confidence seemed a world away

◀ Palace of Electricity, 1900

from the 1889 Exhibition, when some tourist brochures issued by Thomas Cook (another Midland enterprise that benefited from this world event) included a diagram showing where the Eiffel Tower might fall. But importantly they were benefiting from the long years of experiment, invention and sheer courage of the Midland engineers.

Youtube will also give you a glimpse of another image that seems to sum up the spirit of the times, that of the "Trottoir Roulant" or moving pavement, which would transport you from one end of the exhibition to another at varying speeds depending on your preference and, perhaps, age.

The popularity of this novelty overrode social concerns: it was " a railway without weight, noise or smoke; without cinders, smells or jars; where crowding and waiting is unknown; on which passengers cannot be knocked down by cars or have their legs cut off by wheels; on which there is no switching or obstructing of trucks, no delays at stations and on which collisions are made impossible..."

The Railway Age had brought speed and movement to society, but it had come at a price, and there was evidence that people might prefer a mode of transport with less pollution, fewer accidents, less congestion. The picture of the moving pavement shows a few of the passengers using this ideal railway, which seems to give them a peaceful transition between stations from which you can watch the world go by with a cup of coffee. Above all, the impression is that people are relaxed and having fun.

It was a paradigm of the advances expected to be made in the new world heralded by the Exhibition; a world dominated by physics rather than chemistry, by light rather than heavy industry. It would appear to be a world in which a steam engine would appear to be a bit of an anachronism, especially when this was the first time that the diesel engine appeared on the world stage; except when you remember that all this transformational electricity had to be produced by a power station run by steam. And when the engine was the "Princess of Wales" by an engineer who was also an artist, it was by no means out of place.

There were three concentric platforms on the Trottoir: the first was static, the second travelled at 2.25 mph, and the third at 4.50 mph. It became so popular that seats were eventually fitted. On the middle pavement someone appears to be setting up a camera.
National Gallery of Art Washington

▼ Social upset? The pavement as seen by Le Figaro.

The Midland Railway itself was also on show, and the advertisement here preserved in the Midland Railway Study Centre shows some views of destinations such as Matlock and Edinburgh as well as informing the reader of the Midland's agent in Paris, a Mr. Henry Johnson. The background is embellished in a style that at least echoes the "biological romanticism" that was Art Nouveau and which provided the decorative touchstone of this Exhibition. The most prevalent use of this decoration was in glassware, much of it used to enhance the coils of the Fairy Electricity; this was the year that the name of Emile Gallé first emerged on to the world stage. So what was Art Nouveau, this "new art?"

Wikipaedia has this definition:

"The unfolding of Art Nouveau's flowing line may be understood as a metaphor for the freedom and release sought by its practitioners and admirers from the weight of artistic tradition and critical expectations."

Interestingly for our study of a locomotive designed and made by craftsmen in Derby, the style was an outgrowth of two British art movements, the Arts and Crafts Movement and the Aesthetic Movement. The former, inspired by William Morris, emphasised handcraftsmanship and traditional techniques, while the latter, with its rallying cry of "Art for Art's sake", was a reaction to the art education of the time, industrialised mass production and the debasement of historic styles. The Nirvana for an artist in this style was the synthesis of art and craft, the "Gesamtkunstwerk" or "total work of art" which embraced a variety of media. Thus its most successful examples are complete buildings such as Charles Rennie Mackintosh's

Hill House near Glasgow, in which furniture and decoration are a completion of the whole "work", or the decorative style of the Paris Metro which is one of the few survivals in the city which brought the style to life. This art form was supposed to be applied to the environment rather than simply to the walls of an art gallery or those of a private collector, and the social concerns of William Morris and John Ruskin were very much part of its impact.

Some of the literature on the Paris Exhibition of 1900 stresses its failures rather than its successes, such as the fact that visitor numbers were disappointing and it did not make money (in fact few did, after the triumphant success of the 1851 Exhibition and Paxton's cheap and successful construction methods). Even the famous historian of the Midland railway, Hamilton Ellis, is downbeat on the subject:

"It was not ...a very happy exhibition: the Engineering Annexe was so far away that many people never went to see it.

Furthermore, we were at that time a very unpopular nation, Continental and American sympathy being almost solidly for the Boers in South Africa." However, the Princess did go to the ball, and she came back with a prize that I think meant something quite significant. If she was not necessarily a work of "Art Nouveau", she was nevertheless imbued with many of its ideals, and perhaps in the terms of the definitions above she came as close as anything to the "total work of art". She had not only the handcraft techniques of generations of Midland craftsmen in her DNA, but the sinuosity of the "flowing line" derived from nature prized by the artist as well as the triumphant bonus that she moved with grace, speed and power. And in a year that celebrated the achievement of over a hundred years of progress in engineering design, what more could you ask for?

Porte Monumentale (Porte Binet), ▲
Paris Exposition 1900.
National Gallery of Art, Washington

▼ St. Pancras station, platform 3; 4-2-2
No. 2601, Princess of Wales, waiting
with express; Harold Hopwood pic;
LCGB Nunn H1866

A GREAT DEGREE OF ELABORATION

"His designs were invariably characterised by as great a degree of elaboration as the essentially utilitarian character of the object aimed at would permit."

That was the conclusion reached by the Derby Daily Telegraph's obituary writer in his tribute to Charles Trubshaw, the former Chief Architect of the Midland Railway, following his death at the age of 76 in Derby on 15th February 1917.

Charles Trubshaw had been born in 1840 in the village of Endon on the eastern fringe of the Potteries. His father, also named Charles, was the Architect and Surveyor to the County of Stafford and one of several generations of Trubshaws, dating back to at least the middle of the 18th century, who had chosen architecture, surveying or civil engineering as their profession. Charles Trubshaw junior was no exception in following the family tradition. His great uncle, James Trubshaw had built the Grosvenor Bridge spanning the River Dee in Chester (1833), the bridge across the Trent linking the Derbyshire villages of Repton and Willington (1839) and the original Exeter Bridge in Derby (1847).

After completing his formal education, Charles junior began his professional training under the tutelage of his father. However, by the age of 23 he felt that he had gained sufficient experience to seek employment elsewhere and this resulted in him landing a post on the staff of the London & North Western Railway's Engineering & Architectural department based at Birmingham New Street. The following year (1865) saw his talents confirmed by his election as an Associate of the Royal Institute of British Architects.

In his teens and early twenties Charles developed a passion for cricket which he retained for the rest of his life. As a player he reached a sufficient standard for three of the games he participated in to be recorded on the remarkable Cricket Archive website.

In 1860 and again in 1861 he was selected by the Earl of Lichfield to appear in his Shugborough Hall team against no less an opposition as an All England XI. Back then the rules of the game were somewhat different to the ones we know today. For a start, only four balls were bowled per over and the two

games against England at Shugborough were very one sided insomuch as the Shugborough team fielded 22 players against the All England XI's eleven men! Trubshaw hardly covered himself in glory in the first match being run out for 2 in the first innings and was bowled out for a duck in the second. In spite of being outnumbered England won the game by 9 wickets. Trubshaw's batting did not improve in the game the following year. He was bowled for a duck in the first innings and was not out without scoring in the second, but he did take 2 wickets for 20 in the match which the home side won by 5 wickets.

Charles is again mentioned in the Cricket Archive's report of the game between North Staffordshire and Cheshire at the County Ground at Chelford in May 1862. Once again, his batting statistics took a hammering being not out for 1 in the first innings and run out for 0 in the second. But this match did highlight his skills as a both a bowler and in the field because he took four wickets and three catches. This time the numbers were equally matched (11 players on each side) as was the result, a draw.

Trubshaw's career with the LNWR spanned the years 1864 to 1874, after which his long association with the Midland Railway began. In the meantime, in August 1870, he had married Caroline Hill in Oswestry. Their first child, a daughter, Edith was born three years later at Edgbaston whilst Charles was still working for the LNWR in Birmingham.

Charles's initial job title with the Midland was Northern Division Architect. His opposite number, the Southern Division Architect, was John Holloway Sanders. Sanders had been involved with the MR since around 1850, but it is not clear if he was an MR employee from the beginning or if he was contracted out by an independent architectural practise to the Midland before taking on the role as Chief Architect. However, by 1869 the Midland system had expanded to such an extent that the board decided that Sanders needed assistance. But curiously, rather than appointing a deputy, it was decided to split the responsibilities and made Sanders the MR Southern Division Architect and give the new man the title Northern Division Architect. Certainly today it would appear that Sanders was given a "sideways promotion" in the reorganisation.

John Sanders is credited with developing the Midland's distinctive 'twin' and 'triple pavilion' style station buildings. Indeed, the building style is sometimes referred to as Midland (or Derby) Gothic. Examples could be found all over the Midland system from Armathwaite on the Settle & Carlisle line to Weston in Somerset (the first station on the line out of Bath).

The first appointee as Northern Division Architect was William Lees, but there are no MR buildings that can be attributed to him and the reason for him leaving the company after a relatively short period is unclear. The decision to employ Trubshaw was made at a meeting of the Way & Works Committee on 5th May 1874 when it was "resolved that Mr Charles Trubshaw be appointed architect (under the Engineer) to the Northern Division at a salary of £400 per annum, his whole time be given to the Company and that he resides in Derby, also that arrangements are made for his services to be commenced as soon as possible." The wording of the minute is intriguing. One wonders if Lees been caught 'doing foreigners' in company time and been dismissed? At least Charles would have been under no illusions in that respect.

▼ Although out of context chronologically, this is the scene on the morning after the disastrous fire that destroyed the Trubshaw building on Ambergate Platform 3 on 20th March 1899. Only the masonry chimney remains. As mentioned in the text, originally planned as a waiting shelter, it had been adapted to also accommodate the station staff. In the middle distance to the left of the chimney is the back of the waiting shelter on Platform 5, with the mostly hidden, but identical shelter on Platform 6 beyond. The difficult terrain can be easily appreciated. According to press reports, it was a bitterly cold day with the temperature barely above freezing but work has already started on rebuilding the wooden platform. No doubt Charles Trubshaw is one of the bowler hatted gentlemen surveying the scene. To complete the story, a new, but smaller waiting shed was subsequently provided further along Platform 3 and a new permanent building for the station staff was built in the bottom left of the photograph. Photo by courtesy of the National Railway Museum DY1687

Unlike Lees. Trubshaw soon began making his mark. One of his first, if not his first, assignments for the company was the design of the buildings for the new triangular station at Ambergate. As related in the chapter entitled The Golden Triangle, this was the third station to serve the local community and opened on 10th December 1876. Because of its elevated position, five out of the six platforms were built on embankments. For these Trubshaw designed five identical timber waiting sheds with low profile, hipped slate roofs so that the relatively lightweight structures were easily supported on timber piles. He proposed to locate the main station building on the one area of solid ground at the south end of the Up Sheffield line platform. (No.4)

Knowing that a major economy drive was imminent, when the Way & Works Committee considered the proposals in April 1875 they decided to postpone the construction of the main station building until the financial situation improved. To provide temporary accommodation for the Station Master, booking clerks etc., Trubshaw was instructed to adapt the waiting shed on Platform 3, but still retain waiting facilities, both for ladies and for the general

Part of the approach side of Skipton station photographed in 1965. It can be accurately dated by the far right poster board which is announcing the new "arrows of indecision" logo which was introduced that year. Note also the Ford Consul Classic on the far right. As mentioned in the text, this was Trubshaw's first really big project for the MR but interestingly it already displays what would become two of his signature features. The first on the left, is the rectangular panel just above the corbels supporting the chimney. Carved into this panel is a Wyvern, a dragon like creature which was the Midland's logo. Believed to originate from the ancient Saxon Kingdom of Mercia, a Wyvern was used in the arms of the pioneer Leicester & Swanington Railway and was appropriated by the Midland when it absorbed the line. Time after time, various versions of Wyverns would appear in Trubshaw's designs. The other interesting feature is the canted bay on the right. As we shall see later, Trubshaw seemed to have an obsession for 135° angles, be it in bays like this or in octagonal towers or columns. Photo by courtesy of the Ian Howard Collection

A close up of the decorative cast iron brackets and spandrels supporting the platform canopy at Hellifield photographed in September 2015. In 1994, British Rail, English Heritage and the Railway Heritage Trust raised £500k towards the restoration of the station buildings and awnings and Network Rail spent a further half a million pounds on refurbishing the canopies in 2013. Note the Wyvern (with two legs) cast into the right hand spandrel flanked by four Yorkshire Roses, also the MR towards the right side of the bracket supporting the cantilever. The canopy structure is handed so that the MR and the Wyvern are facing the correct way when viewed when looking in the direction of travel. The station was rightly listed by English Heritage as a Grade 2 structure in 1977. The canopy supporting structure is a wonderful example of Victorian foundry artistry and craftsmanship at its finest. The ironwork was cast by Walter MacFarlane & Company at their Saracen Foundry in Glasgow.
Photo: Steve Huson

public. Although the Midland's finances did improve, Trubshaw's proposed main station building never did materialise and for the next 22 years the station staff had to make do with the 'temporary accommodation' in the waiting shed.

Following on from Ambergate, Trubshaw's first really major project was the new station at Skipton. Only 13 miles south of the start of the Settle & Carlisle line, the new station opened on 30th April 1876, the same day as passenger services began on the S&C. At Ambergate, Trubshaw's architectural talents were restricted by the nature of the site, but at Skipton he was obviously determined to break the Midland Gothic mould and stamp his own personality on the design. The result was a fairly complex, but pleasing, frontage which has survived the test of time and is still a familiar sight to passengers approaching the station from the town. Another departure from Midland Gothic was the provision of platform canopies to give waiting passengers some protection from the rain.

Canopies were also a significant feature of Trubshaw's second major project, the new station at Hellifield which opened on 1st June 1880. Hellifield was one of several MR interchange stations whose size was completely out of proportion relative to size of the community they served. The raison d'être for building the new station was the opening of the Lancashire and Yorkshire Railway's line from Blackburn so that passengers from Manchester, Liverpool, Preston, etc., could use the MR's new Settle & Carlisle line in preference to the existing LNWR routes to Carlisle and Scotland. Unlike his elaborate design to welcome the residents of Skipton to the station, Hellifield villagers have to access their station through a subway and up a ramp to the single island platform which originally had bays at both ends. The simple, rectangular station building on the island platform provided every necessary convenience to the Victorian traveller, but what the building lacked in ornamentation was more than compensated by the delicate ironwork supporting the canopies. These were supplied by the celebrated Glasgow ironfounders, Walter MacFarlane & Co., who had earlier cast the ironwork for Skipton.

In spite of having the title Northern Division Architect, it will be recalled that one of Trubshaw's terms of employment included that he lived in Derby. The 1881 census shows Charles and his wife Caroline residing at 3 Grove Terrace on Osmaston Road in Derby. By then he had three children. Edith, (who had been born in Charles's LNWR days) was now aged eight. Her sister, Mabel was six and the girls had a two year old brother, who was named, seemingly in according with family tradition, Charles. Charles (senior's) salary was sufficient for the family to employ two female servants, Elizabeth Lee an 18 year old nurse for the children and a 24 year old maid, Harriet Meakin.

Due to ill-health, John Sanders took early retirement but sadly his retirement was short lived for he passed away on 16 October 1884 aged 59. Charles Trubshaw does not appear in the list of mourners at the funeral, but the list does include an A. Wheatley. The author presumes that this is Alfred Wheatley, who without the kudos of

Hellifield is an example of one of several Midland Railway interchange stations whose size bore no relationship to the size of the community it served. Other classic examples include Ambergate, Chinley, Miller's Dale and of course, Trent. The original station at Hellifield was replaced by this new one in June 1880 as a consequence of the opening of the Lancashire & Yorkshire Railway's line from Blackburn. Thereafter it became an obligatory stop for expresses between Leeds and Carlisle. This view, taken in the early years of the 20th century is looking north along the Up platform with the loco shed in the background. Opened at the same time as the station, the shed is no doubt the work of Charles Trubshaw. The delicate detailing of the cast iron columns can be appreciated in this view, but note the reversed MR lettering and Wyverns in the ironwork above as the camera is facing away from the direction of travel.
Photo: Steve Huson Collection

an official title, took over the senior architect's role after Trubshaw retired in 1905. Curiously, it was not until a month after Sanders' death that it was announced that Charles Trubshaw had been appointed as Chief Architect on 21st November 1884.

Returning to 1882, this was the year that Trubshaw successfully applied to become a Fellow of the Royal Institute of British Architects. One of the three existing RIBA Fellows who seconded his application was his erstwhile colleague, John H Sanders. Trubshaw was obviously proud of his new stations at Skipton and Hellifield because he mentions both specifically in his application as being "executed in stone with iron and glass roofs, costing about £15,000 and £11,000 respectively."

As mentioned earlier, the development at Hellifield was a result of the L&YR opening their line from Hellifield to Blackburn from whence their lines continued to Preston, Liverpool and Manchester. As a result Hellifield, suddenly expanded from a small agricultural hamlet into a compact railway community. In addition to the new station, a loco shed and a separate carriage shed were built along with cottages to accommodate employees and a handsome house for the Station Master and his family. Although non of these ancillary buildings can be directly attributed to Charles Trubshaw, they were designed during his tenure as Northern Division Architect. Additionally, his FRIBA application mentions his involvement in the design of dwellings for staff, goods, grain and bonding warehouses, engine shops and sheds &c. So, if not designed on his own drawing board, he would have closely supervised the work being carried out by his assistants and signed off their completed plans and specifications. Hellifield station was listed Grade 2 by English Heritage as early as 1977; Skipton had to wait until 1991 to be listed, which also included the separate Trubshaw canopy on the island platform.

1882 saw two more Trubshaw stations opened, this time nearer to home in Nottinghamshire on the Bennerley and Bulwell line. The MR had opened the line three years earlier in order to compete against the GNR for traffic from the collieries that were linked to the latter's Derbyshire Extension Lines. Passenger services from Nottingham to the market town of Ilkeston via the Bennerley and Bulwell were something of an

Kimberley Station with six members of the staff and two female passengers posing on the platform. Judging by the style of ladies' costumes the photograph was taken in the early 1900s. Passenger traffic ceased on 1st January 1917 as a wartime economy. Photo: Steve Huson Collection

MIDLAND STATION, KIMBERLEY NOTTS.

after thought and Trubshaw was tasked to provide stations at Watnall and at Kimberley. Both opened on 1st September 1882.

Kimberley Station which was built in the Arts & Crafts style, bore more than a passing resemblance to John Sanders' twin pavilion design. The main difference is that the pavilions were spaced much further apart thus increasing the length of canopy. Trubshaw also added some attractive, but restrained detailing. It cost £2,496 and the contractor was E. Wood, a well known Derby builder.

Kimberley and its smaller neighbour at Watnall must rate as Trubshaw's shortest lived stations. Both were closed after just over 33 years of service when passenger traffic on the line was suspended on 1st January 1917 as a wartime economy measure. Passenger services were never reinstated. That said, Kimberley station building although derelict and in a very dangerous condition was still standing at the time of writing (July 2016) having been used as a social club in its latter years.

Kimberley station was flanked by two separate breweries, one of which, Hanson's, can be seen towering above the station in the coloured postcard on the previous page. An equally large brewery, Hardy's, is out of sight to the left of the photographer. The first brewery on the site was established in 1832 by Samuel Robinson which was bought by the Hardy Brothers in 1857. Ten years earlier Stephen Hanson had begun brewing nearby using water from the same spring. From small beginnings some 60 years later the brewery occupied the impressive building in the background. When the original spring began to run dry both concerns agreed to share water from the Holly Well spring for brewing. There was friendly rivalry between the two firms until 1930 when due to commercial pressure, they decided to merge to become Hardy's and Hanson's. Their range of Kimberley Ales were much enjoyed in pubs throughout the East Midlands until the brewery was taken over and closed in 2006 and brewing transferred to the new owner's brewery in Suffolk.

Following on from what had been a relatively local assignment, Charles Trubshaw found himself back in Yorkshire, this time his project was to provide a new station at Keighley. The original station had been built by the Leeds & Bradford Extension Railway the first section of which opened as far as Keighley in March 1847 and finally reached Colne in October 1848. The opening of the "Little" North Western the following year created more traffic through the station as did the branch line along the Worth Valley to Haworth and Oxenhope which began in 1867. There was a significant increase in traffic following the opening of the Settle & Carlisle in April 1876.

The situation promised to get worse after the MR granted the Great Northern Railway running powers over the final half mile or so of the Worth Valley branch and use Keighley's passenger facilities for GN's so called Queensbury Lines services from Halifax and Bradford (Exchange). It was this that probably was the catalyst to provide the new station.

The 1847 station was located on the north side of the bridge that carried Bradford Road across the line. Trubshaw elected to widen the bridge and locate the new main buildings on the south side above the lines and provide four platforms; two for main line services and two for the Worth Valley and GNR trains.

▼ Looking east across the Station Bridge at Keighley, with the MR goods yard on the left and the GNR's yard on the right. The tall building in the centre background is the Midland owned Queens Hotel. Much of the station buildings are hidden by the wall and advertising hoardings on the right. The windows in the passageway leading to the ramp down to the down K&WVR/ GNR platform can be seen above the wall on the right. Photo MRSC 68529/ John Alsop Collection A99131

STATION BRIDGE
KEIGHLEY

However, rather than flights of steps from road level to platform level, Trubshaw provided the easier option of long enclosed ramps. As at Skipton and Hellifield plenty of wet weather protection was provided by platform canopies, but this time a cantilever canopy also ran along the front of the station exterior.

The new station came into use on 6th May 1883 which gave plenty of time to settle down before the Great Northern's Queensbury Line services began using the station in the November of the following year.

With the new Keighley station up and running Trubshaw's next major project was just 9 miles away in Bradford. The Midland's first station in the town had been built by the Leeds and Bradford Railway and had opened in 1846. It soon proved to be inadequate and was quickly replaced by larger premises on Market Street after the L&B was absorbed by the Midland in 1851.

By the early 1880's further increases in traffic levels at Bradford prompted the Midland Board to instruct Trubshaw to draw up plans for not only a new station but for an integral five-star hotel alongside the existing Market Street terminus. Work on the site, between Cheapside and Kirkgate, began in 1885 and took five years to complete, but long before work started, Charles and his team would have been busy preparing and costing various schemes until they produced one that the MR Board, and in particular the Chairman, Matthew Thompson, would find attractive.

Matthew Thompson, in addition to his chairmanship of the MR, was chairman of the Glasgow & South Western Railway and a former chairman of the Forth Bridge Company, in which the Midland held a 30% shareholding. In recognition of his services to the Forth Bridge project, a baronetcy was conferred on Thompson by the Prince of Wales at the opening ceremony of the bridge in 1890. Thompson was also major political figure in Bradford life. He was an Alderman, a former MP and had been Mayor of the borough on two occasions. Anything less than the best in a town that already had many fine buildings would have seriously harmed his standing in the community.

A view looking north along Keighley Platform 2, the down main line platform, with part of the up main line platform visible on the right. The long ramp from the platform up to street level can be seen in the centre background. Note the suspended signs including "To Worth Valley And Great Northern Trains""Cross the line by the Subway" and over the bottom of the ramp "Midland Railway Hotel and adjoining Station" Midland Railway Study Centre 68528/ John Alsop Collection A98631

Although the project was a quantum leap for Trubshaw, he responded by producing an hotel and station that in the opinion of the Bradford Daily Telegraph, "must take rank amongst the leading railway centres in the Kingdom."

No doubt Thompson was delighted not only with his Chief Architect's designs but also by the glowing reports in the local press. Both the Bradford Daily Telegraph and the Bradford Argus were full of praise for the station, when it opened on 1st March 1890 and found even more superlatives to describe the hotel when it began receiving guests three months later. The hotel is fully described in the chapter "The Experienced Traveller."

Sadly, Sir Matthew Thompson, passed away in December the following year, but his determination to provide excellent facilities for Midland passengers at Bradford paid dividends. One of the pioneer railway commentators, E. L. Ahrons reported that he truly believed the claim that more passengers were booked at Bradford than any other station on the Midland line. That said, Ahrons could perhaps have been a little biased as he had been born in Bradford and educated at Bradford Grammar School.

For the new terminal station Trubshaw provided an impressive ashlar facade between which and the station itself was an area covered by a fully glazed roof to protect passengers arriving by cab from the weather. Incorporated towards the top of the some of the pilasters of the façade were carved the coats of arms of Bradford itself, Carlisle, London, Bristol and Peterborough. Peterborough perhaps seems a curious choice, but at the time it was the most easterly point of the MR empire. The station buildings contained first and third class booking halls, waiting rooms and all the usual offices. Beyond this was the circulating area and six terminal platforms, the five main ones being 450 feet in length. As seen in the photograph of the interior on a later page, the whole area was spanned by an iron and glass roof which was supplied by the Stanningley based Butler Foundry. From the beginning, the station was lit by electricity which was installed by the MR's own engineers, but as electricity was still in its infancy, the bets were hedged by providing gas lighting for emergency use!

▼ Close up of detailing on cast iron canopy support bracket over Platform 4 at Keighley. Steve Huson

Close-ups of the city coats of arms carved in the façade of the Midland station at Bradford photographed in June 2016. Each one has been carved in three separate stones, some ▼
of which have proved to be more weather resistant than the others. Compare the still crisp carving on the upper stone of Carlisle, with the badly eroded top stone of Bristol.

Bristol

Peterborough

Bradford

London

Carlisle

▼ Judging by the lack of smoke staining on the stonework, this view of the façade of the Midland Station in Bradford with the Midland Hotel rising behind it was not very old, so
it must date from around 1900. The presence of overhead electric tram wires is not much help as Bradford was one of the pioneers of electric tramways which began in 1892.
There is some controversy regarding the station's name. Following the grouping in 1923, it became Forster Square, but prior to that some sources claim that it was named
"Market Street" but this is not borne out by the signage in this photograph or by other official documents that the author has seen. The main entrance to the hotel is marked by
the massive square porch at the left hand end of the façade. Above the porch is an octagonal tower and dome, variations of which were to be a hallmark of many of Trubshaw's
subsequent buildings, including the new station frontage at Derby, the Railway Institute in Derby, the new station at Leicester and the Midland Hotel in Manchester.
Photo: Steve Huson Collection

▲ The interior of Charles Trubshaw's Midland Station at Bradford seen here in this postcard view from the early years of the 20th century. The 174 feet wide, ridge and furrow iron and glass roof over the six platforms was supported in mid span by a row of tall Corinthian cast iron columns. The sign for platform 1, which was set back a little, can be seen on the left although the platform itself is off camera. A well patronised local train has just arrived at platform 2 headed by a Johnson 0-4-4T, which is more than likely one of several examples of the class that were based at Manningham. The train is a typical hodge-podge of carriages that characterised many secondary MR services at the time. First is a four wheeled first, followed by two six-wheelers and an early Clayton bogie clerestory. Next are three unidentified four wheeled vehicles with a six wheel clerestory brake bringing up the rear. A slightly less motley assortment of rolling stock is standing on platform 4. The make up of the local trains contrasts sharply with the five uniform clerestory vehicles standing on platform 3 which will be departing later, probably on a service to Leeds and beyond. Note the electric lights which were installed by the Midland's own electrical engineers. Note also in the right foreground the octagonal roof lights over the Telegraphic Office and the adjoining bookstall. Photo: Steve Huson Collection

L. Trubshaw
may. 6. 1891.

▲ Charles Trubshaw's signature authorising the payment of an invoice for various building works carried out by a contractor on the Birmingham to Bristol line MRSC 21343

The LMS added "Forster Square" to the station's name in 1924 to differentiate it from the former LYR/GNR station, Exchange, in the city. Trubshaw's station closed in 1990 when the line was truncated and part of the original site is now used as the car park for the Midland Hotel. Fortunately, half of Trubshaw's façade was left in-situ whilst the remainder has been sympathetically rebuilt at right angles to its original alignment. The original main entrance to the hotel was marked by a robust square porch at the end of the façade. Above this porch is an octagonal tower topped with a cupola, a feature which along with 135⁰ canted bays, octagonal columns and other eight sided details became Trubshaw's signature in many of his later designs.

By the time of the 1891 Census, the Trubshaw family had moved to 123 Osmaston Road, a large, handsome, double-fronted villa the garden of which looked out over the extensive grounds surrounding the new Derbyshire Royal Infirmary. This time, only Charles, Caroline and their eldest daughter Edith, appear on the register, together with Harriet Barnes, a 22 year old domestic servant and Myra Wood, their 23 year old cook.

The early 1890s proved to be a very busy time for Charles and his team with several major projects running concurrently including new stations at Bingley and Leicester, major alterations to Derby station and a new Literary Institute in Derby.

The first of these major works passed a significant milestone when the booking and parcels offices at the new station at Leicester London Road opened on Sunday 12 June 1892. It would be another two years before the station was finally completed but even the incomplete facilities were a marked improvement on the facilities at the previous station on Campbell Street. The Campbell Street station had been built by the Midland Counties Railway in 1839 and half a century later it had become totally inadequate. The Leicester Chronicle described it as being "cramped and dingy and has too long has been a reproach to the large and prosperous borough."

Having successfully constructed a medium sized station building on a bridge at Keighley, Trubshaw decided to repeat

the exercise, but on a much larger scale at Leicester. Here, the bridge which had carried the main London Road over the MCR lines was not only widened, it was also extended so that the goods lines could bypass the station's platforms. But unlike Keighley which only has a canopy along the frontage, Trubshaw designed an imposing 250 feet long brick and terracotta façade behind which, as at Bradford, was an area covered by a fully glazed roof to protect passengers arriving by cab from the weather.

Such was the urgency of opening the new facilities that only half the façade had been built and much remained to be done when the station opened its doors. It had been decided that an official opening would not be appropriate at this stage, but to show some civic appreciation of the Midland's efforts, the Mayor, Alderman Wright, arrived at 8 o'clock and purchased the very first ticket, a first class single to Humberstone Road. The ticket was issued by the Station Master, Mr Mitchie, who then gave His Worship a quick tour of the new buildings.

The next edition of the Leicester Chronicle reported that the Mayor was well impressed with what he had seen and had spoken "in the highest terms of admiration of the handsome and spacious booking hall which he regarded as one of the finest in the kingdom."
A few weeks prior to the first part of the station being opened, a reporter from the same newspaper had been given a preview of what the town's inhabitants could expect from their new station. One of the conclusions of the report, written in typically verbose Victorian prose, was that the Midland Company was

Clock Tower ▲

▲ A view looking north along platform 2 which was principally used for express services to Manchester, Liverpool, Leeds, Carlisle and Scotland. On the right a train of close-coupled six wheelers is standing on the London platform 3. The centre road was used for storage and for relieving locomotives to stand to await the arrival of the incoming train. Midland Railway Study Centre 23540

▼ Looking south along Leicester platform 3 soon after the station was completed with an unidentified 2-4-0 on station pilot duties on platform 2. A three bay roof such as this was traditionally supported by rows of intermediate columns below the valleys, but to achieve a clear span, massive horizontal struts between the apexes were required. Note the enamel sign on the left advertising the long forgotten Compo washing powder. Photo by courtesy of the National Railway Museum DY393

"thoroughly and generously fulfilling its pledge to provide Leicester with a station at least commensurate with its growing wants." The article did express disappointment that the MR had not followed up on the highly successful electric lighting experiment at Bradford station and that gas lighting was being used at Leicester.

It will be recalled that at Keighley, Trubshaw had used ramps between the road and platform levels, at Leicester the two island platforms were linked to the upper level by conventional stairways supplemented by 25 cwt. capacity hydraulic luggage lifts.

The description of the new Booking Hall is interesting. "Measuring some 90 by 70 feet the walls and the offices were lined to a height of eight feet six inches from the floor with Minton tiles arranged in a very artistic style. The prevailing colour was cream, but chocolate, old gold and dark green were "harmonised with an exceedingly pretty effect." In the centre of the hall was a large octagonal structure which was the MR

Booking Office. It had two ticket windows for first class passengers and three windows for third class passengers.

Trubshaw's seeming obsession with 135⁰ angles had manifested itself once again!

Over the next two years the local newspapers carried occasional reports on the station's progress. In February 1894 it was reported that the gas lighting had been replaced by electricity and the final report that your author has found, dated 26th April 1894, said that the considerable progress had recently been made and that 5 out of the 22 main lattice girders to support the roof spanning the main line platforms, 2 and 3 had been erected. The outer platforms, mainly used by secondary services were provided with canopies for weather protection.

To have built the station without causing major disruption to services was a considerable achievement. Credit for this is due to very careful planning by Charles Trubshaw and the Midland Railway Engineer, John McDonald. For the citizens of Leicester stoically putting up with the building works until the new station was completed seems to have been a small price to pay to relieve their many years of suffering "the misery of being cribb'd, cabin'd and confin'd" in the Campbell Street Station."

Hard on the heels of the opening of the first part of the new Leicester station in June 1892 another of Charles Trubshaw's projects, this time the new station at Bingley, opened its doors to passengers at 6.00 am on 24th July 1892. The replacement of the original Bingley station, along with the one at Keighley, was first mooted in 1871, but as we have already seen, Keighley was not replaced until 1883 and it took until September 1889 before the Midland Board decided to go ahead with Bingley.

The new Bingley station, which was south of the original and located on Wellington Street, was, like Kimberley, another variation on the twin pavilion theme.

The new station was built immediately beyond the north end of the 151 yards long Bingley Tunnel; in fact, the south ends of both the platforms abut the tunnel's north portal. As can

The exterior of Bingley photographed in 1904. The pleasing symmetry of this elevation is somewhat spoiled by the canopy, but the latter feature would be much more appreciated on rainy days than Charles Trubshaw's delicate detailing. MRSC/KRM 60158

be seen in the photograph, from the forecourt it appears to be a single storey building, but as the building is set into a cutting, when viewed from the platform it is a two storey structure. Thus, the wide, elliptically arched main entrance in the centre leads onto the footbridge over the line.

For the main part of the structure Trubshaw opted to use thin coursed York stone with the roof line of the pavilions noticeably higher than that of the central section. The pavilion gables projected on the approach side but were flush on the platform side. The top section of both the gable walls on both sides feature typical Trubshaw carvings and are garnished with stone ball finials.

The Midland also provided a new detached house for the Bingley Station Master, adjacent to the station, on the corner of Wellington Street and Park Street

With the new Bingley station opened, Charles Trubshaw could concentrate on the ongoing work at Leicester and the two

▼ The down platform of Bingley Station thronged with excited excursionists on 4th May 1904. Presumably it is an outing for employees and their families of one of the local mills. Even though it is a Wednesday everyone is dressed in their 'Sunday Best'. The men are all wearing either cloth caps or bowlers; the ladies a variety of bonnets and hats. Everyone's boots and shoes are positively gleaming!

Once again Trubshaw has made extensive use of canopies on both platforms and as can be seen in the previous photograph, the outside of the station too.. In spite of the rear elevation of the building being mostly hidden from view, Trubshaw has not skimped on the detailing. Midland Railway Study Centre 67386 /John Alsop Collection A70458

projects in Derby. With Leicester being only about three quarters of an hour away by train and the works at Derby taking place more or less outside his office, Charles could spend more time at home with his family.

The original station at Derby had been designed by the North Midland Railway's architect Francis Thompson. As the Midland Railway grew, so did the requirements for office accommodation in Derby and over the years Trubshaw's predecessor, John Sanders, carried out several extensions to the original building including the porte cochère (1855) the Shareholders' Room (1857) and the Boardroom (1873). By the 1890s office space was at a premium once again and Trubshaw was tasked to carry out further extensions and alterations.

To create the necessary space for the extension, the bold decision was taken to move the covered cab approach about 70 feet forward which involved the Derby Tramways Company having to realign their tracks and alter the position of the terminus. On this blank canvas, Trubshaw created two matching three storey pavilions in front of the existing Shareholders' Room on the south side and the Secretary's Block on the north side. Between these was a two storey block, 42 feet wide, the first floor of which provided twelve new much needed offices for the General Manager and his staff. At street level a new arrival hall was provided with a new third class booking office to the right, beyond which again was the first class booking office. This arrangement would become familiar to rail travelling Derbians for the next 90 years. W.H. Smith's bookstall (where your author regularly bought his Trains Illustrateds and Ian Allan ABCs in the late 1950s), stood between the arrival hall and the third class booking hall. Completely hidden beneath the new block additional cellars were provided for use by the Midland Hotel who supplied wines and spirits to all the company's other hotels. By 1895 the demand was such that catacombs beneath the hotel and the station contained eye watering quantities of alcohol; 100,000 gallons of bonded Whisky, 150,000 bottles of vintage Champagne, and between 300,000 and 400,000 bottles of Claret and Burgundy.

The new extension was built in red brick and stone. The rebuilt original façade and the cab circulating area concealed a lot of the new front elevation, but what was visible above roof of the cab rank displayed some elaborate Trubshaw detailing. Along the top of the outer wall of the central block was a balustered balustrade, punctuated symmetrically by three false 135° gables. The outer pair were plain; but the central one contained a clock, supported by carved stone Wyverns with a further Wyvern surmounting the apex. Following the wanton demolition of the station by BR in the early 1980s, the central gable was preserved and somewhat incongruously relocated at the north end of the station car park.

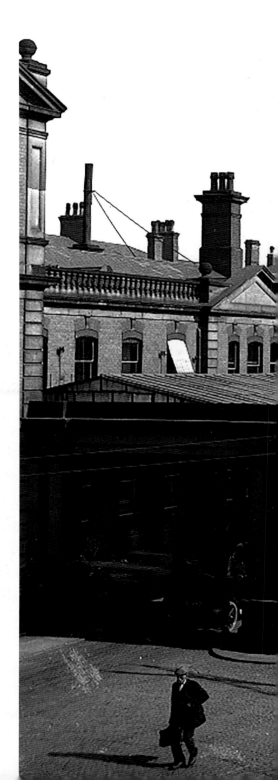

At each end of the central block Trubshaw added his subtle signature in the form of rather squat semi octagonal towers each capped with a cupola and flagpole. Although it is perhaps a little difficult to appreciate with buildings on each side, taken in isolation Trubshaw's 1893 frontage must surely have represented the ultimate in the Midland twin pavilion style.

The post 1892 Derby station facade has been photographed from the first floor windows of Midland Railway Institute on a number of occasions. This one, which which has rarely been published previously was taken on 16th May 1924 and shows a mixture of early motor vehicles, but horse power has not yet been completely replaced. On the right is the Midland Hotel connected to the station by an overhead canopy. Behind and beyond the hotel are the Goods Manager's offices. In front of the hotel a Derby Corporation tram is waiting to depart for Kedleston Road (Route no.1). Note the semi octagonal tower with a cupola and flagpole at the far end of the office block.
Photo by courtesy of the National Railway Museum DY13437

THE MIDLAND RAILWAY INSTITUTE DERBY

The history of the Institute goes back to September 1851 when the MR Board acquiesced to a request by a group of employees anxious to improve themselves by providing two cottages in the railway village (8 & 9 Leeds Place) for the use of the Derby Railway Literary Institution. By the following year membership had grown to almost 200 and evening classes were established teaching the "three Rs" and English grammar. By 1857 membership (which cost 1 penny a week – the same as a pint of beer) had increased to such an extent that MR Board allocated some rooms on the ground floor of the station below the Shareholders' Room for the use of the Literary Institute. By 1890 with a embership of over

▼ The Midland Railway Institute, including the 1901 extension, are seen here from one of the first floor offices seen in the previous photograph. It is a scene that is still very recognisable today. To the left is Midland Place and on the right, beyond the Institute are the railway cottages on Railway Terrace, the far end of which is the Brunswick Inn. There are still trees opposite the Institute, to the right of these cabs are waiting to be called forward. This is now the station car park. The horses on the carts on the left are waiting patiently for the return of their drivers who are no doubt enjoying a pint in Wright's Vaults on the left hand corner, or the Victoria Inn next door on Midland Place. Note, in pole position, Trubshaw's signature semi octagonal tower with its cupola, lantern and flagpole. Photograph by courtesy of the National Railway Museum DY1785

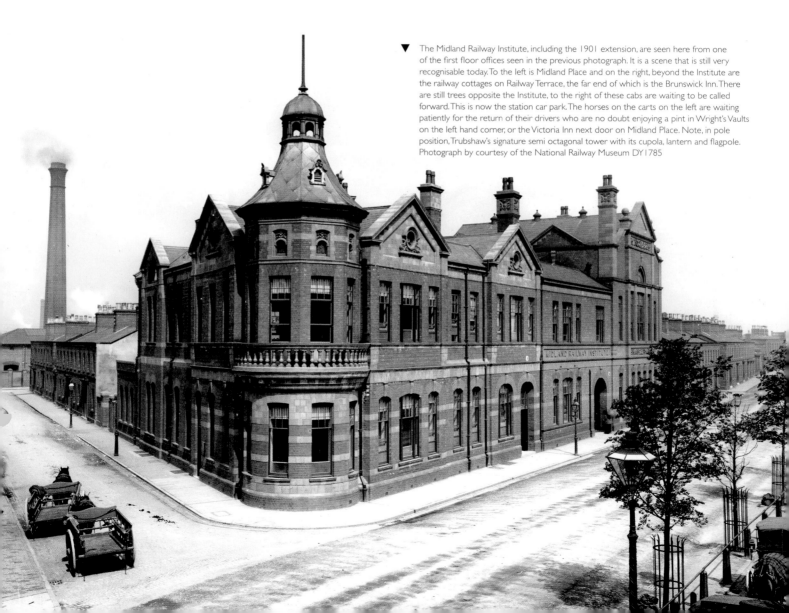

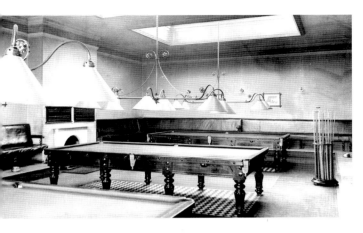

The Billiard Room at the Midland Railway Institute in Derby with three of the five tables in view. Note the large skylights and the ample provision of electric lighting for playing after dark. Note also the comfortable leather seating for the spectators on raised plinths to give a better view of the tables. Photo by courtesy of the Ian Howard Collection.

A delightful little vignette that illustrated the programme for the first concert. The Institute was opened by Ernest Paget at 4.30 pm on Thursday 15th February 1894 and the inaugural concert began at 7.30 pm the same day. The programme is now in the care of the Midland Railway Study Centre reference 18915.

1,100 these rooms had become completely inadequate and the Directors agreed to provide new, purpose built premises. The initial site on the narrow strip of land between

Calvert Street and Derby Canal was not favoured by the Institute Committee and led by its dynamic Hon. Secretary, George J. Pratt, an alternative site on the corner of Midland Place and Railway Terrace was agreed by the company. It was a bold decision for it involved the demolition of 15 valuable residential properties in the railway village,

The first section of the new Institute, which was built in brick with terracotta decoration was opened on 15th February 1894 by the Midland Railway Chairman, George Paget, (later Sir Ernest Paget).

Its facilities were available to every MR employee who paid the modest subscription which was still one penny per week, payable quarterly. The main entrance was on Midland Terrace. On the ground floor was a library that grew to contain over 17,000 books, both fiction and non fiction, which were all available to loan. In addition there was a reference section containing 1,250 rare and expensive volumes, which included a special section devoted to railway literature.

The Billiard Room on the ground floor contained five tables, two of which were for snooker. As can be seen in the accompanying photograph, comfortable raised seating was provided for spectators.

On the first floor was the Reading Room where members could peruse 22 daily newspapers, 36 weekly periodicals and 54 monthly or quarterly magazines. Well lit, warm and comfortable, smoking was allowed in this room which was also available to the wives and daughters of members provided that they were in possession of a Ladies' Ticket. These cost two shillings and six pence (12½p) and were valid for a year.

The Institute attempted to cater for the widest possible audience, including theatrical and musical events which were held in the Concert Hall which was also on the first floor. Capable of seating up to 400 people, there was a stage at one end behind which were separate dressing rooms for male and female performers.

A glance at a map of railway owned hotels in the north of England as the nineteenth century drew to a close would reveal a rather surprising gap – Manchester. Even more surprising is that the city, nicknamed the "Cottonopolis," did not even possess an independently owned hotel of any quality. The majority of the many merchants and businessmen visiting the city who required overnight accommodation opted to catch a train to Liverpool, or sometimes even to Leeds or Bradford, to find overnight accommodation rather than spend the night in one of Manchester's inferior hotels.

The reluctance of the railway companies serving the city (LNWR, LYR, MS&L, CLC and the Midland) to build a quality hotel adjacent to one of its main stations could perhaps be traced back to 1866 when Manchester Corporation's attempt to build an up-market hotel had been a financial disaster. Alternatively, another factor might have been that all the city's main stations were 'shared' in one form or another and no one was willing to be the first to build an hotel for fear of upsetting the status-quo. That said, the CLC (Cheshire Lines Committee - a three-way partnership of the Midland, MS&L and the GNR), did have a plan to build an hotel and offices in front of their Central Station, but the scheme never came to fruition.

Although the Manchester Central train shed roof is nearly 140 feet shorter than Barlow's great roof at St. Pancras, it is almost as wide, and almost as high, and in the author's view, equally as impressive. The CLC operated regular expresses from Central to Liverpool (Central) as well as numerous efficient commuter services, but these tended to be rather overshadowed by the glamorous arrivals and departures of the Midland's magnificent London expresses. Perhaps the thought of a Grand Hotel fronting the station à la St. Pancras would identify Central as being Midland rather than CLC owned. But, whatever the reason, the bottom line is that the plans never got beyond the drawing board and the wooden buildings erected to provide a temporary booking hall, waiting rooms, etc., until the hotel and offices were built, continued in use for 89 years until the Central closed in 1969!

Passengers leaving Manchester Central Station either by cab or on foot could not fail to notice the tall building directly opposite. Although the main entrance to the hotel was on the opposite side of the building on Peter Street, this elaborate glazed terracotta decoration adjacent to the rear entrance on Windmill Street would not have left anyone in doubt of the purpose or the ownership of the building. Note the Wyvern surmounting the Midland coat of arms, embellished with garlands, cherubs and fancy scroll work. Photograph; Steve Huson

The impasse was finally broken by the Midland in 1896 when they purchased a 2 acre plot of land bounded by Peter Street, Lower Moseley Street, Windmill Street and Mount Street. The purchase price of £365,000 was further complicated because amongst the existing buildings on the site was The Gentlemen's Concert Hall owned by Charles Heywood. It was a popular venue, membership of which was limited to 500 who were required to pay an annual subscription of five guineas a year to be a member. The hall's popularity may be judged by the fact that the waiting list of prospective members numbered around 200. In spite of the title, ladies were allowed to attend concerts, provided that they were the guest of a member. In the past musical legends like Frédéric Chopin and Felix Mendelssohn had given recitals on its stage and the great pianist and conductor Sir Charles Hallé (founder of the world famous orchestra) had performed in the hall after moving to Manchester from London. To ensure that his concert parties would continue on the site Charles Heywood made it a condition of the sale and demolition of his neo classical Concert Hall, that the Midland must provide a similar size concert and theatre facility in their new hotel.

Although the site was bounded by four streets, the new hotel building was, in geometric terms, an irregular pentagon because a slight dog-leg in Peter Street meant a similar offset in the hotel. The two thoroughfares flanking the building, Lower Moseley Street and Mount Street taper towards each other such that the fifth side, facing Windmill Street was comparatively short. It was this Windmill Street elevation that looked out on Central Station, but Trubshaw chose to locate the main entrance to the hotel on the opposite side of the building, in the Peter Street elevation. This was the side that faced the heart of Manchester and its magnificent town hall and effectively announced to the city that here was more than just a railway hotel, but an hotel that the city could be proud of. But, railway travellers were not forgotten. There was an entrance opposite to the station on Windmill Street and bearing in mind Manchester's reputation for rain, a walkway with a glazed roof between the hotel and the station was provided. The roof was raised across Windmill Street to allow trams to pass beneath.

As mentioned in The Experienced Traveller chapter, before much design work took place the MR board sent Charles Trubshaw and William Towle (Midland Hotels Manager) on a fact finding mission to North America during the winter of 1896. The pair had already collaborated on the design of the Midland Hotel at Bradford. Successful and popular though Bradford was with travellers and locals alike, the new Manchester hotel had to eclipse both Bradford and the recently acquired Adelphi in Liverpool in every respect.

The hotels on Messrs Towle and Trubshaw's itinerary in America included the Arlington in Washington DC and the new Manhattan and the Waldorf in New York City. The pair then journeyed south to Florida where they were courteously received by the industrialist and oil magnate Mr Henry Morrison Flagler, the president and proprietor of the 100 mile Florida East Coast Railway. Flagler, who is much better known in the US than he is in the UK, had been the influential force in the development of both Palm Beach and Miami. In Palm Beach, Flager owned the iconic Royal Poinciana and Breakers Hotels. Such was the Midland Railway's reputation on "the other side of the pond" that Flagler not only placed his private train at the deputation's disposal, he and most of his officials accompanied them on their tour of inspection.

The challenges facing Towle and Trubshaw on their return from North America were enormous. For Trubshaw the new hotel was to be his magnum opus. For Towle, although the completion of the hotel was still in the distant future, he had to plan that when he did eventually receive the keys, he had to quickly establish the Midland Hotel Manchester as not only the leading hotel in the north, but the most complete hotel in the world.

The dream come true! Soon after the Midland Hotel, Manchester opened in September 1903, the company published a series of postcards featuring delightful water colour portraits of their hotels including several of the latest addition to their family. This one shows the main entrance on Peter Street, one of the city's main thoroughfares, and is marked by the two wide semi circular arched openings leading to and from the cab court. The dog-leg in the Peter Street side of the hotel, mentioned in the text, is indicated by the more muted colour to the left of the entrance. The monogram "EWH" towards the bottom left hand corner suggests that the artist was Ernest William Haselhurst (1866 – 1949). Midland Railway Study Centre 07144

Building work commenced in 1900 and took three years and an expenditure of £1.25 million before the hotel was ready to receive its first guests. It opened to the public on Monday 7th September 1903, but there had been a private opening celebration for civic officials and the great and good of Lancashire on the previous Friday. Trubshaw's ten storey Renaissance style building, parts of which soared to above 100 feet, incorporated two large light internal wells so that areas such as the Winter Gardens and the Octagon Court on the ground floor could, in the daytime, be illuminated by natural day light.

As we have seen in a number of his earlier works, in addition to his predilection for 135^0 angles, Trubshaw also liked to incorporate a few intricate details into his designs. For the Manchester project he seems to have developed what might be described as design diarrhoea. I do not mean that in any way disparagingly because it is a building that I greatly admire. But like Sir George Gilbert Scott, who squeezed every possible Gothic revival detail into the exterior of the Midland Grand at St. Pancras, so Charles used every possible Trubshavian detail in the design of the Midland Manchester.

The main contractor, Messrs William Brown & Son of Salford employed over 1,500 men during the building of the hotel. It was during December 1902 that the scaffolding began to be removed and Mancunians got their first glimpse of what was, and still is, one of the city's iconic buildings. For the exterior of the hotel Trubshaw chose red bricks, copiously decorated with similar coloured Burmantofts' faience (glazed terracotta) modelled by a sculptor named Edward Caldwell Spruce. For added opulence the entire ground floor was clad with polished red and grey Aberdeen granite. The elaborate exterior concealed a steel frame that carried fireproof and soundproof floors.

Rather than provide the more usual type of porte-cochère, the two large tunnel like openings (one entry, one exit) seen in the illustrations above were connected by an inverted "U" shaped carriageway so that cabs could drop off or pick up guests within the hotel. This worked well whilst guests arrived by horse drawn vehicles, but as equine power was replaced by internal combustion engines, fears about the effects of toxic exhaust fumes caused the cab court to be abandoned in the 1930s.

▼ Another view of the front of the Midland Hotel, Manchester, this time from the opposite side looking down Lower Moseley Street on the left towards Central station. Peter Street is running left to right in the foreground. Towards the right hand side, two horse cabs wait outside the entrance to carriage court to collect their next fares. Trubshaw's frequent use of his 45° set square when drawing the floor plans is very apparent. Even the boiler chimney was octagonal. Not so obvious in this view is his intricate detailing in the terracotta tiling. Midland Railway Study Centre 07384

In addition to the Concert Hall, of which more anon, the hotel had 400 bedrooms, 3½ miles of corridor and 23 lifts. All the bedrooms had electric light, telephones and most had private bathrooms. Every bedroom had a clock, synchronised with the hotel's master clock. At night guests could illuminate the clock dials from their beds. Other in-house novelties included a Post Office, a bank, Thomas Cook ticket office, ladies and gents hairdressers, Turkish baths, a flower stall, and a book stall. At various times there was also a tailors, a chemist's shop and even an haute-couture milliners. No doubt some of these features had been noted when Towle and Trubshaw were on tour in the US. Perhaps the most revolutionary feature was the air conditioning system. Two powerful electric fans pumped 80,000 cubic feet of air per minute though a series of linen and coke filters which it is reported were remarkably efficient in cleaning the air. The cleaned air was warmed in winter and cooled in summer.

It will be recalled that incorporating the Concert Hall was a condition of sale of part of the land to the Midland. The MR honoured that agreement and in executing it Trubshaw chose a Louis XIV style décor with the plasterwork picked out in gold. The first performance took place in March 1904. The hall had seating for 850 but could accommodate a further 100 plus standing patrons. It was in this theatre in 1907 that Annie Horniman (the tea family heiress) founded the first British repertory company.

However, the new theatre was not welcomed by many of Manchester's other theatre owners. They were soon petitioning the city council to have the new theatre closed down on the basis that it contravened the local bye laws with respect to the number of external exits. The Midland argued that as many of the patrons would be hotel guests the bye laws were not applicable in this case, which the council

The Concert Hall, or as the postcard title refers to it "The Beautiful Hall" in the Midland Hotel, Manchester. The main drawback was the level floor which rather restricted the audience's view. The painted panels on the front of the VIP boxes represent scenes from A Midsummer Night's Dream. Midland Railway Study Centre 07143

Terra cotta Wyverns beneath the cill of one of the windows looking out towards Peter Street ▼

Midland Hotel, Manchester
Garden & Terraces

▲ Another of the series of official Midland Hotel
postcards, this one featuring the Winter Gardens
and Terrace which for many years was THE
in-place in Manchester to be seen. This postcard
together with those of The Concert Hall and the
Roof Garden all carry the monogram PR which
your author believes is the artist Percy Robertson.
Midland Railway Study Centre 07145

▼ The Roof Garden of the Midland Hotel in the
early days with the distinctive clock tower of Alfred
Waterhouse's Town Hall visible in the background.
There is no doubt that idyllic scenes such as this with
elegantly dressed Edwardian ladies and gentlemen
taking tea beneath gaily decorated parasols and
serenaded by an orchestra did occasionally take
place, but equally, for many days of the year the
roof garden was a somewhat less uninviting place
as illustrated in the next postcard. Midland Railway
Study Centre 07142

Midland Hotel, Manchester
Roof Garden

accepted. Ironically, Charles Heywood, on whose
insistence the concert hall was provided, never did revive
his concert parties and with growing competition from
cinemas, the curtains closed for the final time in 1922.

The hotel was decorated and furnished throughout by
Waring and Gillow in various styles such as Jacobean,
Georgian and Adam. Hungry Mancunians and visitors
to the city had no less than five different restaurants to
choose to satisfy their appetites. One of the restaurants
was the Grill Room where on the 4th May 1904, a
mutual friend introduced The Hon. Charles Stewart
Rolls to Frederick Henry Royce. The result of that
meeting, as the saying goes, is history. Another of the
hotel's restaurants, the German Restaurant, not only
served continental food and delicacies but also genuine
Müchener Löwenbräu and Erste Pilsen Brauerei beers.

Trubshaw's pièce de résistance was undoubtedly the
hotel's Roof Garden. It has been suggested that the
architect got the idea whilst he was inspecting the
latter stages of the construction of the roof. He was so
impressed by the view over the city's rooftops with the
Pennine hills in the far distance, that he decided to create
the roof garden so that the hotel's guests could share the
vista.

In reality, bearing in mind the heavy atmospheric
pollution that prevailed in industrial towns and cities
at the turn of the 20th century, the number of days in
a year that seeing anything much more than half a mile
away could probably be counted on the fingers of one
hand. Add to that Manchester's reputation for rain,
and whilst novel, it was probably the least used of the
hotel's facilities. The smoke from the chimneys serving
the hotel bedrooms below the roof gardens as seen in
the photograph would have made the roof untenable
on cooler days. That said, the Roof Garden was the
venue for wedding reception in 1910 of Rebecca Marks,
the daughter of one of the founders of the Marks &
Spencer empire. No doubt the happy couple and their
guests would have been serenaded by Herr Drescher's
Orchestra. Robert Drescher, from Vienna, was the
hotel's musical director.

Although Trubshaw's detailing may not be to everyone's taste, no one can deny the quality of the Burmantofts faience around the outside of the building The decision to use vitrified terracotta to resist the corrosive effects of the Mancunian air has proved to be a wise one when compared to the degradation of some of the natural stone carvings at Bradford and Leicester.

The Grade II* listing by English Heritage / Historic England is well deserved and it is certainly worth walking around the whole of exterior of the building to study the detailing at both low and high levels.   We have already seen the name panel on the back of the hotel on Windmill Street. Just around the corner on Lower Moseley Street above the windows of the original Banqueting Hall are four semi circular panels, technically known as lunettes, each one illustrating a different

A somewhat bleaker view of the roof garden without the patrons, the parasols and most of the pot plants but photographed from pretty much the same spot as the artist sat when painting the previous illustration. Note the white and brown glazed brick chimneys and Charles Trubshaw's intricate wrought iron balustrade. The Town Hall Clock Tower which as the crow flies is 250 yards away is fading into the mist. Midland Railway Study Centre 19915

branch of the classical arts; literature, sculpture, architecture and painting. As mentioned earlier, the terracotta was modelled by Edward Caldwell Spruce, Burmantofts Chief Designer who had been born in Altrincham and had grown up in Knutsford.

Given the subject of this chapter, the architecture panel commemorating Palladio and Wren would seem to be the most appropriate one to illustrate, Equally, the sculpture panel is also very relevant as its creator, Spruce, was also a sculptor. Angelo, is presumably Michelangelo, but the choice of John Flaxman (1755 – 1826) is interesting for he too spent part of his career as a modeller for Wedgewood. Spruce's pride in the finished panels resulted in him signing each one "E C Spruce Modeller" in the bottom left and "Burmantofts Faience Leeds" in the
bottom right.

▼ One of the four semi-circular terracotta panels (or lunettes) commemorating the arts over windows looking out over Lower Moseley Street. This one represents sculpture and was executed by Edward Caldwell Spruce of Bermantofts Pottery Leeds.

The main entrance on Peter Street with "MIDLAND HOTEL" in large gilded art nouveau style letters with a Wyvern in a circular niche below has been photographed too many times to warrant another one here. However, much less noticed are the four large terracotta lions rampant guarding the north west corner of the hotel at the junction of Peter Street and Mount Street. Each lion is holding a shield between its paws; the shields of the outer pair of lions carry the letters M and R intertwined, whilst the two inner beast's shields bear the coats of arms of Manchester and the Midland Railway respectively.

A third public entrance to the hotel was located midway along Mount Street and was marked by another fine example of Burmantofts' craftsmanship adorned with yet another Wyvern and a third style of lettering.

Further along Lower Moseley Street near the Peter Street ▼ corner is this riot of terracotta decoration on one of the gables containing the seventh and eighth floors. Located some 70 to 80 feet above street level, few would have appreciated the detailing in the hotel's early years. Trubshaw however musthave anticipated future architectural trends, so that today with similar height buildings opposite the hotel on Lower Moseley Street and Mount Street, the intricate mouldings can be appreciated by a somewhat wider audience.

▲ The Mount Street entrance to the Midland Hotel, Manchester.

As reported earlier, the Midland Hotel Manchester opened its doors to the public for the first time on Monday 7th September 1903, but the official opening ceremony had been carried out the previous Friday in front of invited guests only. At the ensuing banquet, a former Lord Mayor of Manchester, Alderman Sir James Hoy, proposed the toast "To the success of the Midland Hotel" and spoke of the wonders of the new hotel and said that he had been told that "in it there was the best of everything that could be had on the face of the globe."

The report of the junket in the Manchester Courier on the following day only mentions Charles Trubshaw as being the architect, with no reference to him being present at the opening ceremony. On the other hand William Towle seemed to delight in basking in the limelight and made a well received speech extolling the new hotel and its facilities.

Perhaps the absence of the architect was due to the fact that early years of the 20th century were an emotional roller coaster for Charles. I have been unable to establish if he was present at the opening of his magnum opus or not, but if he had, any euphoria would have been rather tempered by the death of his wife Caroline at the age of 57 on 5th July the previous year. They had been married for 32 years.

Mrs Trubshaw would also have been sadly missed at the wedding of the couple's youngest daughter, Mabel Caroline to Richard Oakes of the Royal Engineers in Derby on 22nd April 1903. But more tragedy awaited the family. After just ten months of married life Mabel died in Pretoria, South Africa on 21 February 1904. She was 29 years old.

Less than a fortnight after the Midland Hotel in Manchester opened, what must surely be Trubshaw's smallest work, the memorial to the Midland Railway employees who had been killed in the South African War, was unveiled in the entrance hall at Derby station. It look the form of a simple rectangular bronze plaque surmounted by a Wyvern. Under the heading "In memory of the following members of the Midland Railway Company's staff who lost their lives in the service of their Country in the War in South Africa 1899 – 1902" were the names, ranks and regiments of each of the 68 men who died which are listed in four columns. Fortunately, when the station was rebuilt in the 1980s the plaque was relocated on platform 1.

The North Midland Railway between Derby and Leeds which opened in 1840 bypassed Sheffield completely due to the insistence of George Stephenson (who engineered the line) that the maximum gradient should not exceed 1 in 330.

Arguably this was a very serious error of judgement by Stephenson, a situation that the MR compounded by not rectifying it until the direct line from Chesterfield opened in 1870. In those interim 30 years, the Midland's presence in Sheffield was confined to the cramped and inadequate station at Wicker, the terminus of a branch line from Rotherham. In those 30 years, the Steel City had grown exponentially. The new through line required the construction of a new station in Pond Street. However, Sheffield's growth continued apace and by the early 1900s traffic had grown to such an extent that not only the line southward to Dore & Totley needed quadrupling, the 1870 station also required enlarging.

This proved to be one of Charles Trubshaw's swansong projects when it was completed in 1905.

The new platforms and facilities were constructed on the western side of the existing Sheffield station with the new booking hall, refreshment rooms, etc., located on the new platform 1. Most of the original 1870 buildings were retained for other uses, but the area where horse drawn cabs had once stopped to allow passengers to board or alight now became a running line, (platform 2). Trubshaw's new station buildings which cost £215,000 were fronted by a 300ft long porte cochère with a glass and iron ridge and furrow roof.

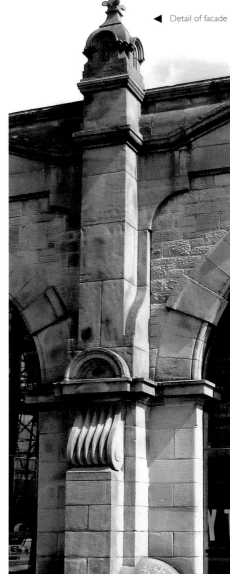
◀ Detail of facade

▼ The Yorkshire Rose

▼ The Wyvern

MR monogram

The northern end of Trubshaw's façade to the enlarged Sheffield station seen soon after the extensions were completed in 1905 and before the large sign was added. Numerous horse drawn cabs patiently wait for custom, whilst on the left an open top electric tram is working route H. The smaller twin arches towards the right hand side mark the passenger entrance, the roundel above the central pillar contains a carving of a Wyvern. The façade is slightly asymmetrical with five bays to the north (left) of the passenger entrance and six bays to the south (right). In the background are the rows of terraced houses on Park Hill with the skyline dominated by St.Luke's Church, on South Street. To many, the church was known as the Sale Memorial Church. To the right of the church is the chimney of the Norfolk Brewery owned by William Greaves & Co. Midland Railway Study Centre 67957/John Alsop Collection A70531

Soon after it opened the MR decided to make sure that the citizens of Sheffield were in no doubt as to its ownership the new station by erecting a sign some 70 feet in length over the entrance. Taken only a few years after the first photograph, the stonework is already showing the effects of the smoke and grime in the atmosphere. Midland Railway Study Centre 67954/John Alsop Collection A 3915

The twelve bay gabled façade built in Derbyshire gritstone, had bays with two semi-circular arched openings in each end and a similar bay towards the centre which marked the passenger entrance. On the north side of this were four bays with a single elliptically arched opening in each, with five identical bays on the south side.

Compared to the exuberant detailing of his designs for Manchester Midland Hotel, the new Sheffield station seemed very muted. Even Trubshaw's signature 135 angle corners are conspicuous by their absence except, subtly, for the included angle at the apex of the gables of the façade and the glazed roofs behind. That is not to say that the station and the façade or the station building are entirely devoid of decoration, or more to the point, lack character. The repeated features in each of the bays of the façade, such as the keystones and every third voissoir projecting outwards and the stepped corbelling below the gable copings are perhaps beginning to reflect a new and simpler approach to architectural detailing in the 20th

The southern end of the Sheffield façade photographed on 13th May 1912.. Two different styles of Midland Railway horse drawn Express Parcels vans (2110 on the left and 4138 on the right) are awaiting their next turns of duty. The back of a third unidentified van is parked under the porte cochere. Photo by courtesy of the Ian Howard Collection

▲ A view looking into the north end of the porte cochère which was taken on the same day as the previous photograph (the parcels vans can be seen on the right had side). On the left is a dray owned by E. J. Jeffs whilst in the centre are a mixture of horse drawn cabs and early motor cars Note the large electric clock showing the time is 2-22 pm. Photograph by courtesy of the Ian Howard Collection.

century. Inevitably, a Wyvern featured in the roundel over the passenger entrance, but the roundels in outer bays both exhibited a stylised representation of a Yorkshire rose.

Behind the façade, each bay of the station building had two semi circular arched openings with projecting keystones, except the entrance to the booking hall which was a single arched opening. The stone spandrels flanking the arch were intricately carved with floral pattern with MR in a circular motif whilst the lintel above was similarly decorated with a central Wyvern.

Charles retired in 1905 and in appreciation of his outstanding work for the MR, the Board resolved to allow him the keep his silver pass for Midland Lines.

Much of his leisure time during the summer months of his retirement was spent at the Derbyshire County Cricket Ground on Nottingham Road in Derby supporting the home side. His silver pass no doubt proved useful to enable him to travel to watch the other Derbyshire home games played at Queen's Park Chesterfield and perhaps also to travel to away games with neighbouring counties such as Nottinghamshire, Leicestershire, Warwickshire and Yorkshire. The outbreak of the First World War brought a premature end to the 1914 cricket season and did not resume in Charles's lifetime for he died at his home, 123 Osmaston Road, Derby on 17th February 1917 aged 76. The Derby Daily Telegraph reported that latterly he been in indifferent health. His simple funeral service was conducted by the curate of St. Andrew's church and took place in the chapel at Nottingham Road Cemetery prior to internment. The Derby Daily Telegraph reported that the chief mourners were his daughter Edith, his son, Charles and his wife, Gerald, one of his brothers, and of two of his nephews.

Space precludes this chapter from being a catalogue raisonné of Trubshaw's many works but the author hopes that his selection of some of the architect's projects will have focussed some greater attention on an important Midland official whose career with the company was concurrent with both Samuel Johnson and Thomas Clayton.

It is perhaps ironic that the few examples of Johnson and Clayton's work that have survived and are now revered museum exhibits; whereas many examples of Trubshaw's work, albeit sometimes much altered, are still very much in use today. None more so than his hotels in Bradford and Manchester and his stations at Skipton, Keighley, Leicester and Sheffield. The latter has been most sympathetically updated in recent years so that the once draughty porte cochère has been transformed into a comfortable, multipurpose, circulating area simply by dint of glazing the openings and the ends in the façade. Also, after many years of disuse, neglect and vandalism, the former first class refreshment room, complete with its original tiles, counter front and bar back have been beautifully restored and in 2010 re-opened as the Sheffield Tap which is now a Mecca for real ale enthusiasts.

The former first class refreshment room on platform 1 at Sheffield station has been sympathetically restored and reopened in 2010 as the Sheffield Tap. Some original features such as the front of the bar counter, the bar back and the wall tiles have been incorporated into what has become a place of pilgrimage for real ale enthusiasts. Photo; Steve Huson

POSTSCRIPT

In 1922, the Midland Hotel in Manchester underwent several changes which are really outside the scope of this chapter. However, one change which cannot be avoided noting was that the former German Restaurant, was prophetically renamed the Concorde Bar …

Charles's younger brother, Ernest, decided to not to follow the family tradition of a career in architecture or civil engineering but instead established a successful tin plating business in Llanelli. Subsequently he became a highly influential figure in the Welsh steel and tin plating industry. Ernest's son, Harold, continued in his father's footsteps, but Ernest's grandson, who was also named Ernest, decided on a career in aviation. After service as a pilot in Bomber Command during WW2, he was transferred to the King's Flight and flew Their Majesties King George VI and Queen Elizabeth on several Royal tours. After leaving the RAF, Ernest, who was Charles Trubshaw's great nephew, and who preferred to be known by his second name, Brian, subsequently became a distinguished test pilot and achieved world wide fame on 9th April 1969 when he flew the prototype British Concorde, 002, on its maiden flight from Filton to RAF Fairford and indeed on many subsequent test flights.

FULLY
QUALIFIED
SURVIVOR

Out of the many disputed reasons for the First World War, one constant emerges: it was a war where armies of millions were involved from the start, and the sheer bulk of those troops meant that they had to be transported by rail. Built into the German plan for success was the ideal that their rail system would allow troops and support to be switched if necessary between the Eastern (Russian) and Western (French) Fronts on which conceivably they could be fighting at any time.

Perhaps not surprisingly, as a railway enthusiast I have always been attracted to the historian A.J.P.Taylor's "RailwayTimetable" theory for the start of WW1. According to this theory, the diplomatic "face-off" in July and August 1914, basically a game of bluff and counter-bluff, led to the Russians (then led by the Tsar) threatening to mobilise. This in itself need not have started the war since it would simply mean that the troops would be sent to mobilising centres in Russia, not to cross a border on to German soil. As if to emphasise the fact, the Tsar went on holiday after giving the order. The act of mobilisation by itself was seen as a deterrent, not a green light for war.

However, the German approach to planning was somewhat different, and their mobilisation plan (the "SchlieffenPlan") ended firmly in Belgium and Northern France. The British at that time had an alliance with both of those countries as well as Russia, and the feeling was that they might well feel called upon to do something, although such was the diplomatic dithering at the time this was not at all clear. The Germans needed to move fast because they did not want to fight both east and west, and thus their initiation of railway timetables made war inevitable. The German plan laid down the first 40 days of the German invasion of France and none of it could be altered because if it did all the timetables would go wrong. Serbia and its assassination of Archduke Ferdinand, and Austro-Hungary which apparently started the war were forgotten by now; the whole thing came down to "if the Russians mobilise, then so must we."

Anyone who is familiar with railways will know how long it takes to develop a timetable, and the seeming intractability of

The title of this chapter is the title of Michael Chapman's famous album of 1970. See www.michaelchapman.co.uk I am grateful to Michael for his very kind permission to use it.

The moment when No.2717 is discovered alive and well in Mons. Colonel Speir, later of the LMS, who found it, is thought to be the man standing on the footplate.

wagons did sterling service on the Western Front, and nearly 23,000 of its workforce took part in the fighting.

However it is also true that one of its locomotives was the only British one captured by the enemy in the course of the war. That in itself is perhaps surprising when we consider that over a thousand locomotives took part, but it is also an indication of how static the Western Front became after the initial mobilisation by the Germans failed to make the expected breakthrough to Paris and got stuck along a 500-mile front along the French and Belgian borders. So how did the capture occur?

Writing in the Railway Magazine of July 1933, an author with some experience of footplate work in France calling himself only "Loco" has this to say about the event in 1917: "When the British advanced on Cambrai in October, 1917, the Peronne-Cambrai railway, which was quickly repaired, ran up the centre of the new salient. Early on the morning of the German counter-attack (November 30) No. 2717 took a working party and several wagons of chalk to fill a crater near Marcoing. Their progress was delayed by heavy shelling, and before long retiring infantry advised them of "Jerry`s" close approach. Ordered back, they went some 3 miles, the engine being finally left near Gouzeaucourt level crossing, with one injector working and the other tender water-valve open. The Germans were then in sight on the flank."

He goes on to say: "After the Armistice her driver, J. Woodhouse, Oxenholme, was working a supply train to Germany, and at Charleroi was surprised to find his old steed; she was included among a batch of engines handed back by Germany. The cab had been extended and other alterations made..."

them is still something we are familiar with today, so all of that rings true. However, I am not sure whether anyone has found out yet what the Belgian signalmen thought when hundreds of trains started moving east to west in front of their boxes. The Belgian army slowed the Germans up more than they expected by sabotaging infrastructure.

The Midland Railway made a considerable contribution to the war effort; seventy-eight of its engines and 6,000

He might have added that before being so kindly restored No.2717 was being used as a machine-gun post "practically in no man`s land", and that when it was finally withdrawn after doing further service after the war it had run a total of 1,223,630 miles, having been built in 1871. Truly a giant among engines, with an incredible story behind it. This essay is an attempt to piece together what we know about it, and in the centenary of this important battle of the First World War to shine some light on this battered old warrior and the action that caused it to be captured.

▲ Tanks loaded up and ready to be hauled
(quietly) to the front line, Battle of Cambrai
1917. The engine on the right is a Great
Western Dean Goods. No.2717 would
have been involved here at Plateau station.
The unpleasant conditions the troops had
to endure are in evidence here.
Imperial War Museum

THE ROAD TO CAMBRAI

Cambrai was the first major success for tanks in the First World War, and if November 1917 seems late in the day for that, then it does need to be remembered that they were invented specifically to overcome the inertia of a static war which no-one was winning and which was causing horrendous numbers of casualties in every attack. Famously, there were nearly 60,000 British casualties of the first day in the Battle of the Somme in July 1916; over a million died overall in that battle. Railways could feed people into the front line, but then they contributed to them getting stuck. Lt.Col.J.F.C. Fuller, tank staff officer and expert on mechanisedwarfare, had this to say in the Tank Corps Journal in April 1922:

"Before its outbreak…the effect of the strategic utility of railways on tactics was not generally considered. What do we see? We see the railways like great cataracts pouring millions of men…we then see a strange sight – millions of men facing each other – gathered in armies like bloated pumpkins hanging on their slender stems. Then from time to time, like obese monsters, we see these armies struggling forward – every yard they advance from their railhead making supply more difficult… While in civilian life the railway had increased the power of movement many hundreds of times, on the battlefield it had reduced it to zero."

The "millions of men" from Germany got quite close to Paris before a French counter-attack on the Marne on September 6th. drove them back closer to the Belgian border. The decisive French action was made possible only because on the evening before, 600 Paris taxis were emptied of their fares to transport reinforcements to the front. Unfortunately the commentary of the not usually shy taxi drivers of Paris is not recorded, but the issue of movement of large numbers of men after they had got to railheads was seen to be critical.

The German Army started to dig in on the line of the river Aisne, and Field Marshal Sir John French informed the King that in winning the war, "the spade will be as great a necessity as the rifle." Not long afterwards a colonel on the front line was amazed to hear the sound of music coming from the German trenches among the woods and ridges. They were settling in for siege warfare with on the one hand the bourgeois home comforts and on the other, the deadly firepower that only comprehensive railway transport could provide.

The British Army had been equipped with the Maxim Gun since 1889, four years after Hiram Maxim invented it in Hatton Gardens.* However, even by 1914 the British Expeditionary Force only had four hundred of these weapons which were changing the face of warfare; the Germans had more than twelve thousand, and were prepared to use tactics such as interlocking fire zones that would make them even more deadly. The attitude among British officers seemed to be that they were rather an unsporting weapon. Nevertheless the power of the gun itself used by either army made it clear that shocking numbers of casualties were inevitable in any attack.

By December 1914 the German strategy seemed to be to hold the line so that the allies would have to give in eventually and the land that was in their hands at that point, much of it valuable industrial belt, would be incorporated into the Reich. They only deviated from that strategy three times; Ypres 1915, Verdun in 1916, and Spring 1918 at Cambrai.

Meanwhile they laid siege to Antwerp, a matter of concern to the British Government since it would give them access to the coast at Ostend from which they could launch U-boat raids. To raise the siege a brigade of marines was despatched to Dunkirk closely followed by a fleet of London buses which were supposed to provide the marines with the mobility they needed on the ground. In the event the buses got to Antwerp just in time for them to help with a fairly organised retreat, still bearing destination boards for Hendon and advertisements for Dewar`s Whisky and Iron Jelloids. They left the city looking "shipshape and warlike" according to an eyewitness, although this impression may have been spoilt by the "schoolchildren climbing on to the rear platforms."

This is of relevance if only because it shows one of the low points in trying to break the stalemate of trench warfare. It became increasingly obvious that mobility was needed, particularly after the Battle of Loos in September 1915. Here the new and unpleasant weapon was poison gas, a new element in transportation was the use of Holt caterpillar tractors from America to haul guns, and three new armoured trains were deployed, but still the old infantry slogging match produced little in the way of advance and 43,000 British casualties. Buses were still being used to transport the men up to the front line, as they were throughout the war, but as they got closer to the front lines they tended to get bogged down.

Cue the railways, which were of course designed to overcome the problem of transporting heavy material through mud and other debris. One railway company had arrived with the British Expeditionary Force in France on 15th August 1914, but their effectiveness was limited by the lack of rolling stock and the use of mainly single lines. In January 1915 it was decided to send Railway Operating Division (R.O.D.) troops to France, the first five units consisting of maintenance engineers and footplatemen. Cecil Paget, the then General Superintendent of the Midland Railway, was chosen as the man in charge of the R.O.D. As a railway man first and foremost he was apparently reluctant to accept any higher rank than that of major; eventually the authorities had to talk him into accepting something more commensurate with his responsibilities.

* In a book on steam power it only seems fair to mention that Maxim spent the vast fortune he made trying to develop a steam powered aeroplane.

This was typical of a man all of whose energies went into making the Midland more efficient. The Midland directors had reason to thank him for introducing permissive block working at a time when many coal trains remained in loops alongside the main line for many hours, the crews sometimes booking off without turning a wheel. While working out the new system he lived for months in an inspection coach watching the congestion spots and formulating the remedy. He apparently did his own cooking in the coach kitchen and was very good at it, unusually for the times. He was also responsible for other efficiencies, including a general tidy-up and redecoration of the offices in Derby that led to far fewer minor ailments being reported. His first job for the Midland had been to supervise the construction of the Schenectady engines for the Midland, and he had developed a heavy freight engine largely at his own expense. You would need such "hands-on" people on the Western Front.

One of his first jobs was to double the track on the Hazebrouck-Ypres line. The French were nominally in charge, but in 1916 they allowed the British to be in control of lines within their own area.

In 1916 also an assessment of the situation by Sir Eric Geddes led to a strengthening of the R.O.D's resources in France. 20,000 trucks and 350 extra locomotives were sent at this time, plus 1,000 miles of track and the relevant maintenance personnel. By October 1918 there were 1,376 locos working on the Western Front behind the lines. Closer to the trenches, a system of narrow gauge lines was starting to be developed which could be laid quickly over rough ground and quickly repaired. The light rolling stock meant that less damage was likely as supplies were moved up to the front line.

So supply to the front was becoming more efficient, but how to break through the miles of barbed wire and concrete defences set up by the Germans, and how to cross the British front line before you got there? At Loos the Holt caterpillar tractors pointed to some way of using a tracked vehicle, but beyond that, agreement was in short supply. In December 1914 a proposal was put before the Cabinet for a vehicle consisting of large numbers of heavy rollers propelled from behind by a tractor, the idea being to crush the barbed wire through sheer weight.

▼ Cecil Paget. He was one of the 7,521 Midland employees who had signed up for war service by 14th November 1914. He was awarded the DSO in 1915 and the CMG in 1918. The French made him an Officier de la Legion d`honneur and the Belgians also awarded him a high honour.

This was followed by a number of ideas from patriotic inventors, including a fleet of armoured lawn mowers with wire cutters powered by compressed air; portable bullet-proof infantry screens; a travelling armoured field fortification with a two hundred-man crew; a rotating machine designed to spin a giant explosive-loaded flywheel before launching it at the enemy at 100mph; the substitution of tobacco snuff in shrapnel shells was at one point suggested.

Winston Churchill, at this time the First Lord of the Admiralty, was the most proactive supporter of the mechanical, rather than the military, solution. On 5th January 1915 he sent a memorandum to Lord Asquith, proposing the fitting up of

"a number of steam tractors with small armoured shelters in which men and machine guns could be placed...used at night they would not be affected by artillery fire. The caterpillar system would enable trenches to be crossed quite easily. 40 or so of these engines prepared secretly and brought into position at nightfall would advance quite certainly into the enemy`s trenches smashing away the obstructions and sweeping the trenches with machine gun fire..."

The problem was succinctly put and understood at the highest level, but the optimum engineering solution would take somewhat longer to realise. The first attempt was to lash two municipal steamrollers together and launch them at a dummy trench near Wormwood Scrubs. They broke apart within three yards of starting and even when on their own their rollers spun uselessly in the mud, so they were sent back to work on the roads. The problem remained, though, and if the Germans did not want to move from their increasingly concreted-in positions, they had to be moved. It was crucial to capture the railheads and junctions that supplied them, and Cambrai was the centre of a vast network of railways.

A small supplier of agricultural machinery called Foster`s based in Lincoln, (they are credited with making the last steam traction engine in 1942) with Admiralty advice, finally came up with a design for a vehicle with tracks running round a "quasirhomboidal" frame, with a sharply-angled prow ideal for climbing trench walls. The big track would have a footprint

Surprise! This view from a trench under attack shows the sort of effect the British expected from its new weapon. **IWM**

equivalent to a fifty-foot wheel. The armament was to be in side-mounted turrets called "sponsons". On 29th September 1915 an acceptable prototype was demonstrated, called HMLS (His Majesty's Landship) Centipede. When Haig took over as C-in-C from French at the end of the year he put a member of his staff, Major Hugh Elles, on to organising a division to operate the new weapon. It was early understood that surprise was of the essence if it was to be effective. Trials were held in the Breckland in south Norfolk, far away from prying eyes, and the very name, "tank" was invented to call the least attention to it.

Training of the new Tank Brigade was to take most of the early part of the next year, but by September some new element was felt to be necessary to push the Germans out of their well established lines on the Somme. The grim realities of this epic battle which started on 1st July 1916 have already been mentioned, but the new capabilities of the tank were tested in the offensive of Flers-Courcelette on 15th-22nd September. The British Army eventually took Morval, Lesboeufs and Gueudecourt, and combined with the French to encircle Combles. The strategic objective of a breakthrough was not achieved, but the tactical gains were considerable, the front line being advanced by 2,500–3,500 yards (2,300–3,200 m) with many casualties inflicted on the German defenders. The talk in the papers thereafter was of a stunning new weapon that had helped to turn the tide. Historians are naturally more cautious, and the consensus seems to be that the launch of the tank upon the world stage was a mixed success. The tank commanders such as Elles were concerned that the fleet such as it was was not ready yet for such an assault, if only because of breakdowns for which other tanks had to be cannibalised, but Haig and the rest of the staff seemed to feel that it was "now or never" and flung them into the fray, perhaps with the idea that experience was the best teacher. The infantry that marched with them, or behind them where possible as they were supposed to lend some sort of cover, either seemed to have thought they were hilarious, particularly when they ground to a halt, or that they were useful if the tactics employed were right. One tank, C22, was disorientated enough coming out of Chimpanzee Valley to start shooting at its own men from the Norfolk Regiment. Captain Crosse of the 9th Norfolk stopped this by banging on the side of the tank under fire, but:

Tanks being loaded at Plateau Station. The curious bundles on top that make them look like prehistoric monsters are fascines, a tightly-bound bundle of wood used for trench-crossing; by this time the Germans were making their trenches much wider. **IWM**

"It was many months before the 16th Infantry Brigade wished to have anything to do with tanks...not until the Cambrai show", reports Major Weyman".

Some tanks got well on the way to their objective, including D5 Dolphin, which penetrated nearly to Gueudecourt, and D17 got to Flers. However, both turned back on realising that they had gone well ahead of the infantry and were in danger of counterattack.

Second Lieutenant William Stadden had also gone ahead to Flers, but on finding that he was on his own, walked back to the village to find only 28 of his men still alive, with no tank cover.

His verdict was " I don`t personally believe anybody was frightened of them, nor indeed interested in them – they were too thin on the ground. It would have been different if they had been field kitchens..." He would seem to have put his finger on the problem. However, it was always the contention of Lt.Col. Fuller, second in command of the Heavy Brigade as it was now called, that the tanks would work best in bulk and preferably in "unicorn formation", one out in front and two staged behind on each flank with a company of infantry walking in file behind them. Fuller claimed it was based on a battle drill devised by King Cyrus of Persia in his wars against the Medes, but either way it was at least a plan.

He was stung into producing a paper on how tanks should be used by the action at the Third battle of Ypres, sometimes called Passchendaele, which started on 31st July 1917. The first offensive involving tanks that year had been at Bullecourt, where a dozen tanks had gone in in support of an Australian division but were beaten back with heavy losses. The second was at Messines in early June. Sixty-two brand new Mark IV tanks were employed and twenty-five reached their planned objective on the opening day. All was looking well for the main assault towards Ypres, which was intended to close the railway junction at Roulers, a vital supply line for the Germans. Unfortunately on the afternoon of the 31st it began to rain, and tanks foundered in the resulting morass. Eighteen floundering tanks were destroyed by shellfire near Hooge as they tried to engage a strong point called

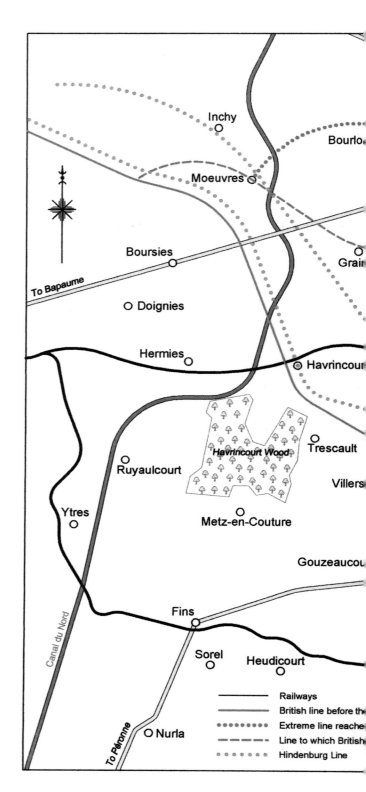

Raillencourt

CAMBRAI

taine

Proville

taing

Noyelles

Neuf
Wood

Marcoing

Rumilly

Masnières

urt

Les Rues
Vertes

Crêvecoeur

Les Rues-
des-Vignes

St. Quentin Canal

Bonavis

Vacquerie

Banteux

Banteouzelle

elieu

Villers-
Guislain

To Douai

To St. Quentin

| 1 | 2 | 3 | 4 |

Miles

er

Le Catelet

"Clapham Junction". It became known as the "tank graveyard".
As Fuller had stated at the outset, it was all effectively over
for the tanks as soon as it had begun. On 6th November the
Canadians finally took Passchendaele Ridge, but it was at a
cost of a quarter of a million British casualties. The famous
Menin Gate stands as a record of their heroism.

On the face of it, things were not looking good for another
attack so soon after this. Artillery and tanks did not work as
combined weapons, and tactical surprise seemed as far away
as ever. But before the Battle of Cambrai, it is said, the staff
officers at GHQ (and chiefly "Bungo" Byng the Third Army
chief) finally listened to the voices of the "men on the ground",
the artillerymen and the tank men who knew the technology
they were dealing with and knew what it could and could not
do. The country round the Flesquières Ridge was fairly flat and
well drained for a start, which would suit the tanks, and it had
waterways on each side which would make it less susceptible
to an attack from the flanks.

Fuller suggested that the tanks should be used as a "hit and
run" force to go in and scoop up prisoners and guns, and to
keep on doing it until the enemy was tired. The artillery, under
Brigadier-General Tudor, backed him up with a plan to sustain
the element of surprise for as long as possible by the technique
of "map shooting" and "silent registration". Observation from
the air and new ideas of sound ranging and careful appraisal
of shells, barrel wear and meteorology meant that the method
of starting a battle by finding range through a massive barrage
from the artillery was no longer necessary. The stage was
set. All that was needed was for the tanks to be brought into
position by the railways from Plateau. It was thought to be a
"quiet sector" by the Germans, a place where their regiments
could go and recover from the hell of other areas, so again it
had the element of surprise. The whole of the tank corps was
to be employed, and the offensive was to be in three stages,
the first to break through the German line between the Canal
du Nord and the Canal de l'Escaut using tanks and infantry.
Stage two would capture Cambrai and its railway junction and
the wooded Bourlon Ridge using the cavalry, and stage three
would advance northwards taking the German lines from the
rear and flank. After recent setbacks Haig was not sanguine
about results, and said he would abandon theoperation unless
there was a decisive outcome by forty-eight hours.

DAYBREAK, 20TH NOVEMBER 1917:

The predictive fire on the Hindenburg Line and key points to the rear caught the Germans by surprise. As the men and tanks advanced, a creeping barrage was laid down to precede them. Not everything went to plan – the 62nd Division advance had started without their tanks. 51st Division found advancing with tanks difficult when the German trenches were too wide to be crossed – the tanks became ditched as the fascines were not wide enough. The other divisions advanced over open farm land and had few problems. 12th Division advanced as far as Bonavis and Lateau Wood, 20th Division captured La Vacquerie and advanced onto Masnières where a tank broke a canal bridge over the St Quentin canal, resulting in the cavalry crossing in single file. 6th Division, after crossing the Hindenburg Line, captured Ribécourt and advanced to Marcoing. The 36th Division advanced up the dry canal bed of the Canal du Nord and reached the Bapaume-Cambrai road by nightfall. 51st Division became stuck on the Flesquières ridge when their tanks were destroyed by an artillery group which had had previous training in using their guns in anti-tank warfare. Unfortunately Major-General Harper, CO of 51st division, was too far back to advise on the infantry being deployed in a pinching-out operation. 62nd Division fought their way onto the Bourlon Ridge having taken Havrincourt and Graincourt.

The English attack at Cambrai for the first time revealed the possibilities of a great surprise attack with tanks...the infantryman felt that he could do practically nothing against its armoured sides. As soon as the machine broke through our trench-lines, the defender felt himself threatened in the rear and left his post.
- Field Marshal Paul von Hindenburg

The cavalry were not having the same effect and, where they crossed the St Quentin canal, they did so in small numbers which were not sufficient to cause the Germans problems. The cavalry support of the 6th Division did advance as far as Noyelles but were pushed back.

By the end of the first day the advance into German held territory was three to four miles deep but the Flesquières ridge was still in German hands. Before the second day dawned, the Germans vacated Flesquières ridge and the 51st Division advanced to Fontaine Notre Dame, where they were held

▼ A British tank of F Battalion after it had crashed into St Quentin Canal destroying the vital bridge at Masnières. IWM

▲ A little girl rescued from Masnières with a British soldier at Gouzeaucourt, 22nd November.

up by fire from the wood. Few tanks were available on this second day so the infantry had to advance alone. 62nd Division continued in their attempt to take Bourlon Wood. One action, before the village of Anneux, was particularly costly: 186 Brigade led by the gallant Roland Boys Bradford took many casualties. 51St Division advanced on Fontaine Notre Dame, coming under enfilading fire on their right flank. This caused them problems all day. III Corps had difficulty bringing up their artillery, so predictive fire was not available.

At 8.00 pm Haig's 48 hours were up and decisions had to be made. Byng closed down the offensive of III Corps on the Eastern side, their job was to hold the salient against any German counter-attack. Haig advised Byng to take Bourlon Ridge and 40th Division was brought up to replace the 62nd. They attacked through ground mist in the morning of 23 November but were met by machine gun fire and were unable to take the wood. On their west flank, 36th Division made little progress against strengthening opposition. 51st Division were pushed out of Fontaine Notre Dame and 40th Division became stuck trying to take Bourlon village.

By 23 November, fresh troops were required and the Guards Division was brought in to bolster the attack on Bourlon wood and Fontaine Notre Dame. The Germans pulled back out of the wood and their artillery swamped the vacated space until the English forces had to withdraw. By nightfall the Guards had taken heavy casualties and had been pushed back to their starting line. At this point Haig instructed Byng to close down the battle and prepare to withdraw troops on 27 November.

By Peter Palmer of The Western Front Association – with grateful thanks for permission to reproduce this account of the battle of Cambrai.

COUNTER ATTACK

No. 2717 was one of the engines helping to take all 36 trains loaded with tanks up the line from the 15th to the 18th November. In his memoir "A Company of Tanks," William Watson describes the eerie atmosphere of the night before the battle:

"...the slow dark trains, the sudden lights... the lorries that bumped through the night...Quiet railwaymen, mostly American, went steadily about their business...I found a hut with a fire in it and an American who gave me hot coffee and some wonderful sandwiches made of sausage and lettuce..."

More on the Americans later, but suffice it to say that the fate of 2717 and the USA`s 11th Engineering Corps are inextricably intertwined at this point. A Corps formed mainly of New Yorkers (hence the delicious sandwich?) only in March of 1917, they had been on the ground at Plateau station near Braysur-Somme since August, the first US troops on the Western Front, and the first to face enemy fire also, in September. Details of the work they did is supplied by H.J.Farmer, writing in the LMS Magazine of 1929:

"...special precautions were taken by the railway construction engineers to ensure that the track was capable of carrying trains of exceptional weight, and that all facing points were provided with a special clamp to hold them over firmly (military lines were not provided with any point locking arrangement). Ramps for unloading from the height of a wagon to ground level were also constructed at the buffer end of various sidings at certain advanced stations."

Farmer also gives a useful insight into railway working behind front lines:

" Any reference, whether by telephone or otherwise, to the destination station was to be by code letter only, because telephone conversations were liable to be picked up by enemy listening posts. The trains themselves were invariably to be referred to as Fish, and the speed was not to exceed 12 miles per hour at any stage of the journey, with a maximum of six miles per hour going round the S-curve between Leaze Wood and Les Boeufs. Furthermore, there was to be an absolute minimum of noise and lights, and above all, strictest secrecy was to be observed."

At least they had the use of telephones; the tanks only had pigeons to set free at crucial moments, and there is a story of one tank commander feeling so sorry for his pigeon that he let

*In what was possibly the most dramatic "what if" in history, Private Henry Tandey, VC, of Coventry, spared Adolf Hitler`s life at Marcoing on 28th August 1918 when the village was retaken for good. Tandey first took out a machine gun nest, then laid planks across a gaping hole to allow troops to roll across. Finally he led a bayonet charge against outnumbering enemy troops. As the bitter action wound down that day, and the Germans were surrendering or retreating, a soldier limped into his line of fire. The battle weary man, unable to raise his rifle, just stared at Tandey. "I took aim but could not shoot a wounded man", said Tandey, "so I let him go." The young German soldier nodded his thanks, and disappeared.

Later on the earlier bravery of Tandey at Ypres was immortalised in a painting by the Italian artist Matania. Hitler had a copy of the painting and when Neville Chamberlain asked him about it on his visit in 1938 Hitler said: "That man came so near to killing me that I thought I should never see Germany again. Providence saved me from such devilishly accurate fire that those English boys were aiming at us".

Tandey had reason to regret his magnanimity when he watched the firestorm unleashed on Coventry. He tried to join up again, "to see that Hitler didn`t escape a second time" but at 49 he failed the physical. He spent 38 years working at the Standard Motor Company, and his ashes were buried in the cemetery at Marcoing.

it go without a message at all, which somewhat puzzled HQ.

After the outbreak of the battle, it seems that the engines and their men lay low for a while at Sorel, one of the advance posts of the ROD. The absence of shelling, says Farmer, gave cause for optimism that all had gone well, and from the 22nd they started ferrying refugees and prisoners of war to behind the British lines. Cross-reference of material from the 11th Engineers and Mr.Farmer suggests that the next move was to extend the standard gauge lines to follow up the advance, and 2717 would have been involved in carrying trainloads of material together with American and Canadian engineers up the line towards Marcoing*.

The map of Gouzeaucourt on 30th November 1917, shows the level crossing where 2717 was left just east of the town. The mill shown also on the east was where the British headquarters had been set up. The Germans swept in from the east with surprising speed, and it was only the intervention of the Guards that held them to the old British lines. The tanks were still being rested up and serviced behind the lines, and arrived too late to make much impression.

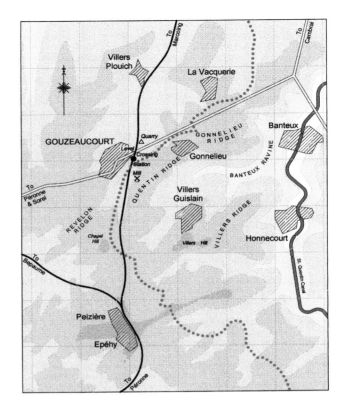

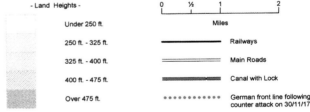

- Land Heights -		
	Under 250 ft.	
	250 ft. - 325 ft.	
	325 ft. - 400 ft.	
	400 ft. - 475 ft.	
	Over 475 ft.	

0	½	1	2
		Miles	

Railways

Main Roads

Canal with Lock

German front line following counter attack on 30/11/17

"Sgt Frank Haley from the city explained how they had laid the railway for the tanks and then helped unload and assemble the tanks before the battle.

Once the battle had commenced they had followed the British Army repairing the railways that the Germans destroyed in their own retreat. Part of the British plan had in fact been to link up their track at Gouzeaucourt to that of the Germans...a few kilometres away."

The morning of the 30th , therefore, would seem to have been a settled one for the engineers. They had their jobs to do and there was no reason to think that their plans for the day would be upset.

However, unknown to the British Army, after the initial shock of the 20th, the Germans had reinforced their lines around Cambrai with fresh experienced storm troops from the Eastern Front, recently released from their duties as a result of the Decree on Peace recently signed by Lenin, who was now in charge of Russian affairs following the Bolshevik revolution.

In the days after the battle of the 20th, consolidation of positions moved swiftly. Here is the C. O. R. C. C. (Canadian Overseas Railway Construction Company) on the Achiet-Marcoing line (Hermies Diversion) with their tracklaying train on the 22nd November 1917. It would appear to be a Dean Goods in charge, and they are laying down an interesting sleeper formation, perhaps for greater stability. Below, further up the line an LNWR Coal Engine with a continental guards van steams across a trestle bridge, presumably the two gentlemen pictured are checking to see that the bridge remains intact. Both photos IWM.

The massively concreted Hindenburg line was not expected to be a point of weakness, which was why it was staffed largely by weary and less effective troops, but now that the need arose, the railways did the job of transporting from east to West with great efficiency, and the Germans were ready to strike back.

On the morning of the 30th therefore, No.2717 hitched up to its train of wagons full of chalk and coaches full of US engineers, and headed off towards Marcoing. H.J. Farmer appears to have held a senior position and was in charge of despatch; it appears that 2717 had been working up the line all night, and appeared at Sorel in the early morning.

"At half-past six a.m. that morning I despatched 2717 again. This time her load consisted of material, together with four American officers and 280 men for Gouzeaucourt, where they were to commence tracklaying with the Canadian engineers."

He appears to have been able to verify the times because the incoming train driver had handed him a token for that section, called a "Bulletin de Penetration" on French railways, and *"being occupied at the time"* he had put it in the gauntlet cuff of his greatcoat and forgotten about it. It only came to light about six months later when he was on leave and wanted to send the coat for cleaning. What would we give to have that souvenir now?

Farmer ends his account with the following:

"At quarter past seven, however, a barrage of German fire moved on Gouzeaucourt, and fifteen minutes afterwards a general retirement was ordered, the enemy having cut our lines. Many hours later the driver and fireman of 2717 returned, but alas, without their locomotive. They had had to take cover for a long time in a shell hole, leaving their engine behind disabled..."

So what had happened? One moment the front seemed stable and consolidation was well under way, the next all was chaos and for the only time in the war, a locomotive was left to be captured and used by the Germans. What happened to the Americans is hard to piece together. It seems most probable that they had been dropped off at Gouzeaucourt and were working on the track when the Germans broke through. This was apparently at about 7.30 a.m., and such was the speed and ferocity of the attack that there were stories of officers running about in pyjamas trying to organise a fightback.

Major General de Lisle was the Commander of the British 29th Division. He had just been forced out of his own headquarters in the Mill and set about rallying everyone that he could get his hands on, including the Railway Engineers. There were rifles around but many lacked the time to get hold of them and they set about the Stosstruppen, highly trained fresh men from the Russian front, with mattocks, shovels, spades and anything else they could lay their hands on. One engineer, Harold T. Andrews, was killed, and eleven others were seriously injured but the rest, under the leadership of Lieutenant Paul McLoud, managed to get back to the old British trenches where the line was at last held with reinforcements from the Guards regiment. McLoud was later awarded the American Distinguished Service Cross and the British Military Cross.

The 11th Engineer Regiment was thus the first to fight, albeit with pickaxes and shovels, of all the American troops engaged during the war. Private Charles Geiger, among others, had been wounded and captured in the attack by the Germans on Gouzeaucourt and spent the day as a prisoner until the British Guards Division stormed back into the village forcing the Germans to leave their prisoners behind.

No such luck for No. 2717, which stayed in the hands of the enemy. H.J. Farmer puts the feeling eloquently:

"Railwaymen will understand the feeling, almost of affection, with which a locomotive comes to be regarded by those for whom she works, and realise the genuine grief with which we heard that 2717 was out of action and captured by the enemy."

The hero repatriated. It was built as No. 861 by Dubs & Co. in July 1871, rebuilt with a Johnson B Class boiler in September 1887, renumbered 447 in July 1905 and then 2717 in November 1907. When built it was stationed at Staveley then sometime between May 1908 and April 1014 it was moved to Hasland. Sent to France May 1917. After returning to traffic in Britain it was allocated to Sheffield until it was returned to Derby where it was assessed in June 1919 before being restored to Midland condition and taken back into MR stock in March 1920. After returning to traffic in Britain it was allocated to Sheffield until withdrawal in late 1932. **Notes by Dave Hunt MRSC.**

BACK TO BLIGHTY

The story of No.2717 might well have ended there. After all, not too many elderly engines could have survived several months as a machine gun emplacement- perhaps it was the famous Kirtley double frame that did it. However, the next we hear of it is a report that:

" in November 1918, during the great advance, Engine No. 2717 was found [at Mons]by Colonel McMurdie, of the 13th R.C.T., and Colonel K.R.N.Speir, who by a curious coincidence is an ex-Derby pupil and an officer of the LMS."

This report is printed in the LMS magazine under the heading of "War Veteran No.2717" by one "E.J.L." Members of the Midland Railway Society have identified this as Ernest Lemon, who at the time was in a very senior position in the LMS, hence his careful identification of another LMS officer.

Kirtley No.2733 at Bergrette, Belgium. ▲
Photo Midland Railway Trust.

Of our other authorities, "Loco" writes in the Railway
Magazine of July 1933:

"After the Armistice her driver, J. Woodhouse,
Oxenholme, was working a supply train to Germany and
at Charleroi was surprised to find his old steed."

H.J. Farmer does not go into detail, but once again stresses the
emotions when the engine is found again:

"Our grief was turned to joy, when, twelve months after
her loss, she was recovered in the great British advance."

So what had happened after Cambrai? There is no doubt that
when 2717 was captured, the army was caught quite literally
with its trousers down, and the tanks, which had basically
done the job for which they were originally designed and
by their weight and surprise factor had punched their way
through four or five miles of enemy territory, had been stood
down for repairs and were too far in the rear to be effective
when the counter-attack came. It was left to the Guards to
plug the gap at Gouzeaucourt, and then the winter

set in and the war of attrition continued. Official opinion, which up till that point had claimed the biggest success of the war and had led to the bells being rung back home for the first time, now gravitated towards asking what went wrong. However, a lot had gone right, and lessons were learnt, particularly in the case of "all arms" battle tactics, which were later to be used effectively in the battle of Le Hamel and Amiens the following year and ultimately led to the end of the war. Here a lighter tank, the Mark V, was found to be useful in consolidating the initial attack which only took 93 minutes instead of the two months of a similar attack at the Somme only two years earlier. The heavier tanks were used for supply, and proved their worth in that respect. Above all, the Australian troops which led the charge were reconciled to the tanks by training together beforehand; their suspicion had been dictated by the disaster of Bullecourt the year before. Signage and better communications, including the use of wireless for the first time, also helped in this success.

There are no indications that there were special celebrations for No.2717 on its return to British hands. That may have been because whatever its status, it was in working condition and therefore was put back into service immediately, apparently working the first train between Mons and the German frontier. It was a minor celebrity on repatriation obviously, since there is a special photo of 2717 in ROD livery reproduced above, as well as others which also served in France, suggesting that the Midland regarded all of its war heroes with equal affection.

The biggest surprise, for the Midland and others perhaps, was the extent to which No.2717 had been looked after and even enhanced by its captors. A list of the modifications that had been made is in the Midland Railway Study Centre. It describes alterations and additions such as these:

"The copper boiler tubes were taken out and replaced by steel, the firebox ends being beaded.*

The underside of the boiler barrel was renewed. Cast iron firebars were renewed and replaced by built-up steel bars.* M.R. drop fire-door and fittings were removed and replaced by a firedoor of enemy (sic) manufacture hinged at the side, with an arrangement for adjusting door on opening, and locking automatically when fully open for stoking purposes.

* Steve Huson comments:"My take on this is that both non ferrous materials and railway locomotives were in short supply . No. 2717 was therefore an important POW. From the German point of view, replacing the non-ferrous tubes and spectacle frames on an otherwise serviceable locomotive with ferrous equivalents was not a big deal."

A lubricator has been fixed on top of L.H. leading splasher admitting oil to cylinder steam chest. This lubricator is similar in principle to our sight-feed lubricators.

The pipes used with the fittings added by the enemy are in all cases steel.*

The cab roof and sides have been extended, the roof being carried by two additional pillars."

The modifications and alterations seem all in the direction of greater efficiency, and indeed comfort for the crew in the latter instance. Perhaps this is not to be wondered at too much if you read an account by ex-Sapper J.Harries of the R.O.D. who took the first staff train into Cologne:

"On arrival near the Nippe engine shed, we backed off our train, and ran on to an electric turntable capable of holding six locomotives...we were run off on to the shed roads...the fumes and smoke from the huge round shed were drawn by funnel clamps up to a single flue and into a high smokestack, which compared favourably with the low chimneys and smoke clouds of many British sheds. Slipper baths and a full-sized swimming bath were located at the far end of the shed, all done in white tiles – and how we enjoyed ourselves in them! There were electric turntables and small trams running in the pits and alongside the firedroppping pits, for smokebox, firebox and ashpan ashes. These were hooked on to an electric crane and hauled up above, to tip down a long chute into wagons. Everything seemed a considerable advance on the old-fashioned shovel system of ours."

Obviously the British crews thought they were in heaven! However, the relief of survival and getting "back to Blighty" must have wiped out any lingering envy of a German driver`s lot. And No. 2717, its adventures over, was in for a few more years shunting on the Midland before its extraordinary history came to an end after over sixty years and nearly a million and a quarter miles.

Here the new ashspray in the smokebox is highlighted, a refinement that did not catch on, perhaps to the chagrin of future firedroppers.

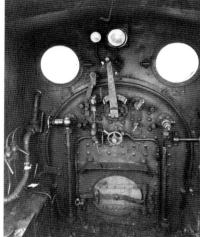

The caption to this photograph reads: "Cocks and pipes for ashspray, carriage warming and firehole door". The no nonsense Kirtley cab looks the same despite all this sophistication, but even here the Germans were determined to make it more comfortable by extending!

No.2717`s dome cover on repatriation. It had 13 patches, nearly as many as the entire engine, suggesting it was perhaps a tempting target. This and the other photos on this page are part of a series of notes and photographs in the Stephen Summerson collection, now in the care of the Midland Railway Study Centre, ref.no. 77-11586. It is not clear whether Stephen made up the album himself from collected material, or acquired it from a third party.

FROM OUT OF THE SHADOWS...

Two remarkable pictures emerged when researching this book. The first shows No.2717 in May 1918 actually behind enemy lines, apparently when it was in for repairs at the factory of "Zimmermann-Haurez et Cie" in Monceau sur Sambre. The results of being used as a machine gun post for several months are plain to see, but a testimony to its builtin Kirtley solidity perhaps is that it is not nearly as damaged as you might expect. On the cab sides "Bw. Cambrai" is written; the number is still intact on the smokebox. The photograph is copied from a German magazine from the 1970s, but despite extensive enquiries I have not been able to track down its original. I am grateful to Adrian Tester for bringing it to my attention.

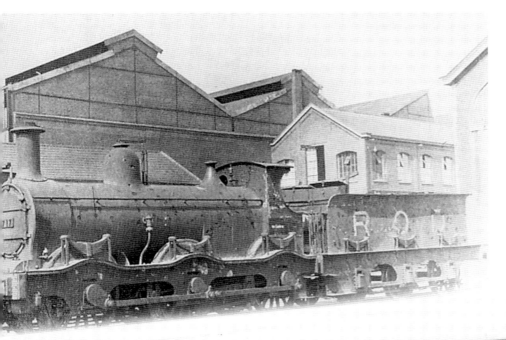

▼ The second picture is the only one I have seen of No. 2717 in LMS livery. The cover on the funnel suggests that it might actually be on a siding waiting to be scrapped. It looks a little forlorn, but the brightly highlighted number on its side suggests that someone recognised its importance. Photographer unknown.

THE EXPERIENCED TRAVELLER

The EXPERIENCED TRAVELLER Stays at

"Take Note of it"

MIDLAND HOTELS

"THE EXPERIENCED TRAVELLER is the keenest judge of a hotel and he is quick to appreciate a first class Hotel when he finds one. To the experienced traveller a really good Hotel is an oasis in the desert; a place to which he will return to again and again, and will recommend to his friends."

So begins the opening paragraph of a 1920 brochure extolling the virtues of Midland Railway's Hotels, the cover of which featured the Art Deco style image of the young lady reproduced here. The unknown, but obviously talented artist however appears to have used rather too much artistic licence when it came to locating the Midland's hotels. Whilst London, Derby, Liverpool and Manchester are more or less geographically correct, Bradford and Leeds seem to have moved very close to the Scottish border, whilst Morecambe has definitely been exiled into Caledonia!

But forgetting those artistic shortcomings, at the end of a comfortable journey on a Midland train a passenger could be assured that there would no shortcomings in the standards of comfort and service at any one of the company's several hotels. The company tended to regard the Midland Grand at St. Pancras as the jewel in its crown, but the same high degree of quality, comfort and service could be expected at its hotels en route such as the Midland at Derby, or at the northern termini in Liverpool, Manchester, Leeds and Bradford and even on the sea front at Morecambe. At various times the company also owned hotels at Normanton, Keighley and Heysham as well as four in Ireland.

The histories of the Midland Grand, the Liverpool Adelphi, and the Midland Hotel in Manchester have already been well documented, so this chapter will concentrate on four of the lesser known hotels; that is those at Derby, Morecambe, Bradford and Heysham and of course, the genius behind their success, Sir William Towle KB.

MIDLAND HOTEL,
DERBY.

The first of the Midland's hotels opened in Derby in 1841, three years before the Midland Railway Company itself came into being. The concept of a railway providing overnight accommodation for its passengers had been picked up by the building contractor, Thomas Jackson of Pimlico. Jackson, in collaboration with Francis Thompson, the architect employed by North Midland Railway, had already made an indelible mark in Derby as the main contractor for both the Tri-junct station and the adjacent railway village and Brunswick Inn. Jackson's offer to build, at his own expense, an hotel on land adjoining the Tri-junct station entrance was accepted by the North Midland's board in December 1839. The NMR acquired the necessary land, which it leased to Jackson and the resulting hotel, designed of course by Francis Thompson, received its first guests in May 1841. The Midland Hotel, as it came to be known, was only the second purpose built railway hotel to open and following the demise of the hotel at Euston in 1963, it has become the oldest railway hotel in continuous use.

▼ A lithograph, showing the original Tri-Junct station at Derby on the left with the twin, three storey blocks of the Midland Hotel on the right. The original hotel consisted of the left hand building, the right hand block and the single storey connecting corridor being added in 1842.

Both the station and the hotel were built by Thomas Jackson of Pimlico to the designs of architect Francis Thompson. The station, which had been extended several times, was controversially demolished in the 1980s and replaced by a modern building, but the hotel is easily recognisable today.
MRSC/KRM 60483

G. Rowe. Cheltenham

DERBY RAILWAY STATION & MIDLAND HOTEL

Published by W. Adam Matlock

Chambermaid

In the early days neither the NMR or Jackson any had thoughts of running the hotel themselves and initially it was managed by Joseph Hall, the proprietor of the station's refreshment room. Within a few months of opening the hotel's reputation was given a major boost when it received its first royal guest, the Queen's favourite uncle, HRH Prince Augustus Frederick, the sixth son of George III, who stayed overnight on 27th September 1841.

The hotel became popular with travellers to such an extent that in 1842/3 a second three storey block had to be built on the west side of the original building to satisfy the demand. The two buildings were connected by a single storey corridor which incorporated the main entrance.

By April 1843 the hotel was being managed by a Londoner, John Cuff, under whose watch the Midland gained an even better reputation for the high quality of its service. This was reflected by it becoming known unofficially as Cuff's Midland Hotel.

In August 1844 the hotel again entertained royalty in the form of the Duke and Duchess of Cambridge accompanied by the Hereditary Grand Duke and Duchess of Mecklenburgh-Strelitz and their entourage who lunched at the Midland en route to visit the Earl of Shrewsbury

at Alton Abbey in Staffordshire. The relationship between the royal families in Europe in the 19th century is a complex subject in its own right and not one which your author intends to delve in to too deeply. Suffice to say here therefore that the Duke of Cambridge, Prince Adolphus, was a younger brother of the Midland's first royal guest (the Duke of Sussex). Their mother, before her marriage to George III had been Princess Sophia Charlotte of Mecklenburgh-Strelitz from which I conclude that the Duke of Cambridge and the Hereditory Grand Duke were cousins.

Just two days later the Midland received its next royal guest, Prince William of Prussia, the heir presumptive to the Prussian throne and his entourage who were en route to Chatsworth. But the best was yet to come ...

On 28th September 1849, Her Majesty Queen Victoria, Prince Albert and their four eldest children (The Princess Royal, The Prince of Wales, Princess Alice and Prince Alfred) chose to break their journey from Scotland to Osborne to stay overnight. Derby was en fête for the occasion, with crowds gathered at the station to greet their Queen and her family who had travelled over Midland metals from Normanton. The following morning they continued their journey south on the Midland as far Gloucester, where no doubt Her Majesty was not amused at having to change trains owing to the infamous break of gauge.

However, the Royal party must have been very satisfied for they returned for another overnight stay at the Midland whilst travelling from Osborne first to Holyrood and then to Balmoral on 30th August 1852. On this second occasion Victoria and Albert's fifth child, Princess Helena, joined her elder siblings. As in 1849, the Royal Train was driven on the MR lines by the Locomotive Superintendent, Matthew Kirtley.

The surprising twist to the story is that just six weeks after entertaining the Queen and her family, John Cuff, his wife, four sons and four daughters sailed out of Plymouth on the ship Minerva bound for a new life in New Zealand.

The Cuffs were a very hard act to follow and it seems that the next manager perhaps fell somewhat short of expectations. Certainly by August 1855 the Midland was being managed by Mrs Susan Chatfield, who in the 1851 census was recorded as being the hotel's housekeeper. Mrs Chatfield who was in her mid 50s seems to have been a rather feisty lady who did not suffer fools gladly. In September 1855 she welcomed her first VIP guest in the form of the Earl of Cardigan. The Earl, otherwise Lieutenant-General James Brundenell, KCB, had commanded the Light Brigade during the Crimean War and had led the Charge of the Light Brigade at the Battle of Balaclava.

In April 1856 it was the turn of members of the French royal family in the form of their Royal Highnesses, the Prince and Princess de Joinville and the Duke and Duchess of d'Aumale who stayed overnight en route to Chatsworth. The relationship this time is an easy one to explain; the Prince, François d'Orléans, and the Duke, Henri d'Orléans, were brothers.

In 1859 Thomas Jackson found himself in serious financial difficulties due to the non payment over £210,000 for work that he had undertaken during the construction of the Riga & Dunaberg Railway in the Baltic. It resulted in him being declared bankrupt and his assets, including the Midland Hotel being put up for sale. By this time the Midland board had woken up to the desirability of having the Hotel under its control. However, before buying the hotel, the company needed to obtain Parliamentary approval and were thus powerless to take immediate advantage of Jackson's bankruptcy. However the problem was neatly overcome by the MR board who appointed a group of trustees to purchase the hotel on the MR's behalf for resale to the company as and when Parliamentary approval was granted.

The Parliamentary approval to purchase the Midland Hotel was contained in the Midland Railway (Additional Powers) Act 1861. Although it received the Royal Assent on 28th June 1861, it was not until the 1st March 1862 the MR finally bought the hotel for £10,600. Included in the sale was the Rutland Brewery which adjoined the hotel and was another of Thomas Jackson's enterprises. Thus, for a short period at least, the Midland Railway Co. owned a brewery!

Concierge

THE MIDLAND HOTEL, DERBY.

▲ (Plate H2) A view of the Midland Hotel as seen from Midland Road with the station in the left background. The main entrance is visible between the two blocks. Behind the wall on the right was the hotel garden which included a tennis lawn for the use of visitors. The illustration is taken from page 56 of the 1898 Guide to Midland Railway Hotels entitled "Travel and Entertainment" MRSC 02430

The earliest reference to the brewery that the author has found is an advert in the Derby Mercury in October 1850 seeking a brewer to manage a four-quarter plant. Such a brewery had the potential for producing 4,000 (36 gallon) barrels of beer per annum. It seems however that in the period between Jackson's bankruptcy and the Midland taking full control, the hotel's Trustees decided that the brewery would be leased. The subsequent details are sketchy, but by 1868, after at least one other occupant, it was being operated by Hooson & Brothers, who also ran two breweries in Sheffield. However, in November the following year the entire contents were put up for sale by auction. It appears from the list of items to be sold that by then the Rutland Brewery had developed into a reasonably large undertaking. Amongst the lots offered were a 900 gallon copper and 4,000 gallons of ale in individual casks. The buildings were subsequently demolished by the MR to allow the hotel to be extended.

Although the Midland now owned the Midland Hotel, they did not seem to be very anxious to actually manage the establishment which they sub contracted to the well known caterers, Spiers & Pond. Information about the hotel during next few years is rather sparse. Susan Chatfield remained as manager during the transitional period, the last reference I have for her is February 1863. By then she had passed her 60th birthday and was probably looking forward to a well earned retirement.

Mrs Chatfield seems to have been replaced by Mr and Mrs Plock. Frederick Plock who was born in the German state of Hesse-Kassel in 1841 does not seem to have made very much of an impression during his tenure as manager. The highlight seems to have been In November 1869 when Her Royal Highness Princess Mary of Teck and His Serene Highness the Prince of Tech stayed overnight. Princess Mary, a granddaughter of George III was affectionately known to the British public as 'Fat Mary' because she was small in stature but weighed around 18 stones. Having reached the age of 30, her chances of her getting married seemed rather slim until some serious match making by her cousin, Queen Victoria, found her a husband in the form of the Duke of Teck. (Teck was part of the old German kingdom of Württemburg). The couple's daughter, also named Princess Mary of Teck subsequently became the Queen Consort of George V.

One other very significant event however did occur during the Plock era when in 1864 the 14 year old son of the blacksmith of the tiny south Derbyshire village of Twyford was employed by the Midland Railway. The young man's name was William Towle.

Several generations of the Towle family had been farmers and blacksmiths in Twyford and no doubt it had been assumed that the young William would follow in his father's footsteps. However, it seems that the thought of spending his life forging white hot pieces of iron over an anvil did not appeal to William, but a career on the railway certainly did. Although most biographies claim that he was employed at the hotel from the start, in an interview that he gave to the St. Paul's magazine in 1895, Towle stated that initially, he had been employed in the MR Accounts Office and that after a while the Accountant, Mr. Hodges, had sent him to keep the books at Midland Hotel. For the Midland Railway, for rail travellers in Victorian Britain and for William himself, sending him across the road to the hotel proved to be a very foresighted decision. Just seven years later, the newly wed 21 year-old had impressed his superiors to such a degree that he was appointed not only as manager of the Midland Hotel, he was also put in charge of the Refreshment Rooms on Derby Station. His wife Edith was also employed to look after the housekeeping and the female staff. It was the first step on the ladder that would take William Towle right to the very top of the catering profession and earn him a knighthood.

Interestingly, three more of the additional powers granted to the MR in the 1861 Act reflected the company's growing interest in providing accommodation. The first authorised the company to purchase the Normanton Hotel near the former North Midland station at Normanton in the West Riding of Yorkshire. The second provision allowed the MR "to erect an Hotel, Refreshment Rooms and other Conveniences therewith on Land belonging to the Company at or near the Station of the Company in Leeds in the West Riding of the County of York." This was to be the first hotel that the company built itself and opened on 10th January 1863 as the Queen's Hotel. The third, but rather curious provision of the 1861 Act allowed the company to subscribe and contribute funds towards an hotel etc., near the

company's station in Sheffield. At the time the Midland's station was the inadequate former Sheffield and Rotherham Railway terminus at Wicker. This remained the case until February 1870 when the new through station at Pond Street on the new direct line from Chesterfield opened. By this time plans for a Sheffield hotel seem to have been quietly abandoned.

Waiter

MIDLAND HOTEL,
MORECAMBE.

The Midland's fourth hotel, on the promenade at Morecambe, had been opened on 11th September 1848 by the "little" North Western Railway. The NWR's intention was to build a line from Skipton to Low Gill on the Lancaster & Carlisle near Tebay. Having got as far as Ingleton, 18¾ miles from Low Gill, the company changed tack and headed towards Lancaster instead. From Lancaster, the short lived Morecambe Harbour and Railway Co. had built a line westwards to the harbour at Poulton-le-Sands. The MH&R was soon absorbed by the NWR

The NWR was described by one contemporary observer as a "ramshackle affair." Having run out of money building the line, it could not afford to buy either locomotives or rolling stock, which it had to hire, until the Midland took on the responsibility of working the line from June 1852.

In view of the NWR's parlous finances, building an hotel must, at the time, seemed to have been a harebrained decision. In retrospect, it proved to be a shrewd investment as the land was close to the harbour at Poulton-le-Sands, which was then in the very early stages of developing into the holiday resort that we now know as Morecambe. The NWR commissioned a local architect, Edward Paley, to design the hotel which cost a modest £4,795, including the furnishings. Built of stone, with green painted wooden window shutters, the NWR decided to name their new 40 bedroomed hotel, the North Western Hotel.

In addition to the embryonic Morecambe becoming a popular holiday resort there were ambitious plans to develop the harbour into a major port, not just as a route to Ireland, but possibly for trans-Atlantic traffic too. Thus, as well as catering for holiday makers, there was the potential for the North Western Hotel to provide accommodation for maritime travellers too.

▼ Another illustration from the 1898 guide book "Travel and Entertainment" this time from page 60. The artist seems to have deliberately foreshortened the distance across Morecambe Bay so that the Lakeland Hills appear closer! MRSC 02430

MIDLAND HOTEL, MORECAMBE.

The Midland leased the NWR for a period of 999 years on 1st January 1859 and then finally absorbed the company in 1874. Included in the deal was the hotel in Morecambe which the MR quickly re branded as the Midland Hotel.

As can be seen in the accompanying advert, in addition to boat trips to local destinations there were daily services to Belfast and Londonderry. The latter however were somewhat handicapped by the shallow waters of the harbour and the consequential dependence on the tides and by the late 1860s the Midland had transferred its Anglo Irish services to the Furness Railway's port at Barrow. As we shall see later in this chapter, the Midland, anxious to have a deep water port of its own, looked south to the fishing village of Heysham.

For some reason, in spite of its diminutive size and perhaps being a little dowdy in relation to the Midland's other hotels, the Morecambe Midland was to be able to hold its own with the 'big boys.'

Yet, in spite of its position on the sea front and views out over Morecambe Bay and no doubt employing the same high standards of comfort and service as in the Midland's other establishments, there were some downsides. With the railway lines to the harbour passing under the windows on one side of the hotel and later part of the harbour being used by Thos. W. Ward & Co., as a maritime scrapyard the hotel's environs could hardly be described as idyllic!

In LMS days it was decided to demolish the old hotel and replace it with a bold, new, state of the art building in the Art Deco style. The architect chosen for the project was Oliver Hill whose iconic curved structure with sculptures by Eric Gill and murals by Eric Ravilious opened in July 1933.

Returning now to William Towle, he quickly began making his mark and just two years after his appointment, the Derby Mercury of 22nd October 1873 carried the following report on the opening of a new dining room at Derby station.

ROBERT HARTLEY,
NORTH WESTERN HOTEL,
MORECAMBE BAY.

THE above Hotel being situated on the banks of the Bay of Morecambe, possesses one of the finest prospects for scenery that can possibly be desired ; in front it commands in one view the entire range of the Cumberland, Westmorland, Yorkshire, and Lancashire Lake Mountains, with the Bay intervening, forming a view unequalled for beauty in the kingdom.

Parties seeking pleasure will find the above establishment replete with every convenience, and fit up with every requirement for their accommodation.

The " North Western Hotel" is within a few minutes' walk of the Railway Station, and close to the Pier, from which the Steamers sail daily.

Wines, Spirits, and Ales of every description, and of the best quality. Hot and Cold Salt and Fresh Water Baths.

Pleasure Boats and Bathing Machines, on the Shortest Notice. Good Coach Houses, and Superior Stabling.

Families supplied with Draft and Bottled Bitter Ales, Porter, &c., &c.

Daily Excursions by Steamers and Sailing Boats to Fleetwood and Grange, to Piel Pier, for Furness Abbey, and Coniston Lake. First-class Steamers daily between Belfast and Londonderry and the Giant's Causeway.

Excursions to the Lakes by Railway during the season.

An advert from the Lancaster Gazette and General Advertiser published on the 7th July 1860. Note the reference to families being supplied with draft and bottled beers!

An early 20th century postcard titled "Promenade and Level Crossing, Midland Station, Morecambe." This suggests that the image probably post dates the opening of Midland's new station in the resort on 24th March 1907. This was located to the left of the photographer. The Midland Hotel with its shuttered windows is on the right. Note the sign "Midland Station Vaults" to perhaps tempt non residents to enjoy a pint heading back from the beach to their unlicensed boarding houses. Note the dome of the Pavilion on the West End Pier (left) and the two unmarked and two MR wagons on the right on the lines leading to the Harbour Goods station. Photo: MRSC 67830 /John Alsop Collection A96199

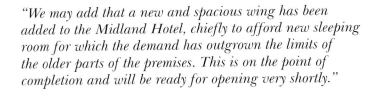

Another postcard from the John Alsop collection ▼ "Morecambe Bathing Sands" with the Midland Hotel in the left background and on the extreme left the tracks leading to the Morecambe Harbour Goods Station. Photo: MRSC 68548 /John Alsop Collection A96317

"Mr Towle whose excellent management of the Midland Hotel has given complete satisfaction to the directors of the Midland Railway saw the evil of the existing system and it is chiefly down to his exertions that the present extended accommodation has been provided."

The report concluded by saying:

"We may add that a new and spacious wing has been added to the Midland Hotel, chiefly to afford new sleeping room for which the demand has outgrown the limits of the older parts of the premises. This is on the point of completion and will be ready for opening very shortly."

It is presumed that this new wing was built on the site of the former Rutland Brewery. The Derby Mercury continued to regularly publish glowing reports of functions held at the Midland, a typical example from the paper of 30th October 1878:

"The Mayor's Invitation Dinner at the Midland Hotel passed off with unqualified success. Good company and genial speeches made the hours seem short. As a specimen of gastronomic art it fell little, if at all, short of absolute perfection and Mr. Towle certainly deserves, en passant his share of the complimentary allusions that were made on all hands to the splendid entertainment."

THE LOUNGE: *MIDLAND HOTEL, MORECAMBE.*

(Plate H7) A view of the lounge of the Midland Hotel ▲
Morecambe. The potted palms, the vases of cut flowers,
the lack of clutter and the furniture style all suggest the
postcard dates from the early 1920s. MRSC 07131

Such reports would not have gone unnoticed in the MR board room and it seems that as a reward, the Midland Hotel Morecambe was added to Towle's responsibilities as per this press announcement in December 1878:

"**MORECAMBE. VISITORS** to Morecambe are respectfully informed that the MIDLAND (late NORTH WESTERN) HOTEL is now conducted for the Midland Railway Company under the superintendence of W. TOWLE, the Manager of the Midland Hotel, Derby,"

The Towle empire was beginning to grow!

In 1885, the Midland Grand at St. Pancras was added to his responsibilities, quickly followed by the Queen's Hotel in Leeds. One contemporary periodical commented:

"Mr. Towle's career so far reflects the highest credit upon himself, and his latest appointment [to the Midland Grand] may be considered the reward of patient merit. He is a pioneer of a good deal of that badly needed refreshment-room reform which is almost everywhere manifest."

The following year Towle had more responsibility put on him when he was instructed to collaborate with the Midland's Chief Architect, Charles Trubshaw, on the internal layout of the new Midland Hotel at Bradford, then little more than a big hole in the ground.

MIDLAND HOTEL,
BRADFORD.

The new hotel at Bradford was part of an ambitious programme of improvements to the Midland Railway's facilities in the town. As related in the chapter on Charles Trubshaw, the impetus for this development began right at the top of the MR hierarchy in the form of the Chairman, Matthew Thompson.

Thompson was one of the main movers and shakers in the political life of Bradford. An Alderman, twice Mayor and a former Member of Parliament for the borough, a cynic might suggest that the new station with its adjoining hotel, on the corner of Cheapside and Kirkgate, was perhaps little more than a vanity project to enhance his standing in the local community. Thanks to prosperity due to its flourishing wool trade, the town was already blessed with many fine buildings, so Trubshaw and his team, including William Towle, were faced with a tough assignment. However, it was a task that they were not only equal to, it was one which they accomplished with style.

▼ One of the delightful series of coloured postcards published circa 1905 by the Midland Railway to promote their hotels. This one shows the façade of the new station at Bradford with the Midland Hotel prominent in the background. The bronze statue on the right is in memory of Richard Oastler (1789 – 1861), a Yorkshire born humanist who was a tireless campaigner against the exploitation of young children by unscrupulous factory owners. By his side are the figures of a young boy and a young girl dressed in working clothes and clogs. The sculptor was John Birnie Philip. The image carries the monogram PR from which your author believes the artist is Percy Robertson. MRSC 07147

Midland Hotel, Bradford
Forster Square

Work on the project began in 1885 and the new station opened on 1st March 1890. The hotel took a further three months to complete to ensure that everything was to the highest possible standard. Sir Matthew Thompson, Bart., as he had then become, must have been delighted with the result. Trubshaw's overall design and the interior detailing were superb.

Built in locally quarried ashlar in the Renaissance style, the hotel rose to a height of five storeys. There were three entrances. One was from Cheapside but the main entrance, marked by a square porch topped by an octagonal tower with a dome and finial, was on Kirkgate. The third entrance was direct from the station concourse.

The entrance hall, lined with white marble had a highly decorative tiled floor and white and gold ceilings. The white marble grand staircase and the main corridors were lined with white marble relieved by bands of Rouge du Roi marble with a plinth and dado of blue marble. Each of the main rooms was panelled in a different variety of wood, for example, oak in the coffee room; the smoke room was walnut and the reading room mahogany. The exception was the restaurant. Capable of seating up to 150 diners, it was artistically decorated with Burmantoft tiles.

The hotel originally had 72 bedrooms which were furnished in light oak with wardrobes, tables etc., in what was termed the "Parisian style," that is a bedroom and sitting room combined. There were seven suites which were described as "remarkably fine," with the two principle suites being "uncommonly large." They were all luxuriously furnished, mostly in walnut and green velvet. Electric lighting was installed throughout the hotel and the writer of a contemporary newspaper report was most impressed that he did not have to leave his bed "to turn it off or on, or even ring the bell as both knobs are fitted at the bedside." The reporter concluded that the sanitary arrangements were "simply splendid."

Having been involved with the project since the early stages of design, the hotel was managed by William Towle, whose popularity the reporter observed, "is on a par with his energy and conspicuous ability." Towle intended that the hotel should

The imposing entrance hall and grand staircase of the Midland Hotel, Bradford photographed just prior to opening in July 1890. The carpet has been fitted from the intermediate landing up to the entre sol and although the stair rod brackets are in situ on the first flight, the carpet remains to be laid. The white marble lining and the Rouge du Roi banding, and the contrasting plinth and dado, mentioned in the text can eaily be seen. Although most of the marble cladding has gone, the scene is still very recognisable today, with the elaborate wrought iron banister and the moulded ceiling hardly altered from the photograph. The reception desk now occupies the dark area on the left, with the Foyer Bar in the centre.
MRSC 61871

Sir Henry Irving

Miss Ellen Terry

become a superior exchange for Bradford's merchants. That ambition received a tremendous fillip when its first V.I.P. guest, only a week after opening, was the great Victorian actor Henry Irving who stayed after a recital of Macbeth at St. George's Hall in Bradford. He was accompanied by his business partner, the actress Miss Ellen Terry, who had spoken the lines of Lady Macbeth in the recital. Behind the scenes and strictly out of the public eye, Miss Terry who, by Victorian standards, had already led a very unconventional private life, was also Irving's mistress ...

Henry Irving and Ellen Terry proved to be the first in a long line of celebrity guests who have stayed at the Midland. Irving was probably accompanied by another of his protégés, Bram Stoker. Stoker, who managed Irving's Lyceum Theatre in London, was also the actor's personal assistant. In addition, Stoker was quite a prolific writer and is probably best known for his novel Dracula, first published in 1897.

The Midland had been open for less than a year when the African explorer Henry Morton Stanley and his wife Dorothy stayed in May 1891. Stanley was in town to give a lecture in St. George's Hall about his experiences during his 23 years on the "dark continent" including his search for the explorer and missionary, David Livingstone. Stanley did eventually find his quarry, the event immortalised, be it fact or be it fiction, by Stanley asking, "Doctor Livingstone, I presume?"

The hotel also claims that almost every British Prime Minister from Lord Salisbury through to Harold Wilson has visited the Midland, either for a meal or an overnight stay. In fairness, it must be said that Robert Arthur Talbot Gascoyne-Cecil, the third Marquis of Salisbury was actually the Leader of the Opposition when he lunched at Midland in May 1895. That said, he had been the PM on two occasions previously and just a month after his Midland lunch, he was back in 10 Downing Street. Standing at 6ft. 4ins., he is reputed to have been Britain's tallest Prime Minister and also the last Prime Minister to lead his administration from the House of Lords.

Sir Henry Irving returned to the Midland in Bradford in October 1905. Since his first visit he had become a knight – the first actor ever to receive such an accolade in the days before such honours were scattered around like confetti. On

this occasion Irving was in town for what was ironically billed as his farewell tour. He was appearing at the Theatre Royal to perform the leading role in four different plays on six consecutive nights. Midway though the week he had been the guest of honour at a civic luncheon and on the evening of Friday 13th he played the title role in Alfred, Lord Tennyson's play Beckett.

On arriving back at the Midland at around 11.15pm Irving was clearly unwell and rested on a chair in the entrance hall. The manager, realising the seriousness of the situation, sent members of staff out to alert local medics. The first two doctors soon arrived on the scene and found Irving unconscious. After giving artificial respiration the actor appeared to recover a little but then faded away and died. It was concluded that the cause of death was a massive heart attack.

Although aged 67, Irving's passing came as a great shock not only to his family and close friends and colleagues, but to the country as a whole. The hotel staff were naturally very distressed too. Many of the actor's obituaries in the press made great play of the fact that his final words on the stage had been "Into thy hands, oh Lord. Into thy hands."

On a much happier note, the hotel was involved in the celebrations that followed Bradford City winning the FA Cup in 1911. The final against Newcastle United which had been played at the Crystal Palace had resulted in a goalless draw after extra time. The teams met again on the following Wednesday, 26 April, at Old Trafford where the match was decided by a single goal by Bradford's captain, Jimmy Speirs. The team arrived later in the day at Bradford Exchange station where they were greeted by an estimated 100,000 fans (about a third of the population of Bradford). Because of the crowds the procession took 45 minutes before it eventually reached the Midland. The team immediately made their way to the first floor balcony overlooking the corner of Cheapside and Kirkgate where the trophy was held aloft by Jimmy Speirs to the delight of the thousands of happy fans below.

In spite of the artist's rather wayward approach to perspective and other inaccuracies, the above image was chosen to portray the Midland Bradford on page 42 of the MR's 1898 Travel and Entertainment guide has been included for the sake of completeness. The most glaring mistake is the impression that the building stands on level ground, whereas in reality, Cheapside (on the left) rises quite steeply. Compare with the 2016 view on the next page MRSC 02430

The Restaurant of the new Midland Hotel, Bradford laid up ready to receive some hungry guests. À la Carte luncheons were served from noon until 3.00pm; ladies could enjoy afternoon tea between 4.00pm and 6.00pm and finally, Table d'Hôte dinners began at 6.30pm and finished at 8.00pm. From the selection of food on the table in the left foreground it would appear that dinner was about to start. A Midland Bradford menu soon after the hotel opened included Consommé Vermicelle, Soles à la Meunière, Gelatin de Caneton à la Parisienne and Filet de Présalé Rôti served with Pommes Lorette and Haricots à la Bordelaise. MRSC 61870

There are a number of curious coincidences. City were the first winners of this particular version of the cup which is the one still in use today. It had been designed and manufactured by the Bradford jewellers and silversmiths, Fattorini & Sons, whose premises were just a stone's throw from the Midland Hotel. The Fattorini family themselves had had a long association with Bradford City and were involved with change of both game and name from Manningham Rugby Club to Bradford City FC. There was a strong Midland connection too. The club held their end of season dinners at the hotel and the MR owned the land on which the club's home ground, Valley Parade, was built.

The rather sad footnote to the story is that the cup winning hero, Jimmy Speirs, by then 31 years old and an army sergeant was killed in action during the Battle of Passchendaele on 20th August 1917. He had volunteered for service with The Queen's Own Cameron Highlanders and had been awarded the Military Medal for bravery.

The Midland had the honour of entertaining a royal visitor in the form of HRH The Prince of Wales (later Edward VIII) who had lunch at the hotel on 13th November 1929. He was in the city to open the new Bradford Chamber of Commerce which is opposite the hotel. Following the ceremony the official party simply walked across Cheapside for a reception at the Midland. The Bradford Telegraph & Argus reported that the hotel had discovered in advance that their royal guest's favourite tipple was a cocktail of white rum and grenadine and several freshly shaken glasses were waiting when the Prince and his party arrived.

Following in the footsteps of Henry Irving, many stars of stage and screen have stayed at the Midland whilst appearing at the Theatre Royal or the Alhambra. One of the mid 20th century's best loved (and highest paid) entertainers, George Formby, and his wife Beryl stayed for a week in September 1940. In those dark days of the war, when the Battle of Britain was at its height, George performed twice daily at 4.15pm and 6.30pm to packed houses in the Alhambra Theatre from Monday 23rd until Saturday 28th September. It proved to be a perfect morale booster in those uncertain days and following his Bradford shows Formby's performances were almost entirely devoted to entertaining our armed forces and

this occasion Irving was in town for what was ironically billed as his farewell tour. He was appearing at the Theatre Royal to perform the leading role in four different plays on six consecutive nights. Midway though the week he had been the guest of honour at a civic luncheon and on the evening of Friday 13th he played the title role in Alfred, Lord Tennyson's play Beckett.

On arriving back at the Midland at around 11.15pm Irving was clearly unwell and rested on a chair in the entrance hall. The manager, realising the seriousness of the situation, sent members of staff out to alert local medics. The first two doctors soon arrived on the scene and found Irving unconscious. After giving artificial respiration the actor appeared to recover a little but then faded away and died. It was concluded that the cause of death was a massive heart attack.

Although aged 67, Irving's passing came as a great shock not only to his family and close friends and colleagues, but to the country as a whole. The hotel staff were naturally very distressed too. Many of the actor's obituaries in the press made great play of the fact that his final words on the stage had been "Into thy hands, oh Lord. Into thy hands."

On a much happier note, the hotel was involved in the celebrations that followed Bradford City winning the FA Cup in 1911. The final against Newcastle United which had been played at the Crystal Palace had resulted in a goalless draw after extra time. The teams met again on the following Wednesday, 26 April, at Old Trafford where the match was decided by a single goal by Bradford's captain, Jimmy Speirs. The team arrived later in the day at Bradford Exchange station where they were greeted by an estimated 100,000 fans (about a third of the population of Bradford). Because of the crowds the procession took 45 minutes before it eventually reached the Midland. The team immediately made their way to the first floor balcony overlooking the corner of Cheapside and Kirkgate where the trophy was held aloft by Jimmy Speirs to the delight of the thousands of happy fans below.

In spite of the artist's rather wayward approach to perspective and other inaccuracies, the above image was chosen to portray the Midland Bradford on page 42 of the MR's 1898 Travel and Entertainment guide has been included for the sake of completeness. The most glaring mistake is the impression that the building stands on level ground, whereas in reality, Cheapside (on the left) rises quite steeply. Compare with the 2016 view on the next page MRSC 02430

The Restaurant of the new Midland Hotel, Bradford laid up ready to receive some hungry guests. À la Carte luncheons were served from noon until 3.00pm; ladies could enjoy afternoon tea between 4.00pm and 6.00pm and finally, Table d'Hôte dinners began at 6.30pm and finished at 8.00pm. From the selection of food on the table in the left foreground it would appear that dinner was about to start. A Midland Bradford menu soon after the hotel opened included Consommé Vermicelle, Soles à la Meunière, Gelatin de Caneton à la Parisienne and Filet de Présalé Rôti served with Pommes Lorette and Haricots à la Bordelaise. MRSC 61870

There are a number of curious coincidences. City were the first winners of this particular version of the cup which is the one still in use today. It had been designed and manufactured by the Bradford jewellers and silversmiths, Fattorini & Sons, whose premises were just a stone's throw from the Midland Hotel. The Fattorini family themselves had had a long association with Bradford City and were involved with change of both game and name from Manningham Rugby Club to Bradford City FC. There was a strong Midland connection too. The club held their end of season dinners at the hotel and the MR owned the land on which the club's home ground, Valley Parade, was built.

The rather sad footnote to the story is that the cup winning hero, Jimmy Speirs, by then 31 years old and an army sergeant was killed in action during the Battle of Passchendaele on 20th August 1917. He had volunteered for service with The Queen's Own Cameron Highlanders and had been awarded the Military Medal for bravery.

The Midland had the honour of entertaining a royal visitor in the form of HRH The Prince of Wales (later Edward VIII) who had lunch at the hotel on 13th November 1929. He was in the city to open the new Bradford Chamber of Commerce which is opposite the hotel. Following the ceremony the official party simply walked across Cheapside for a reception at the Midland. The Bradford Telegraph & Argus reported that the hotel had discovered in advance that their royal guest's favourite tipple was a cocktail of white rum and grenadine and several freshly shaken glasses were waiting when the Prince and his party arrived.

Following in the footsteps of Henry Irving, many stars of stage and screen have stayed at the Midland whilst appearing at the Theatre Royal or the Alhambra. One of the mid 20th century's best loved (and highest paid) entertainers, George Formby, and his wife Beryl stayed for a week in September 1940. In those dark days of the war, when the Battle of Britain was at its height, George performed twice daily at 4.15pm and 6.30pm to packed houses in the Alhambra Theatre from Monday 23rd until Saturday 28th September. It proved to be a perfect morale booster in those uncertain days and following his Bradford shows Formby's performances were almost entirely devoted to entertaining our armed forces and

this occasion Irving was in town for what was ironically billed as his farewell tour. He was appearing at the Theatre Royal to perform the leading role in four different plays on six consecutive nights. Midway though the week he had been the guest of honour at a civic luncheon and on the evening of Friday 13th he played the title role in Alfred, Lord Tennyson's play Beckett.

On arriving back at the Midland at around 11.15pm Irving was clearly unwell and rested on a chair in the entrance hall. The manager, realising the seriousness of the situation, sent members of staff out to alert local medics. The first two doctors soon arrived on the scene and found Irving unconscious. After giving artificial respiration the actor appeared to recover a little but then faded away and died. It was concluded that the cause of death was a massive heart attack.

Although aged 67, Irving's passing came as a great shock not only to his family and close friends and colleagues, but to the country as a whole. The hotel staff were naturally very distressed too. Many of the actor's obituaries in the press made great play of the fact that his final words on the stage had been "Into thy hands, oh Lord. Into thy hands."

On a much happier note, the hotel was involved in the celebrations that followed Bradford City winning the FA Cup in 1911. The final against Newcastle United which had been played at the Crystal Palace had resulted in a goalless draw after extra time. The teams met again on the following Wednesday, 26 April, at Old Trafford where the match was decided by a single goal by Bradford's captain, Jimmy Speirs. The team arrived later in the day at Bradford Exchange station where they were greeted by an estimated 100,000 fans (about a third of the population of Bradford). Because of the crowds the procession took 45 minutes before it eventually reached the Midland. The team immediately made their way to the first floor balcony overlooking the corner of Cheapside and Kirkgate where the trophy was held aloft by Jimmy Speirs to the delight of the thousands of happy fans below.

In spite of the artist's rather wayward approach to perspective and other inaccuracies, the above image was chosen to portray the Midland Bradford on page 42 of the MR's 1898 Travel and Entertainment guide has been included for the sake of completeness. The most glaring mistake is the impression that the building stands on level ground, whereas in reality, Cheapside (on the left) rises quite steeply. Compare with the 2016 view on the next page MRSC 02430

The Restaurant of the new Midland Hotel, Bradford laid up ready to receive some hungry guests. À la Carte luncheons were served from noon until 3.00pm; ladies could enjoy afternoon tea between 4.00pm and 6.00pm and finally, Table d'Hôte dinners began at 6.30pm and finished at 8.00pm. From the selection of food on the table in the left foreground it would appear that dinner was about to start. A Midland Bradford menu soon after the hotel opened included Consommé Vermicelle, Soles à la Meunière, Gelatin de Caneton à la Parisienne and Filet de Présalé Rôti served with Pommes Lorette and Haricots à la Bordelaise. MRSC 61870

There are a number of curious coincidences. City were the first winners of this particular version of the cup which is the one still in use today. It had been designed and manufactured by the Bradford jewellers and silversmiths, Fattorini & Sons, whose premises were just a stone's throw from the Midland Hotel. The Fattorini family themselves had had a long association with Bradford City and were involved with change of both game and name from Manningham Rugby Club to Bradford City FC. There was a strong Midland connection too. The club held their end of season dinners at the hotel and the MR owned the land on which the club's home ground, Valley Parade, was built.

The rather sad footnote to the story is that the cup winning hero, Jimmy Speirs, by then 31 years old and an army sergeant was killed in action during the Battle of Passchendaele on 20th August 1917. He had volunteered for service with The Queen's Own Cameron Highlanders and had been awarded the Military Medal for bravery.

The Midland had the honour of entertaining a royal visitor in the form of HRH The Prince of Wales (later Edward VIII) who had lunch at the hotel on 13th November 1929. He was in the city to open the new Bradford Chamber of Commerce which is opposite the hotel. Following the ceremony the official party simply walked across Cheapside for a reception at the Midland. The Bradford Telegraph & Argus reported that the hotel had discovered in advance that their royal guest's favourite tipple was a cocktail of white rum and grenadine and several freshly shaken glasses were waiting when the Prince and his party arrived.

Following in the footsteps of Henry Irving, many stars of stage and screen have stayed at the Midland whilst appearing at the Theatre Royal or the Alhambra. One of the mid 20th century's best loved (and highest paid) entertainers, George Formby, and his wife Beryl stayed for a week in September 1940. In those dark days of the war, when the Battle of Britain was at its height, George performed twice daily at 4.15pm and 6.30pm to packed houses in the Alhambra Theatre from Monday 23rd until Saturday 28th September. It proved to be a perfect morale booster in those uncertain days and following his Bradford shows Formby's performances were almost entirely devoted to entertaining our armed forces and

munitions workers. By the end of the war it was estimated that George had performed live in front of over three million people. A small brass plaque in the hotel foyer records George's stay at the Midland.

Two more world famous comedy stars in the shape of Stan Laurel and Oliver Hardy stayed at the Midland whilst performing at the Alhambra in Bradford in July 1952. Stan Laurel had been born in Ulverston, (then in Lancashire) just a few days after the Midland Hotel in Bradford opened in June 1890. Born into a theatrical family, he began his stage career as Stan Jefferson, working in both the UK and the USA where he was to meet his long time stage and screen partner, Oliver Hardy. Hardy had been a law student but had an excellent tenor voice and he was soon persuaded to perform on stage rather than in a courtroom. Soon after the pair began working together Stan changed his stage surname to Laurel. Then, as now, Laurel and Hardy just seems to roll off the tongue.

Curiously, the pair appeared at the Bradford Alhambra again two years later but this time they opted to stay in another former Midland hotel, the Queen's Hotel in Leeds which by then had been rebuilt by the LMS.

Mention must also be made of one of Bradford's most famous sons, the writer and broadcaster, J. B. Priestley. He had been born in the respectable Bradford suburb of Manningham in 1894 and was educated locally at the Belle Vue Grammar School for Boys. On leaving, at the age of 16, he worked as a clerk for four years before volunteering for war service in the army in September 1914. After being seriously injured in 1915, he spent many months in hospital but was fit enough to return to France in 1918. After being demobbed early the following year he continued his education at Trinity Hall, Cambridge. Priestley shot to fame in 1929 with his novel The Good Companions. His other popular works include the plays When We Are Married and An Inspector Calls. After a gap of some 40 years, J. B. Priestley returned to Bradford in 1958 and stayed at the Midland whilst taking part in a "grainy black and white" BBC TV documentary about revisiting the city where he had grown up and spent his formative years.

Before drawing a line under the list of the hotel's famous guests, in more recent times these have included the Beatles and the Rolling Stones, Donny and Marie Osmond, Jean Simmons, Benedict Cumberbatch, Michael Palin, and Sir Michael Parkinson, to name but a few from a very impressive list. The hotel has also been featured recently in BBC TV programmes with Michael Portillo, (Great British Railway Journeys) and Len Goodman and Ainsley Harriot (Len and Ainsley's Big Food Adventure).

The imposing architecture of Midland Hotel Bradford photographed ▼ during the author's stay in June 2016. The scale of the building can perhaps be judged by the lady in the centre beginning the climb up the steeply rising Cheapside. The original main entrance on Kirkgate (no longer in use) was through the square porch topped by the octagonal tower on the extreme right. The main entrance today is below the canted bay on Cheapside, but is partially hidden in this view by the pedestrian traffic lights and signs on the adjacent lamp post. The rectangular opening on the far left originally gave access to the ramp down to the fish dock at Forster Square station (closed in 1990) and is now a short cut to the replacement station. For many years the kitchens were located on the top floor of the building and during quiet periods in the afternoon, the junior chefs would while away the time by using silver trays as heliographs to attract the attention of the girls working in the offices opposite. Amazingly, at least one couple, who eventually married, met by this means!
Photo: Steve Huson

Heysham Tower, the Midland Railway's hotel at Heysham, (near Morecambe), was completely different to every other one in the group. For a start it was not adjacent to a railway station or close to Heysham Harbour when it opened and it had not been purpose built as an hotel. It had started off life as the family home of Thomas John Knowlys and his wife, Anna Maria, née Hesketh. The Heskeths were a well known and wealthy Lancashire family and Anna's brother Peter founded the port of Fleetwood. The precise date of construction is uncertain, so suffice to say here it seems to be in the period between 1835 and 1840. It was set in 13 acres of land where, no doubt, the Knowlys's ten children were allowed to let off steam.

As mentioned earlier, in the Morecambe section, some ferry services were operated from the pier there but these were handicapped by relatively shallow waters and the consequential dependence on the tides. By the late 1860s the Midland had transferred their Anglo-Irish services to the Furness Railway's much better harbour facilities at Barrow, but anxious to have a deep water port of its own, the MR turned its eyes southward towards Heysham, (which incidentally is pronounced "Hee-sham"). In the earlier years of the 19th century Heysham had been described as being "a place of fashionable resort for seabathing," adding, perhaps rather snobbishly, that its "visitors are more select than numerous." It was in this very genteel setting that the Knowlys family had decided to locate their home at Heysham Tower. But sadly, Thomas Knowlys committed suicide in 1850 and unsurprisingly, his widow and children soon moved elsewhere.

For many of the years that followed, Heysham Tower was the home of the Bennett family. Alderman William Bennett J.P., was a wealthy Liverpool politician and businessman. When he died in September 1885, as a result of injuries from in a road accident a few weeks previously, his estate was valued at over £267,000. His widow, Mary, continued living at the Tower until her death in 1888. The 1891 census shows that the property was then occupied by Joseph and Mary Cawthra and their 25 year old daughter, Amelia. Joseph Cawthra was a mill owner from Bradford so the clean, fresh sea breezes of Heysham must have contrasted sharply with the polluted air from the mills and factories of his home town.

▼ Heysham Tower as illustrated on page 62 of the MR's 1898 Hotel Guide MRSC 02430

· HEYSHAM TOWER · NEAR MORECAMBE ·

However, by the early 1890s, the winds of change were beginning to blow through Heysham which would culminate in the quiet agricultural and fishing settlement being transformed by the Midland Railway into a thriving port. With the impending development, the Cawthra family decided to vote with their feet and move back to Bradford, selling the Tower to the Midland Railway Company for conversion into an hotel.

The first mention of the hotel being open for business appeared in an advert in the Pall Mall Gazette on the 15th December 1896. Although the advert was primarily to extol the virtues of the new Parisian Restaurant in the Midland Grand Hotel at St. Pancras, it concluded with a list of other hotels under William Towle's management including, last of all, "Heysham Tower near Morecambe."

The "Travel and Entertainment" theme was continued by the MR publishing packs of playing cards the reverse side of which had this curious Art Nouveau image. The cards appear to have been published somewhat later than the 1898 guide book because the Midland Manchester (opened in September1903) is included. MRSC 12918 ▶

A rather impressionistic sketch by an unknown artist of the garden at Heysham Tower reproduced on a commercial postcard. In 1852 the mansion was described as having an entrance hall, dining room, drawing room and library on the ground floor with the Tower room opening into the conservatory. Upstairs, there were eleven bedrooms as well as accommodation for the domestic staff. The description concludes by saying that the house had commanding views over Morecambe Bay and the Cumberland Hills. MRSC 06059 ▼

As mentioned in the preamble, Heysham Tower was certainly a "one-off" when compared to the Midland's other hotels. Because of its commanding but rural position, with views over Morecambe Bay with the Lakeland mountains as a backdrop, William Towle must have seen a potential for catering for a different type of client than those who normally used Midland Hotels.

In 1898, the Midland published an official hotel guide under the title "Travel and Entertainment" which described their newest acquisition as follows:

"This establishment is beautifully fitted up with every modern convenience. ELECTRIC LIGHT throughout the house &c. The rooms, which are well ventilated, are heated with water apparatus during the winter months."

"The House comprises a handsomely furnished Drawing Room, Dining Room, Reading and Writing Room, Conservatory, also Billiard and Smoke Room, all of which are upon the ground floor."

"The stabling is commodious, and visitors may bring their own carriages and horses. A private Landau or 'Bus will, on application, meet intending visitors either at the Midland or L. N. W. Railway Station." (These of course, would be the stations at Morecambe as it was not until 11th July 1904 that the MR branch from Morecambe was opened for traffic). "The house stands in its own grounds of about 14 acres including Vineries, Tennis and Croquet Lawns etc. Excursions can be made from the 'Tower' to the Lake District and other popular resorts returning in the course of the day."

◄ The imposing front of Heysham Tower is shown in this coloured postcard which was used in August 1906 when the hotel had been in Midland ownership for ten years. Note that during the period the mansion was privately owned and indeed, throughout the Midland years, the official name was Heysham Tower. That said, it was occasionally referred to as Heysham Towers in a few MR documents which your author concludes, were typos as it was only in the 1920s that it became Heysham Towers or Morecambe Bay Holiday Camp. MRSC 23789

The Tower seems to have been run on more or less the same lines as a traditional seaside boarding house, with guests being arbitrarily woken at eight o'clock, given 15 minutes warning of meal times and being summoned to the dining room by a gong as shown on the right …

Meal times at the Midland's other hotels were much more flexible; breakfast was usually served between 8.00 and 10.30, lunch from 12.30 to 2.30 and one could sit down for dinner between 6.00 and 8.00. In fairness however, it must be said that "Business Gentlemen" could obtain an early breakfast and also arrangements could be made to convey anyone wishing to travel by an early train to the station. Another concession was that visitors boarding at Heysham Tower could obtain coupons for taking meals at the Midland Hotel in Morecambe.

In spite of the apparent regimentation, a visitor in September 1898 was profuse in his, or her, praise of the hotel.

"The Midland Railway have acquired an immense amount of property including the Heysham Tower Estate. The comfortable mansion is now converted into as cosy an hotel as could possibly exist. From no point of view in the extensive grounds or from the house can the [new harbour] works be seen; the scenery is untouched and the fair prospect of wood and water from the Tower itself suggests a distance from towns and rail altogether disproportionate to the reality. It is now an ideal country house where guests almost forget that they have a modest bill to pay at the end of the each week; they are made at home."

One has to wonder how independent the anonymous reviewer might perhaps have been.

The "modest weekly bill" according to the 1898 tariff was 2½ to 3½ guineas (£2.63 to £3.68) during the winter months, rising to 3 to 5 guineas (£3.15 to £5.25) at Easter, Whitsuntide and during the summer. These were considerably less than individual daily cost of rooms and meals, which were similar to the rates charged at other MR hotels.

However, Heysham Tower's "out of sight" location meant that for many prospective guests, it was also "out of mind" and by 1900 the hotel was only opening for the summer season. The

HOURS OF MEALS . . .

AND

. . GENERAL REGULATIONS.

The Bell rings every morning at 8 a.m., and a quarter of an hour before each meal, and the gong is sounded at meal hours

			Week days		Sundays.
Breakfast	…	…	9 a.m.	…	9 a.m.
Luncheon	..	…	1 p.m.	…	1 p.m.
Dinner	…	…	7 p.m.	…	6.30 p.m.
Tea and Coffee	…	…	8.30 p.m.	…	8 p.m.

The above hours may be altered according to the discretion of the management at any time. Afternoon Tea served at 4 p.m. At any other time it will be charged for.

No attendance to be expected from servants after 10 p.m.

The Billiard Room is open from 10 a.m. till 11 p.m.

Heysham Tower from the south, seemingly from the same series of coloured postcards as the one reproduced earlier. Attractive though this approach is, the main drive to the house was from the north. Photograph by kind courtesy of the Heysham Historical Association.

Chef

Porter

massive construction work taking place nearby was surely another contributory factor to the lack of custom. Yet, even though closed for the winter, the garden apparently supplied flowers and vegetables to at least the First Class Refreshment Room at Leeds. It probably supplied other MR catering outlets too, but the Leeds connection is confirmed by a curt typewritten memo from William Towle dated June 1901 to the manageress, Miss Heywood ...

Heysham Towers Flower Boxes and Hampers.

I have received a complaint that the above when empty are not being returned promptly to Heysham Towers. Please see that no delay occurs in future in emptying these and having them addressed and dispatched to Heysham Towers, Morecambe.

Acknowledge receipt.

W. Towle

Note the two incorrect references to Heysham Towers.

The opening of the new harbour and the railway to Heysham in the summer of 1904 does not seem to have made a significant impact on the number of visitors to the hotel. Ten years later, after William Towle had retired and been replaced by his sons, Francis and Arthur, the Tower still only opened in the summer season, with the weekly tariff unchanged at three to five guineas. By then, the proximity of the Heysham Golf Course (which had opened in 1910) had become an added attraction, being only five minutes walk away. For the more experienced players, the "well known Lancaster Golf Links can easily be reached by train."

During the Great War, the Tower was used as the mess for officers commanding troops stationed in the area, but by the end of the conflict, the Midland had given up hope of the hotel becoming a profitable venture. In July 1919 the MR's Hotels and Refreshment Rooms Committee decided that the Tower's losses were unsustainable and agreed to put the property on the market.

In 1925 it re-opened as Heysham Towers Holiday Camp (note the plural) – although it was sometimes known by the alternative title Morecambe Bay Holiday Camp. In the early days, your author has been told that there was strict segregation of the sexes in so much as female campers slept in dormitories in the house whilst male campers slept in huts in the grounds! What has not been established is if this applied to couples who were married (to each other). If so, it couldn't have been much fun for honeymooners!

Two days before WW2 started the camp was was requisitioned by the Army as an Officer Cadet Training Unit (OCTU). It was returned to civilian use in December 1945 and refurbished as a holiday camp. These were the golden days of the British holiday camps before their popularity was eroded by the more attractive cheap package holidays to Spain and beyond. Heysham Towers also faced stiff competition from the much larger Pontin's owned Middleton Towers Camp nearby. At the peak, Heysham Towers could cater for 500 visitors per week whilst Pontin's were able to cope with six times that number. Inevitably Heysham Towers Holiday Camp closed at the end of the 1972 season and the contents were sold by auction in February 1973. The Towers and other camp buildings were demolished in December 1976.

Heysham Tower must rank as William Towle's most unsuccessful venture in what was otherwise a brilliantly successful career.

As we saw earlier, by the 1880s Towle was controlling all the Midland's hotels and was involved with the design of the new Bradford hotel. A classic example of him never missing a chance to increase the profitability of his empire can be found when the Royal Agricultural Society's Show was held in Derby in 1881. Naturally, the Midland and the other main hotels in Derby were soon fully booked. But rather than turn potential guests away Towle placed the following advert in several editions of the Derby Mercury.

"THE MANAGER of the MIDLAND HOTEL is prepared to receive a limited number of NAMES of HOUSEHOLDERS who would be willing to LET BEDROOMS during the Show Week to Visitors who will be Boarded at the Hotel, the Manager undertaking all the

Lift Boy

Waitress

arrangements except sleeping accommodation. Answers to this advertisement will be treated confidentially, and careful selection will be made of the applicants for rooms who will be in most cases regular customers of the Hotel."

In other words, by subcontracting the sleeping arrangements, he could still make money by providing the overspill guests with their meals etc.

Less than two years after the Midland at Bradford had opened its doors, the MR added the prestigious Adelphi Hotel in Liverpool to its portfolio. The hotel's history went back to 1827 when two adjoining Georgian town houses were converted into an hotel. Several more adjacent properties were added as the Adelphi's reputation grew and by the 1860s it was THE place to stay in Liverpool. However, by the early 1870s demand regularly exceeded supply and the owner took the bold decision to demolish the existing premises and replace them with a brand new, state-of-the-art building. With just under 300 bedrooms, 50 parlours and an army of staff numbering 140, the new hotel opened its doors in 1876. It was this second Adelphi that the Midland acquired in 1892. Needless to say it immediately became part of William Towle's empire, but it faced stiff competition from the nearby LNWR's North Western Hotel adjoining their Lime Street and from the LYR's Exchange Hotel attached to their terminus on the other side of the city.

In 1895 Towle once again began collaborating with Charles Trubshaw, this time on the interior design of the company's new hotel in Manchester. And as related in the chapter on Charles Trubshaw, the MR sent the pair on a fact finding tour of North America to look at the latest hotels in New York, Washington DC and Florida. The tour obviously paid dividends because when the hotel opened its doors in September 1903 it contained such novelties as air conditioning, a concert hall, a roof garden and even its own post office.

At some point after the Midland Grand at St. Pancras came under his wing, Towle relocated his department to the splendid surroundings of the London hotel. He must have left Derby with rather mixed feelings. He possessed a fine bass voice and was a regular member of the choir of the Railwaymen's Church in Derby, St. Andrews on London

Road. On the other hand, moving to London gave him the opportunity to meet the stars of the day and as one of his obituaries commented, there were few celebrities in the world of music who could not be counted as his personal friends.

Although the next nearest hotel in his empire was over 120 miles away in Derby, virtually nothing escaped his attention as he ruled from his lofty eyrie on the top floor of the Grand's West Tower. In today's parlance he would be termed a control freak because he micro managed even the smallest detail. Some of his hundreds of memos have survived by virtue of being pasted into the Guard Books of the establishments concerned. A number of these Guard Books still exist, some of which are held at the Midland Railway Study Centre. They make fascinating reading.

We have already seen the memo to Miss Heywood at Leeds about promptly returning hampers and flower boxes to Heysham. Here are three more random examples, the first dated 10th November 1899.

SALAD OIL

The oil kept in the cruets on the tables must be renewed daily. Every oil cruet must be supplied with not more than one or two tablespoonfuls of oil, as the present practice causes waste and staleness.

MUSTARD

The mustard kept in the cruets on the tables must be renewed for every meal. Every mustard cruet must be supplied with not more than a tablespoonful of mustard previous to each meal, The cruets must be carefully washed and afterwards rinsed out in boiling water previous to being filled.

Two years later there is a memo to his Refreshment Room managers (most of whom were female) regarding sandwiches:

SANDWICHES

I have noticed recently that there is a growing tendency to make the sandwiches out of scrap meat instead of a nice fresh slice of meat.
It is of course necessary sometimes to use the ends of joints for sandwiches, but this practice must be reduced to to a minimum and the sandwiches made with fresh bread and a nice slice of meat as near as possible the size of the sandwich.

Obviously William Towle was trying to ensure that the Midland's sandwiches were not going to be the butt of many music hall jokes as those of British Railways were in the 1950s and 1960s!

In the late 1890s the Towle empire became a dynasty when his two sons, Francis William (born 1876) and Arthur Edward (born 1878) joined the Midland Railway Company. On the surface, this was blatant nepotism, but both boys went on to have glittering careers in the hotel industry. Reference has already been made to an interview that William Towle gave to the St. Paul's magazine in 1895. Later in the interview Towle quoted some interesting statistics:

Every year the company's hotels, in which over a thousand permanent staff were employed, about 180,000 guests were accommodated and around three quarters of a million meals were served in the hotels and dining rooms. In the cellars and stores in Derby they had 100,000 gallons of whisky in bond, 150,000 bottles of 1890 vintage Champagne, and between 300,000 and 400,000 bottles of Claret and Burgundy, all bottled by the company. On a somewhat different topic, he explained that the reason the beds in the hotels are so comfortable is because they made all their own bedding

In 1911 Francis and Arthur Towle were appointed as the Joint Assistant Managers of the Midland Railway Hotels Department, confirming them as the heirs apparent to their father who was then 61 years of age. William retired in on 30th June 1914, but was retained by the MR as an advisor.

William Towle whose genius made the quality and service in Midland Railway Hotels, Refreshment Rooms and Dining Cars second to none is seen here in the Garden Café of the Midland Hotel in Manchester. Although the portrait is a Midland Railway official photograph it was taken by Warwick Brookes, a well known Manchester photographer, possibly on the occasion of the grand opening of the hotel in September 1903. Photograph by courtesy of the National Railway Museum DY8840

However, the storm clouds were gathering over Europe and turbulent times were ahead. Needless to say both brothers stepped into their father's shoes after his retirement, but their double act was short lived because in 1915 Francis volunteered for war service, leaving Arthur in sole charge. Francis was drafted into the Royal Army Service Corps where he achieved the rank of Lieutenant Colonel and found himself as Controller of the Navy and Army Canteen Board at the War Office. He was knighted in 1919 in recognition of his war work.

Arthur Towle also became involved in war work. He was appointed Director of the Ministry of Food in 1917 and following the war he was Controller of Hotels for the Versailles Peace Conference in 1919 and 1920.

The war also interrupted William Towle's retirement. In 1915 he was called up under the Defence of the Realm (Amendment No. 3) Act to serve on a government committee investigating the cause of, and dealing with serious drink problems in army camps and amongst munitions workers.

To put the drink problem into perspective, in a speech in January 1915 the Chancellor, David Lloyd George commented that drink was doing more damage in the war than all the German submarines put together. Amongst the committee's recommendation was the restriction of pub opening hours to 12.00 to 2.30 and 6.30 to 9.30 and the banning of buying rounds. In Carlisle and the surrounding area, where the problem of munitions workers` drinking was particularly acute, the government effectively nationalised the pubs and breweries and a significant number of both were closed. For his war efforts and for services to railway hotels and catering William Towle received a knighthood in 1920.

On returning to civilian life, Francis returned to St. Pancras for a brief period before resigning and joining Gordon Hotels. He became the Managing Director of Gordon Hotels in 1921, a position he held until 1936. In 1931, during his watch, the company's iconic Dorchester Hotel opened with Francis as its Resident Director. Francis Towle also served as the President of

International Hotel Alliance from 1935 to 1938 and in 1946 he was elected as the President of the International Hotel Association which was the equivalent of the pre war body.

Sir William Towle KB passed away aged 80 on 17th September 1929 and was buried in Hampstead Cemetery in London. It is perhaps fortunate that he did not live to see his pride and joy, the Midland Grand at St. Pancras close its doors on 19th April 1935. That task was carried out by Arthur Towle who by then was the Controller of LMS Hotel Services. Arthur rejoined the Midland in 1921 but by then the company had less than two years of independence remaining.

At the grouping, the LMS initially rather fudged the issue of who would be in charge of its hotels by appointing four Area Hotel Controllers. Arthur Towle retained responsibility for the former MR hotels plus the new hotel at Gleneagles which opened in 1924. Finally, the LMS decided to grasp the nettle and from New Year's Day 1925 Arthur Towle took charge of all the company's hotels.

One of Arthur's biggest headaches was the former jewel in his father's crown, the Midland Grand. When it had eventually opened fully in 1876, the 400 bedrooms, the palatial dining room and other public rooms and the high quality of its furnishings and décor, it immediately became THE place to stay in London. Yet, for all the careful thought and detailed planning that had gone into the design and construction of the Midland Grand, it seems that very little provision had been made for the hotel to keep up with the times. Perhaps the best example is that when it opened, the non provision of en suite facilities was not a problem. But as travel habits changed and travellers became more accustomed to en suite elsewhere, the thickness of the George Gilbert Scott's fireproof floors made the cost of installing all the necessary pipework to update St. Pancras, economically unviable. It was the start of the beginning of the end. William Towle did his utmost to keep the Midland Grand attractive. The standards of quality

and service could not be faulted, and Towle introduced
novel features to attract custom such as the provision of a
Ladies' Smoking Room at a time when women smoking,
even in private, was considered very avant garde.

But as better and more modern hotels opened in the
capital and William Towle's previously loyal fan base
either died or defected, the Midland Grand increasingly
became a white elephant. Ironically, perhaps the final
straw was the opening of the Dorchester by his
eldest son!

In spite of moving to London, William Towle never
forgot his roots in the little Derbyshire village of Twyford
on the north bank of the River Trent. From medieval
times until 1963 this had been an important crossing
point of the river for travellers on a manually operated
chain ferry. In 1910, the parish church of St. Andrew,
where William Towle had been christened on 14th
October 1849, was gutted by fire. When William became
aware of this he generously donated new oak pews and a
stained glass window to replace those destroyed in
the fire.

The Midland Hotel at Morecambe and the Queen's Hotel
in Leeds have both been completely rebuilt since
his death.

The Midland Hotels at Derby, Bradford and Manchester,
although no longer railway owned and much altered
internally from Towle's days, all strive to maintain and
improve on the high standards of quality, comfort and
service that he set a hundred and more years ago.

Even the Midland Grand has risen like a phoenix from
the ashes. Although to drag it from the 19th to the 21st
century has reputedly cost an astronomical £150 million,
it once again ranks as one of London's leading hotels

But it is perhaps the simple pews and the stained glass
window in the tiny church alongside the River Trent that
are William Towle's most tangible legacy ...

THE LAST RAILWAY PIONEER -

WILLIAM MARRIOTT 1857 - 1943

Waterland

It may seem a strange way to start a biographical piece, but this photo taken in 2008 at Gunton station in North Norfolk is good introduction to the great Chief Engineer of the Midland and Great Northern Railway, William Marriott. For a start it focuses literally on the nuts and bolts of a railway, the very mundane sleepers, rails, fishplates and ballast without which the fast services, the fine engines and restaurant cars in their gleaming livery that the promoter has dreamed of will never come to life.

For a second, you may notice something about the fishplate that is different; instead of being a thin rectangle, it has a "belly" of extra metal extending down almost to the ballast. You will only find these in Norfolk, if you find them at all, for they are the last remaining examples (nobody quite knows how many) of yet another invention of William Marriott, a man who knew the railway from the bottom up and played a part in the design of everything, largely because he had built most of it and had to "make do and mend" when the money ran out. The fact that it has lasted so long is a testament, like most things of his, to the soundness of his design; the patented plate fits snugly with the chairs and makes a strong lateral bond.

Marriott's is a strange story in many ways because his railway career started in 1881 when most of the great lines had been built and quite a few of them, like the North Eastern, the London and North Western, the Great Western and the Midland, had settled down with their own empires for ten to twenty years. He was trained at the firm of Ransomes and Rapier in Ipswich, a good place for a lad with ambition since one of the partners, Richard Rapier, was very keen on establishing railways abroad, and built the first railway in China in 1875 near Shanghai. R&R later supplied the first engines in Hawaii, again to a narrow gauge, and Rapier was an enthusiastic promoter of light railways in unpromising corners of the world. Not surprisingly therefore, young William was keen to go abroad for his first job, and was all set to go to South America when the call came from a building firm called Wilkinson and Jarvis to get some experience making a light railway in Norfolk.

▼ Fishplate at Gunton Station, Norfolk, 2008. Photo John Earl

So in 1881 Marriott started out in Great Yarmouth and moved north-westwards across deepest Norfolk, stopping work when the money ran out and waiting until the materials and wages had caught up with his platelayers. When the "road" as he called it, was finished in 1883, he was invited to become the first Locomotive Superintendent as well as the Civil Engineer. In that capacity he built an engineering works in the village of Melton Constable, increasing it by over 100 houses. When the Midland Railway bought the line with the Great Northern in 1893 he expected to become Traffic Manager, which might have seemed an obvious appointment considering his encyclopaedic knowledge of the line by then. He was passed over on that occasion, but in 1919 he became Traffic Manager as well, retiring only in 1924 after seeing the line through to the Grouping. He was indeed a master of his domain, and deserves the title of a real pioneer. The Midland and Great Northern was closed by British railways in 1959, well before the Beeching cuts. To this day it can seem a long way across the Fens on a road that is mostly not dualled; there was never really a replacement for the M&GN for travellers from the Midlands, if truth be told.

Possibly to underline that point, in the sixties we travelled that same route to Scout Camp in the back of a lorry. We used to look out for William Marriott's swing bridge at what we called "Sutton Bridge Bridge" (we needed a laugh at that stage of the journey) The big thing was to hope that we could see it opening for one of the small coasters that came up the Nene to load up with sugar beet.

Although probably not as hilarious as we thought, we boy scouts were not entirely inaccurate, as there was a station called Sutton Bridge, shortly after which the train crossed the bridge itself. Long Sutton came three miles or so before that, and it also had a station. To travel the three miles between the two as the ticket shows would cost you the princely sum of three and a half pence in 1914. The chief export of Long Sutton, as with many Fenland villages, however, was not passengers but fruit and vegetables, and the vital necessity of the railways for this enterprise is evident from the label in the Midland Study Centre collection. Fruit was always marked Urgent. Marriott,

Sutton Bridge   The Swing Bridge from Station

The Wrench Series No. 4489

The most visible monument to William Marriott is his swing bridge at Sutton Bridge on the A17 into Norfolk. It was built in 1897 to replace an earlier one by Robert Stephenson. That the railway was always a family affair is evident in this photograph! The bridge is still in use, the railway section here now in use as a road. MRSC 68414 John Allsop collection 1906

▲ No.23 near Long Sutton, 2.3.36, with the 12.05 Spalding to Sutton Bridge. H.C.Casserley

▼ Coming off the swing bridge into Sutton Bridge station, 1931. MRSC John Allsop collection no.68416

with Messrs. Handysides of Derby, built the bridge here for road and rail in 1897, and it is a testament to his skill that it is still carrying an extremely heavy volume of traffic (road only now) a hundred and eighteen years later. It replaced an earlier structure by Robert Stephenson (seen overleaf), which replaced a yet earlier one by two other eminent engineers, Rennie and Telford. The picture gives us a glimpse of the nature of the geography with which Marriott was working. Until the first bridge was built in 1831 and the land drained, this area was called the "Cross Keys Wash" and travellers had to negotiate a two mile stretch of common and marsh from the mediaeval sea wall at Sutton to wait at the Wash House (now the Bridge Hotel) for a guide. This guide would then, for a fee of course, take them across an area of sand and silt sometimes up to their middles in water.

They could then rest at the Cross Keys House on the Norfolk bank before continuing their journey to Kings Lynn and beyond. When horses got stuck the method of freeing them

▲ Where Lines East and Lines West
joined up; King`s Lynn Junction.
MRSC 68389 John Allsop
collection.

was to tramp round a few feet away to force them up by
counter -pressure, but this did not always work and the horses
were left to drown. The area was no respecter of rank, either;
this is the place where famously King John lost most of his
baggage train and the crown jewels. Sadly also, they remain
lost despite the best efforts by archaeologists to find them.

All this might explain why, uniquely for a British railway
system, the M&GN was divided into "Lines East" and "Lines
West". King`s Lynn was the natural break. The Lines West
were owned by the Eastern and Midlands Company, which
E.L.Ahrons tells us "slept with the soundness of a sleeping
partner as far as working was concerned, and woke up only
when any money was due." Before the merger with the Lines
East, it ran one return train each day between Peterborough
and Cromer in the summer months, and that was about it.
The rest of the traffic was left to the Great Northern and the
Midland to sort out between themselves. When in 1889 the
Midland Railway put in a bid for the Peterborough to Sutton
Bridge and the Bourne to Lynn lines, the Great Northern
somewhat naturally objected, and this became the first
section that was jointly worked by the two companies. In
1893 the whole of the eastern section was taken over by this
partnership, and a similar arrangement to the Somerset and
Dorset Joint was instituted, in that the Midland controlled the
locomotive department from Derby, and the great Northern
looked after Permanent Way and Engineering. However, as
Ahrons pointed out, writing in 1926 in the Railway Magazine,
"Mr. William Marriott, M.Inst.C.E., who was engineer and
locomotive superintendent of the old Eastern and Midlands
Railway, still retains the local and real control over both
departments." That phrase, "local and real" really is the nub
of the story, for Marriott knew his workforce very well, and
he also knew the ways of the ground it ran over, ground that
was ambiguous enough to become water at any point, the
"Waterland" of the novelist Graham Swift.

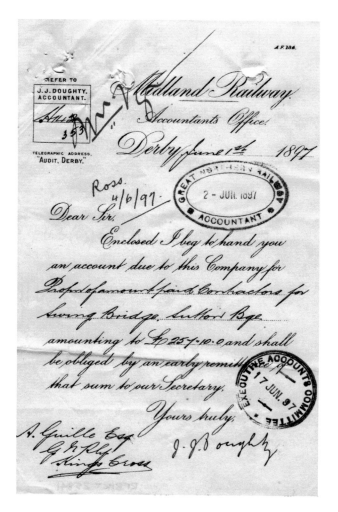

◀ Pay up please! The Midland sends a
bill for Sutton Bridge for the sum of
£257.10s to the Great Northern at
Kings Cross. This is the Joint system in
operation. MRSC

FLOODS AND OTHER ADVENTURES

Luckily enough, we have some insight into Marriott's thoughts and feelings as he wrote a column for the Norwich Chronicle starting in February 1921, detailing his reminiscences of his by then forty years on the railway. A collection of the writings was put together by the Midland Great Northern Joint Railway Society in 1974. Here he is on the flood of 1912 depicted above:

"I had hardly got home when the telephone bells began to ring violently, and messages came in of trains held up at Corpusty, Aylsham ; all over the place banks washed away. I sent for a brougham, and before I got many yards from my house the mat on the bottom of the carriage was floating. I can hardly describe the sensations of that afternoon. We had two bridges washed away on the Norwich Road, three on the Yarmouth line, and several of our biggest banks slid a hundred yards into the fields. Through the mercy of God, all trains were stopped in time.

There was one train at Aylsham which we could not reach for weeks as there was a gap, with the bridge washed away, more than 100 yards long, with the rails hanging like a suspension bridge each side. The water at Aylsham was nearly up to the platform. At Norwich City the platforms were flooded. That night Mr. Colman drove me home, and by the merest hair`s breadth we escaped with our lives. While on the road, another trap passed us and a great limb, almost a tree, fell between the two traps. I was wet through three times that day. For weeks we worked Sundays and weekdays, repairing slips, rebuilding bridges aided by a big slip gang from King`s Cross. That flood cost no less than about £20,000."

He recalls another occasion when he ended up late at night working in evening dress, having been called away from a banquet at King`s Lynn to attend an accident at Honing near North Walsham. He had to catch a Great Eastern train to get there by "a roundabout route", and he arrived there at the same time as the breakdown train from Melton Constable. The wagons "were piled twenty feet high" he says, "and we had a strenuous time pulling the wagons apart. We managed to get away early next morning, and as I was in evening dress and pumps, it was not surprising that I got a shocking cold." This was the kind of "local and real "experience he relied on. He was even open enough to admit that in 1883, when they were working night and day to get the line between North Walsham and Melton Constable open, he fell asleep on his feet while piloting a light engine. "We ran through Bluestone gates," he says, but fortunately no-one was hurt.

It is when you read about the early days of building the railway that the pioneering side comes most to life. In his modest way he recounts some hair-raising tales: "I am afraid that in those days we did things which today would somewhat annoy an urban council. We `snigged` rails along the public roads, ran our tip waggons behind a farmer`s cart to distant cuttings, and we even ran locomotives along the streets, laying rails in front of them. I think people were very good to us.

We were a small, struggling company against powerful competitors, and people will agree with me when I say that honour is due to the men who in face of many difficulties, carried the line through."

▼ The old M&GN station at North Walsham. There were two in this small market town; the old Great Eastern one still survives. MRSC 68399

There were some colourful characters among those early pioneers too, including old Sam Shirt, a "one-armed man" who had worked on the Yarmouth to Norwich line under Thomas Brassey, which would make him a very old man indeed, and Mr. Read, who had been the manager of the Somerset and Dorset line and also connected with other West Country lines such as the Cornwall Minerals and the Bristol Port and Pier railways. Significantly, Marriott gets a little emotive when he writes about those early days.

"I loved the work of opening new ground", he says, and "especially being in charge of the gangs of men, among whom there was feeling of friendship and camaraderie…"

This could break down on occasion however, and he describes an incident in Felthorpe Wood when two trains of muck met…"neither gang would go back, so the point was settled by two champions with fisticuffs, and little Benny Walker, who was a perfect terrier, won and got his train through." More shockingly perhaps, Marriott recounts as fact that one Sunday morning a ballast train went out from Norwich with some men playing cards in the brake van. One of them died suddenly, and they "propped him up in the corner and went on with their game. I often think of the worthies of those times," recounts Marriott: "Spitting Joe, the walking ganger, Diddekoi and Loo Dye, the harum-scarum driver, and a host of others."
The pioneering spirit of the line extended itself to rolling stock. With trains consisting mostly of the stock of the two owning companies in addition to the old teak Eastern and Midlands carriages, the result was a rather "piebald appearance" according to Ahrons. (Observers of the present day scene at Norwich might well retort: "so what's different?") Coaches from the Midland system retained the distinctive red colour, the only change usually being the new lettering of "M&GN".

A smart no.80 leaving Norwich City on 26.6.29 with the 5.10 to Melton Constable. This was one of the 40 Johnson 4-4-0s with 6ft 6in driving wheels delivered in 1894, 1895 and 1896, known as Class C. Midland standards were high, but the M&GN maintained them.
H.C.Casserley

Jack Earl on the old M&GN at ▲ Felmingham, now reverting to woods again.

H.C. Casserley

NORFOLK NAMES AND PANTOMIME DAMES

Locomotives were also distinctive, the ones inherited from the early lines being perhaps the most interesting. The M& GN, it is fair to say, did not do "ordinary" in this or any respect. The two illustrated above, described as "picturesque" in a book by Ronald Clarke, looked as if they were more suited to a narrow gauge line such as the Leek and Manifold or one of Colonel Stephens` light railways.

This is no coincidence, as the Act of Parliament of 1879 that brought the Yarmouth and North Norfolk railway into being stipulated that it was to be a Light Railway. This was a cunning plan to stop the Great Eastern Railway from acquiring running powers over the line. In fact by the time the Eastern and Midlands Railway came into being by the Act of 1882 the whole line was made up to main line standards.

This "Amalgamation Act" joined the Peterborough, Wisbech and Sutton Railway with the Yarmouth and North Norfolk and the Lynn and Fakenham lines to form the Eastern and Midlands Railway in its final form. The Spalding and Bourne sector had amalgamated somewhat earlier in 1866, as had the Lynn and Sutton Bridge. Finally it was possible to have a through run from the Midlands to the East Coast without having to use Great Eastern metals. The exception to this was at King's Lynn, where after several attempts to get into the town on their own account had failed, the M&GN largely used their own station at South Lynn.

Seven 4-4-0 engines worked the line from Yarmouth to North Walsham. They were side tank bogie engines built by Hudswell Clarke with small cylinders 14 x20in. With names like North Walsham, Martham and Great Yarmouth to emphasise their local character, they ran for many years with trains rather too large for their capabilities. Four of them (nos.8,10,19 and 40)were lent to the Midland and sent much further afield to work branch lines, one of them running a push and pull service on the Hitchin branch with a Pullman coach, and others doing similar duties at Wirksworth and Buxton in Derbyshire. Most were withdrawn in the early thirties.

No. 16A pictured here has a different outline again, and was one of the first two Great Yarmouth and Stalham Light Railway engines, initially named Stalham. The other one was called Ormesby and they were built by Fox, Walker of Bristol. An engaging little engine, Stalham is seen here at Melton Constable in 1929 where it was the works shunter; the pride taken in its appearance is plain to see.

The engines with the most fascinating history on this line, however, were eight 0-6-0 tank engines from Sharp, Stewart, the first three of which were called Constable, Reepham and Blakeney, perhaps to emphasise that they were now firmly settled on the East Coast after starting off far to the west on the Cornwall Minerals Railway, another pioneering railway across difficult country from Newquay to Par docks. Their final form was as you can see from No. 15, but it is fair to say that they went through more changes than the average pantomime dame after their transference from the west. Apart from the tapered chimney which was characteristic of the Melton works, all other fittings were Midland style. However, the outside cylinders made them look very un-Midland and were characteristic of the original build, a 30-ton tank designed specifically for the CMR by Francis Trevithick at the St. Blazey depot near Par.

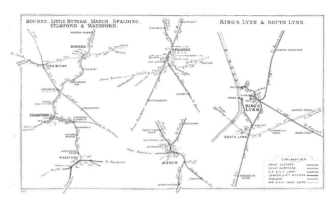

Complex junctions; the M&GN ▲
is in yellow. MRSC

Far from home; a 4-4-0 from ▲
Norfolk on the Hitchin
Branch at Heath Park with a
Pullman coach in tow.

As an indication of how much they had to be adapted by Marriott and the Melton Constable shops, when they first went to Cornwall they were designed to work in pairs, back to back. Coal was carried not in a bunker at the rear but on the side tanks. This meant that with a gap provided in the backplate the loco crews could step between the two engines while working. This made them as close as anything to the curious Double Fairlie "pushmepullyou" type of locomotive which you can still see working on the Festiniog Railway in North Wales. (As an aside, this meant that the engine shed at St. Blazey had an interesting design, because of course the engines being supposed to work in pairs meant that they had to be stabled in pairs also. As 18 engines were bought, there were nine pairs and nine stabling bays. Luckily the shed at St. Blazey still survives, and the turntable is occasionally in use.)

The Allan straight link motion they were equipped with was a hallmark of LNWR practice, and Trevithick had indeed been a locomotive superintendent of the northern division of the LNWR before moving to Cornwall. History does not relate what the Midland Board thought of this evidence of the enemy on their own territory, but the tanks survived a good long while longer than such petty differences, the last being withdrawn in 1940.

▲ 0-6-0 shunter No.15 at Yarmouth, 26.6.28. Note the Midland fittings on the boiler, apart from the funnel, which is a Melton addition. Henry Casserley

CMR No.1. Unfortunately Mr. Treffry`s name is spelt ▼ wrong!

The first transformation; a tender is added and it becomes a 2-4-0 passenger engine

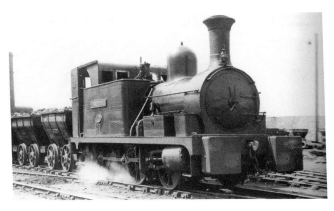

Sporting a large North-Eastern cab to keep out the weather, the last Cornwall Mineral Railway 0-6-0 shunts Hetton Colliery, Durham in 1945, 72 years after it was built for the Cornwall Minerals Railway. It is fitted with dumb buffers because the chaldron waggons it is shunting are lower than normal wagons. This engine is the nearest comparison to the original No 1 on the previous page, and it can be seen how much they were "Midlandised" on the M&GN.

"Double Fairlie" at Blaenau Festiniog, 2011. In their original form, the CMR engines were made to work back to back like this. Photo John Earl

The CMR`s misfortune was the Eastern and Midland`s luck, because by 1877 when the GWR took over operation of the ailing Minerals Railway it was found that some of the locomotives had never been steamed, such was the downturn in traffic. Partly to pay for the CMR`s debts, 9 of the engines were sold back to Sharp, Stewart which neatly paid off a debt still owed. Eight were then sold on to the Eastern and Midland, and one to the Colne Valley and Halstead Railway. This last was only withdrawn from Hetton Colliery in 1948 after 74 years of hard work.

At Sharp, Stewart five of the shunters were fitted with tenders before being sent to the Eastern and Midlands. This was obviously Sharps` solution for making them work independently of each other. However, the first change by Melton Constable further converted four of them to 2-4-0 main line tender engines with new 4ft. 7 inch wheels which gave the class the kind of speed it needed on the long straight run between Lynn and Yarmouth.

After the Midland took over the class was rebuilt between 1897 and 1902, and the result you can see from No. 015, seen demurely shunting the yard at Norwich City on the 14th March 1939. The Midland dome and safety valve are very obvious but typically, in defiance of the ordinary a little hopper has been added to the bunker at the back to make coaling easier, showing Marriott`s inventiveness in little things to the end. The large letters LNER on the side tanks tell their own story, for it was the LNER that eventually took over running of this Midland outpost in 1936. The Joint Committee still met and owned the railway, but administration was passed to Liverpool Street and locomotive supervision was from Stratford. The atmosphere changed, and Melton Works effectively closed in December 1936, causing great sadness and hardship in a sparsely populated area of Norfolk. Many railwaymen were transferred, but some left railway service altogether.

William Marriott had retired in 1924, but his sadness can be imagined as by all accounts the old M&GN had a family atmosphere much of which was fostered by the personality at its centre.

Photo H.C.Casserley 14.3.39

THE "RAILWAY FAMILY"

William Marriott was in fact a friend of my grandfather`s, and my father, Jack, who died in 2015 at the age of 102, remembered vividly his visits to the house when he was a child. The most exciting time was when he brought his signalling engineer with him and for ever afterwards he could boast that the signalling engineer of the Midland and Great Northern had helped him design the signalling on his model railway layout. It was typical of Marriott that he would take the younger members of his staff around with him to make local visits because he realised from early on that a railway was not just about making a profit, it was about serving the people within the community it ran through. That was part of the philosophy that made the M&GN a thoroughly Norfolk railway, and something that has not been forgotten, as is much in evidence on today`s North Norfolk railway based in Sheringham. My grandfather had nothing to do with the railways himself, except that he used them extensively in his travels up and down the country in pursuit of business for the firm of which he was a director. He met Marriott through a common conviction; they were both Plymouth Brethren. I gather from my father that this was not the only thing that provided common ground; he says that they both "thought alike", and this may have been because they had both grown up to be "self-made men", grandad having left school at 14 to support his family and having made his way through the ranks in the clothing industry. Marriott did not have it easy as a child either, having been brought up as an orphan by relatives in Devon.

Undoubtedly part of what appealed to my grandfather, and presumably Marriott also, about the Brethren was their "go it alone" attitude. In keeping with the doctrine of the "priesthood of all believers" they view all Christians as being ordained by God to serve and they are therefore all potentially ministers; there were no ordained clergy. Older members of the church such as my grandfather became Elders, which meant they had quite an extensive pastoral role as well as being expected to lead worship. It was a religion of the times undoubtedly, started in the early years of the nineteeth century and appealing to men who had to be self-reliant when they could look for little help from elsewhere, with no Welfare State to help out.

▼ William Marriott and his wife.

Marriott was a staunch supporter of the Brethren, even to the extent of marching in their processions, although he was sensible enough not to try to impose his beliefs. However, something of his ideals must have percolated down to the workforce:"As I am a great believer in the Iron Duke's dictum that "Education without religion only makes men clever devils", the spiritual side was not neglected." Finding that there were neither church nor chapel in Melton Constable, he organised services in the Hall attended by local clergy from further afield. He also, partly in a bid to attract families to an area which by his own admission "had few attractions", set out to provide "School of Arts" classes for the lads in the village. He also persuaded the directors to provide the old Holt station for a "reading and billiard room", and got up entertainments within the town. In 1921 Marriott states proudly that the classes had been going for thirty years, and

Melton Works, 1908; No.96, ▲
ex-CMR, being overhauled.
MRSC 68395

"I have received many letters from lads all over England, I might say the world, to tell me of their success in life, and saying they owed it to our having insisted upon them attending these classes."

As a postscript, my father who remembers as a schoolboy visiting Melton Works, says that there was a "quiet room" set aside in a corner of the works for anyone who felt the need to use it.

Marriott was well known for looking out for his men in many ways, as was that other famous chief engineer of the Midland, Matthew Kirtley. His view of it was:

"My post was just the size that I could allow all men access and not refuse to see anyone with a grievance...I have had legal affairs, matrimonial difficulties, the choice of a wife, investments, children`s future, medical matters, in fact dozens of private affairs brought to me for advice. I think the strangest request was from a man who asked for a pass to go to the funeral of "his wife`s husband". The matrimonial tangle this revealed cannot be gone into here."

An interesting exchange of letters from 1922-3 survives between Marriott and Sir Henry Fowler, showing perhaps some of the strains and stresses of dealing with issues at a local level when "Central Office" must have seemed quite remote in Derby. Local sensitivities were perhaps aroused at this time by being subsumed into the larger enterprise of the LMS, but a further complication was that at this point the LNER also had a place on the Joint Committee. Headed "Local Locomotive Departmental Committees", Marriott's letter of December 21st 1922 goes as follows:

Dear Sir,

We have one energetic Committee which is putting on its Agenda, matters relating to Signals at some distance from the Station concerned and much nearer another Centre from which one might reasonably have expected the complaint to emanate.

I am inclined to consider that a Local Committee should deal only with affairs that come within the precincts of their Loco. and Station, whilst any subject between the Centres, as a matter of course, should be dealt with by the Sectional Council.

Would you kindly say if, in your larger experience, it has been found necessary to mark out spheres of influence so that there should not be any continual overlapping, etc.?

Sir Henry writes back on the 2nd. January to establish the nature of the complaint, and this is Marriott's response:

...At South Lynn, the complaining centre, there is a Local Departmental Committee but the other (Melton), which is much nearer the signals referred to, has local representatives only.

The men are enginemen and they are asking for white boards to be placed at the back of certain signals where there is an alleged difficulty in viewing. As other items may crop up I want to establish a general principle.

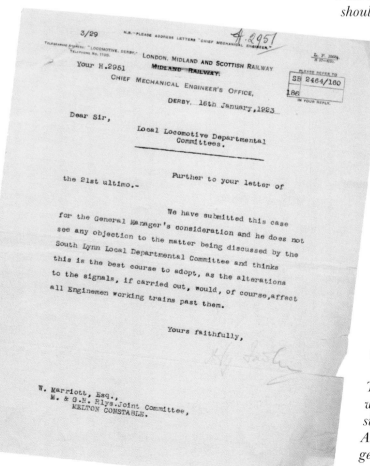

3/29   N.B.—PLEASE ADDRESS LETTERS "CHIEF MECHANICAL ENGINEER."   H.2951

TELEGRAPHIC ADDRESS: "LOCOMOTIVE, DERBY."
TELEPHONE No. 1100.

Your H.2951   **LONDON, MIDDLE AND SCOTTISH RAILWAY**
~~MIDLAND RAILWAY.~~   L. F. 1004.

CHIEF MECHANICAL ENGINEER'S OFFICE,   PLEASE REFER TO
SB 2464/160

DERBY, 16th January, 1923   186
IN YOUR REPLY.

Dear Sir,

Local Locomotive Departmental
Committees.
_____

Further to your letter of
the 21st ultimo.—

We have submitted this case
for the General Manager's consideration and he does not
see any objection to the matter being discussed by the
South Lynn Local Departmental Committee and thinks
this is the best course to adopt, as the alterations
to the signals, if carried out, would, of course, affect
all Enginemen working trains past them.

Yours faithfully,

H. Fowler

W. Marriott, Esq.,
M. & G.N. Rlys. Joint Committee,
MELTON CONSTABLE.

Marriott need not have worried, as Sir Henry writes back with the following response on 16th January:

We have submitted this case for the General Manager`s consideration and he does not see any objection to the matter being discussed by the South Lynn Local Departmental Committee and thinks this is the best course to adopt, as the alterations to the signals, if carried out, would, of course, affect all Enginemen working trains past them.

An amusing detail is that Fowler`s letter is written on Midland Railway headed notepaper, the heading crossed out and London, Midland and Scottish Railway substituted. It shows the Midland right at the point of transition into what became the biggest company in the world at the time and definitely gives the impression that Fowler, who started off as the deputy Chief Mechanical Engineer of the LMS, is very much feeling his way into the new situation, as were all his managers on the outposts such as Marriott. Notably, he does not supply an answer to Marriott`s request for a "general principle".

One of the original Eastern and Midlands engines, no.21 was built by Beyer Peacock and was one of a batch of 15 delivered between 1881 and 1888. To an extent it is "Midlandised" but it still retains its distinctive shape. It was not withdrawn until 1936; here it is at Spalding in 1927. H.C. Casserley

▲ Marriott pioneered the use of concrete in infrastructure, and here is his elegant signboard still at West Runton in 2015. Such was the importance of this advance in technology that in April 1918 he is reported as advising the mighty Great Western that there "should be no difficulty in giving out a licence for the manufacture of concrete signal posts." This from one of the smallest and most cash-strapped outfits in the country! Photo John Earl

It leaves the historian with a puzzle as to what Marriott was after. On the face of it the final answer he receives would seem to be common sense and therefore did not require this incursion into the corridors of power at all. He could have sorted it out at a local level. However, it could be seen as the actions of a man making sure that he was not going to tread on any toes in the giant enterprise that was in the making.

Perhaps this was partly informed by past experience that went fairly deep, particularly when the Midland took over the line in 1893:

" Before I was formally appointed I very nearly lost my post, and I have to thank the late Mr. James Beale and Sir Ernest Paget, the late Chairman of the Midland Railway, that I did not do so."

It turns out that it had been decided that they were not going to keep a resident engineer for the entire line but that it was going to be split into two again. Marriott enlisted the help of his own manager, Mr. Read, who saw Mr.Beale. Mr Beale reportedly grunted: "Midland Officers grasping for power" before going to Ernest Paget to get the decision overturned. In 1900 he similarly came up against wheeler-dealing when Sir Henry Oakley, then the Great Northern chairman, wanted him to become Traffic manager, and had the backing of Paget of the Midland also.

It would seem that Samuel Johnson, his immediate superior, was in favour of the appointment, but he was approached by Mr. G.H.Turner, a Midland manager, who "wanted to put one of his own men in", and suddenly Mr. Johnson"turned round". Marriott says "I actually got as far as the Boardroom door to be appointed when the whole thing fell through." It did not help that Henry Oakley had just retired.

Marriott later met some of the Midland Directors at the Paris Exposition of 1900, and reports that "they were very angry at the way their manager had acted." Typically of William Marriott however, he shrugs it off with: "It was a great disappointment at the time, but I feel sure that all happened for the best." And of course, he eventually became Traffic Manager in 1919.

Few people in the railway era can have had such a wide-ranging influence over one line, but few can have carried out their duties with such grace, energy and good humour. Typical was the way he threw his railway`s energies into the First World War. Here he is after coping with 30 special trains full of soldiers coming down to Melton:

"I was nearly dead when I got home, and went straight to bed, and barely was I there, very cold and tired, when an officer and a sergeant came up the drive, and asked if they could possibly get billets. We took the officer in...we afterwards had half a dozen or more of the Berkshire Yeomanry in the children`s old nursery, as well as two sergeants in the dining room, and very nice men they were. I am afraid that as they went out to Gallipoli many of them never returned."

The war took away from Marriott as well; his youngest son was killed. The railway "family" helped out here too though: " I had heard that our R.O.D. men were running off to Bapaume, which was only five kilometres off the battlefields, so I asked if they would try and find his grave...the village was only a heap of bricks, the road unrecognisable, the battlefield all grown up with weeds so that at any moment you might step into a shell hole or on an unburied corpse (which they did). (Driver) English sent me a sketch of the graves, and would take nothing for their expenses or hire of bicycles. My son now lies in the Guards Cemetery, Les Boeufs."

However it is not at this point I would want to leave him, but at the other end of the waterworld over which he had such an influence. Here is Ronald Clark on the bridge for which he is possibly best known: "The finest of all the Joint structures was the great viaduct crossing Breydon Water where the N&S Joint line to Lowestoft was carried over the estuary. It comprised of five spans...., one of 169ft.8in. being the swing span..." It was a fitting tribute to a man who started small but thought big, and never gave up on the details that mattered.

Bridge over Breydon Water. NRM ▲

Norfolk in the heyday of the ▶
railways... and the system
now. The black lines are
preserved railways.

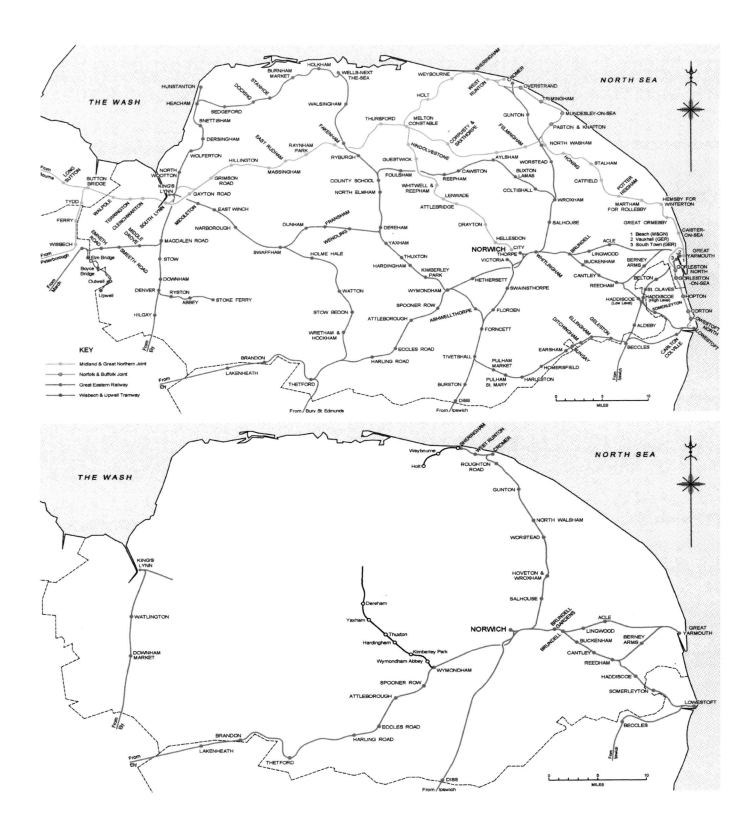

ANY MORE FARES PLEASE ?

THE BURTON & ASHBY LIGHT RAILWAYS

The proliferation of urban electric tramways in the late 19th and the early 20th centuries provided many railways with their first taste of serious competition. This was particularly true for railways whose lines included inner city suburban stations. The Midland was no exception. It was an unequal struggle. For a start, most tramway systems could reach parts of the suburbs that railways simply could not reach. Add to that the fact that many tram systems were subsidised by local ratepayers and that the overheads associated with running a tramway were considerably less than running a railway, the latter soon found themselves on a beating to nothing.

However, the municipal electric tramway system which opened in Burton-on-Trent on 3rd August 1903, posed no such threat to the Midland as its routes were confined within the borough's boundary. But the MR recognised that a privately promoted tramway heading eastwards from Burton to Ashby was a very definite threat.

Between Burton and Ashby is a well populated area roughly bounded by Newhall, Swadlincote, Woodville, Gresley and Moira. Within this area were at least a dozen collieries and a bewildering number of other firms who used the local coal and clay to produce everything from delicate art pottery to house bricks, fire bricks, chimney pots, ceramic tiles, salt-glazed drainage pipes and other items of sanitary ware. Many of these small businesses were connected to the MR lines that served the area.

The Midland's Leicester & Burton line, (which was an extension of the pioneer Leicester & Swannington Railway) opened in 1848 and served Ashby, Moira and Gresley. The remaining towns, Swadlincote and Woodville were originally connected to the Leicester & Burton line by separate branches, opened respectively in July 1851 and April 1859. A rather circuitous link between the two termini, to form what was officially known as the Swadlincote and Woodville Extension opened in September 1884. This involved boring two tunnels and the opening of a new passenger station in Woodville; the original branch terminus being downgraded to a goods depot. The two branches and the connecting link became known collectively as the Swadincote Loop

The amount of freight traffic that the collieries, potteries and other businesses generated, particularly those linked to the mainly single line Swadlincote Loop meant that few paths were available for passenger services. The summer 1903 MR timetable shows only eight up and six down passenger trains used the loop on weekdays and there was no Sunday service. Gresley, on the main line, fared a little better with eight up (Leicester bound) and nine down (towards Burton) services calling daily. On Sundays, there was just one early and one late departure in each direction from Gresley.

The area cried out for a tramway to fill the public transport void.

In 1899, the first attempt to build a tramway between Burton and Ashby, which was supported by the Midland, was unsuccessful due to strong objections by Burton Corporation. In 1902, a second scheme also floundered. This time, although Burton Corporation were in favour, it was rejected due to opposition from the Midland who were concerned about competition with its own services in the area. But realising the potential, the MR applied to the Light Railway Commissioners to build the line themselves. This proved to be third time lucky and the necessary Light Railway Order was granted on 10th October 1903 for four separate lines. Hence the plurality in the line's title, The Burton & Ashby Light Railways.

Beginning in Wellington Street, close to Burton-on-Trent station, the first 2 miles 69 chains of the Burton & Ashby system was thanks to running powers over Burton Corporation Tramway's metals to the Borough boundary. Here at Boundary Junction, the Burton rails made an end-on connection with the B&ALR Railway no.1 which then proceeded through Newhall, Swadlincote and Woodville to terminate in the forecourt of Ashby-de-la Zouch railway station, a total of 10 miles 14 chains from the Burton Terminus. The majority of the route was along public roads but a section, nearly 5/8 mile long, between the Ashby Road at Stanhope Bretby and Newhall was on reserved track.

Railway no.2 ran from Swadlincote Market Place (known locally as the Delph) for a distance of just under 2 miles to Gresley railway station.

Railway no.3 which was 65 chains in length ran from Boot Inn Junction on the Gresley branch to Woodhouse Street Junction on the main line.

Railway no.4 formed the short (37 yard long) spur on the west side of the Delph to complete the triangle and allow through running to the Gresley line from Ashby.

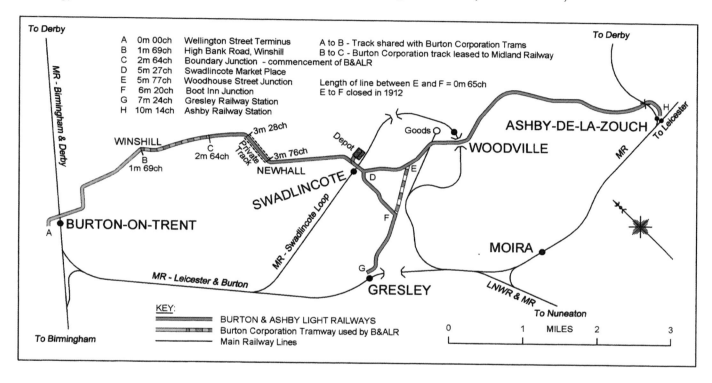

A   0m 00ch   Wellington Street Terminus
B   1m 69ch   High Bank Road, Winshill
C   2m 64ch   Boundary Junction - commencement of B&ALR
D   5m 27ch   Swadlincote Market Place
E   5m 77ch   Woodhouse Street Junction
F   6m 20ch   Boot Inn Junction
G   7m 24ch   Gresley Railway Station
H   10m 14ch   Ashby Railway Station

A to B - Track shared with Burton Corporation Trams
B to C - Burton Corporation track leased to Midland Railway

Length of line between E and F = 0m 65ch
E to F closed in 1912

KEY:
▬▬▬▬ BURTON & ASHBY LIGHT RAILWAYS
▬▬▬▬ Burton Corporation Tramway used by B&ALR
───── Main Railway Lines

The MR appointed Mr C. H. Gadsby MIEE as Consulting Engineer for the Burton & Ashby Light Railways. Gadsby, a Whitworth Scholar and highly experienced tramway specialist had been the brains behind the 1903 proposal, which the Midland had successfully objected to, but then adopted the majority of which for their own application! The MR Board decided that it would be desirable to appoint an experienced tramway engineer to report to the General Manager. The man chosen to undertake this was one of Gadsby's employees, James Toulmin, AMIEE who became an MR employee in March 1904. Toulmin obviously impressed his superiors and two years later was appointed as the General Manager and Engineer of the B&A on 16th March 1906. It was a position he would hold throughout the entire life of the company.

The contract to build the lines, the estimated cost of which was just under £90k, was awarded to tramway specialists, Dick, Kerr & Co. of Preston who subcontracted the electrical work to Callender's Cable & Construction Co. The salt-glazed earthenware pipes which acted as underground cable conduits were manufactured locally. The Light Railway Order specified that where the track was laid along public roads these must have a minimum width of 24 feet. In order to achieve this, the MR had to demolish a number of properties in Newhall and in Ashby.

The MR calculated that 13 cars were required to operate the service and these were ordered from the Brush Electrical Engineering Co., Ltd. of Loughborough. The double deck, open topped cars each seated 57 passengers; 22 on the lower deck and 35 on the upper deck. The full technical specification of the cars appears later in the chapter.

Car No. 3 at Swadlincote in 1915 showing the later simplified style of lining. The overall length of the cars was 28 feet and the maximum width 6 feet 3½ inches. The Brush type AA truck had a fixed wheelbase of 6 feet and was fitted with Hudson Bowring lifeguards. Three types of braking (including magnetic track brakes) were provided because of the steep gradients in parts of the system. The original style of lining can be see in the photograph of Car no.13 outside the depot later in the chapter. Midland Railway Study Centre 25243/The Shelford Archive

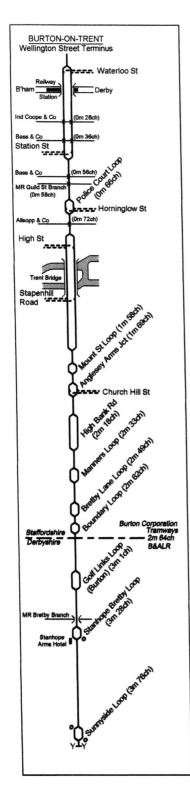
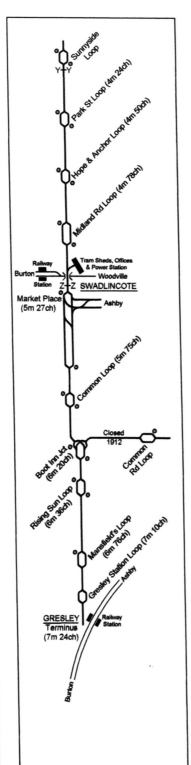
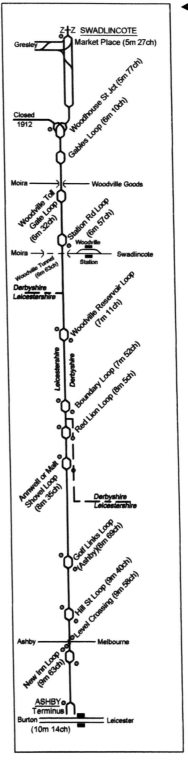

Diagrams showing the passing loops and mileages etc. from Burton are based on diagrams drawn by the LMS in September 1926 and on a detailed survey of the system carried out in July 1920 by the B&ALR General Manager, James Toulmin and F.W. Simmons on behalf of the Midland Railway Estate Agent. Simmons was responsible for keeping the Midland Railway Distance Diagrams up to date. The automatic signals indicating if the section ahead was clear or occupied (shown by red dots on the diagrams) are spaced conventionally and are based on the 1:500 survey sheets of the system.

Swadlincote was chosen as the site for the company's headquarters where its offices, depot, workshops and power station were all were located. The 3'-6" gauge line, was mostly single track, except in Burton and around Swadlincote which was effectively the hub of the system. Between Boundary Junction and Ashby (not counting the double track section in Swadlincote) there were 17 passing loops and there were a further five on the Gresley line. To minimise the number of overhead points, two conductor wires were used – one for each direction.

The Swadlincote depot had eight roads, each long enough to accommodate three trams, giving a capacity for 24 cars, but only 20 cars were ever purchased. A rearward extension to part of the shed accommodated the fitting shops. Alongside to the sheds were the B&ALR offices on the opposite side of which was the power station which supplied the overhead lines at 550 volts, direct current. The supply was generated by two Belgian manufactured 3-cylinder 240 BHP diesel engines which were coupled to Westinghouse 165kw dynamos. These charged a bank of batteries which smoothed out load fluctuations in the system. It is said that towards the end of the B&ALR, the batteries alone were sufficient to provide the power for the afternoon and evening tram services. It is however rather ironic that in a coal mining area, the MR should opt for diesel rather than steam powered generators. The Swadlincote Loop (which was fractionally over 7 miles in length) provided rail connections to six collieries and there were a further half dozen rail connected mines within a five mile radius.

It was originally planned to open the line on 31st May 1906, but this had to be postponed because the contractors installing the machinery in the Power Station had not tested the equipment sufficiently to allow running the cars for testing, training the motormen and conductors and determining a workable timetable. The line was inspected on behalf of the Board of Trade by Major John Pringle RE on the 7th June 1906. The first section of the line between Burton and Swadlincote opened without any ceremony on 13th June with the section from Swadlincote to Ashby following on 2nd July 1906.

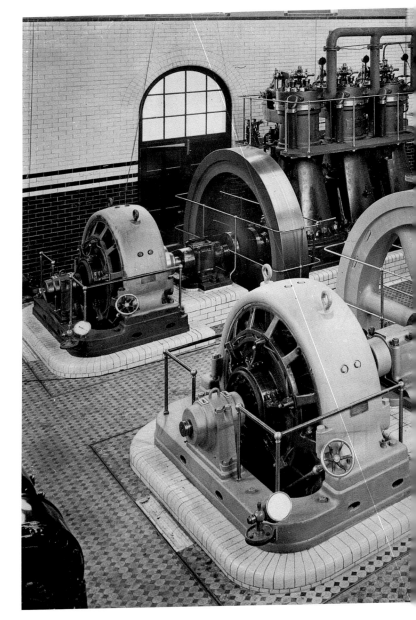

▲ A general view of the B&ALR Power Station at Swadlicote with the two generating sets clearly visible, one was in use, the other on standby. In this photograph the far set was is service. The prime movers were the huge 3 cylinder diesel engines built in Ghent in Belgium. Each of the three cylinders was 15½ inches in diameter and had a 23 inch stroke which in total developed 240 BHP. Each engine was connected to a British Westinghouse 165 kw dynamo via a massive flywheel. Some idea of the enormous size of the engines can be gained by the fact that author estimates that the horizontal exhausts pipes are about 18 feet above the floor! Note also the immaculate condition of both the sets and the power station as a whole. Photograph by courtesy of the National Railway Museum DY9912

Just three days later the first accident occurred. Fortunately, it was not too serious, but never the less it was reported in some detail by the Derby Daily Telegraph. According to the newspaper, the 11 o'clock car from Burton pulled into the loop at Bretby Hollow (later the Burton Golf Links Loop) to allow a Burton bound tram to pass. The Ashby bound car pulled up alongside a stationary horse and cart belonging to Messrs T. G. Green & Company of the Church Gresley Pottery. When the Burton bound car appeared travelling in the opposite direction, the horse took fright with the result that the carter lost control and the animal broke the harness and the shafts and galloped past the approaching car, damaging the catcher at the front.

Apart from from frightening a few horses, the new tram service quickly became very popular with the locals. This seemingly took the MR hierarchy by surprise and the 'spare' cars earmarked to work the Swadlincote to Gresley branch were pressed into service to cope with the demand on the main line. This resulted in the postponement of the opening of the Gresley branch until seven additional cars, ordered in a hurry from Brush, were delivered. Except for some very minor details, the second batch of cars were identical with the first. Having received the additional cars the Gresley branch eventually opened on 24th September 1906 followed by the eastward link from the Boot Inn towards Ashby in October 1906. Compared to the rest of the system, the latter line proved to be rather unprofitable and closed towards the end of 1912 after only six years.

The 10 mile journey from Burton to Ashby, which in the early days cost six pence (2½ new pence), was timetabled to take an hour and twenty minutes. An interesting bye-law allowed passengers to smoke only on the upper deck, and only then if they were seated behind the trolley standard. That said, lighting a cigarette or a pipe as the car bounced up and down and swayed from side to side at speeds that seemingly regularly exceeded the 12 mph legal limit, must have been somewhat difficult.

THE ROUTE - BURTON TO ASHBY

The western terminus of the system was in Wellington Street in Burton. Almost immediately after starting, cars turned right onto Borough Road and soon began the short climb towards Burton station, which then, as now, is located on the bridge spanning the lines. After descending from the bridge the cars proceeded along Station Street as far as the Midland Hotel before turning left onto Guild Street, avoiding the town's main shopping area. (The Midland Hotel in Burton was one of many similarly named establishments up and down the country that had no connection at all with the Midland Railway Co., but which presumably hoped that the MR's reputation for quality, service and comfort would imply that similar standards would be found on their premises!)

After turning into Guild Street the cars entered the first single line section of the journey. Compared with some single sections later, this was fairly short being just 300 yards long. The Police Court Loop began at the north end of Guild Street so that the sharp right hand turn onto Horninglow Road was double tracked. Installing a double track section around a 90° blind corner was a shrewd move which eliminated any chance of a head on collision!

As can be seen on the gradient profile the line though Burton was almost, but not quite level. The minimum quoted on the original diagram was 1 in 8272 – which equates to a rise or fall

▼ The gradient profile of the Burton Corporation Tramway's lines over which the B&ALR had either running powers (0m 0ch to Anglesey Arms Junction, 1m 69ch), or were leased to the B&ALR (1m 69ch to 2m 64ch). The bump at the start marks the bridge over the MR's Derby to Birmingham line. Following that the track through the town's streets is fairly level – the least gradient indicated is 1 in 8272, but the only truly level section was across the Trent Bridge. It could be likened to the calm before the storm! For reasons of clarity only selected gradients are indicated on the diagram.

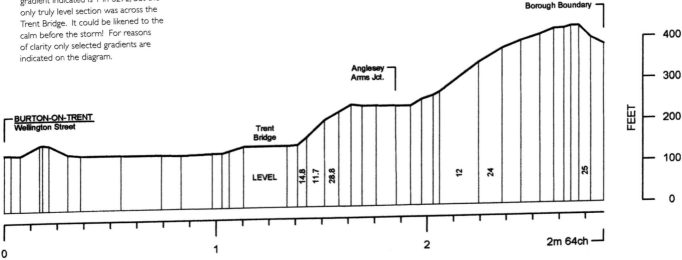

of just over 7½ inches in a mile. However, the only truly level section of the whole system was across the Trent Bridge. The bridge was widened in 1926 which allowed the laying of a second track.

Burton of course was famous for the number of level crossings due to the intricate network of railways that served the town's many breweries. At the zenith there were 87 miles of track which criss-crossed the town resulting in 35 levels crossings where the lines crossed public highways. Five of the crossings were encountered by B&ALR cars on the journey from Wellington Street to Trent Bridge. One of the crossings involved the MR Guild Street branch, the remaining four being brewery owned. Two were part of Bass's extensive system, the other two belonging to the Ind Coope and the Allsopp breweries respectively. The Board of Trade required that the maximum speed for tramcars over all such crossings and 20 yards on either side was limited to 4 mph, but even at that speed it was not unknown for the repeated shocks sustained, particularly from the brewery line crossings, to eventually result in tram axles breaking due to fatigue failure. The same 4 mph speed restriction applied when cars were travelling through facing points.

After crossing the Trent and its flood plain on the bridge, the tram cars faced a formidable climb up Bearwood Hill Road. This commenced at 1 in 14.8, steepened to 1 in 11.7 before easing to 1 in 28.8 and then lesser gradients to Anglesey Arms Junction, (1 mile 69 chains from Wellington Street). For many years, cars had to negotiate a tight "S" bend at the bottom of Bearwood Hill Road before commencing the climb. These caused a very serious accident on 8th October 1919, and after the Trent Bridge was widened in 1926 the lines at this point were completely realigned.

The disaster in October 1919 was caused when Car no.19 lost adhesion as it climbed Bearwood Hill Road and in spite of the motorman's best efforts to prevent it doing so, the vehicle ran backwards, out of control. At the bottom of the hill the runaway tram failed to negotiate the first tight curve resulting in it derailing and rolling over onto its side, Sadly, one of the passengers died from her injuries soon after reaching hospital and nine days after the accident, the conductress, Miss Lillian Parker also succumbed to her injuries. One of the male passengers was bedridden for the rest of his life as a result of the accident

At the Anglesey Arms Junction, the Corporation tracks leading to Winshill veered off to the left leaving the B&A cars to face the long (about ¾ mile) climb up High Bank Road and Ashby Road towards their own metals at Boundary Junction (2m 64ch). Although owned by the Burton Corporation Tramways and leased to the B&ALR, there were no scheduled Burton services on this section.

Mention has already been made about Board of Trade requirements with regard to speed limits over level crossings and facing points. There was also a 4 mph speed limit imposed on trams descending High Bank Hill and Bearwood Hill Road plus compulsory stops at Balmoral Road and at the gates to Woodlands House. At the other end of the scale, cars ascending were allowed to travel at a maximum of 12 mph and similar speeds were permitted on Guild Street and Horninglow Road. Elsewhere on the Burton system the B&A trams were limited to 9 mph.

At Boundary Junction the B&ALR cars not only crossed from Staffordshire into Derbyshire but also from Burton Corporation's tracks onto their own. This, in legal terms, was the commencement of Burton & Ashby Light Railway No.1.

The first part of gradient diagram of Railway No.1 ▼ from Boundary Junction through Newhall and Swadlincote to Woodville.

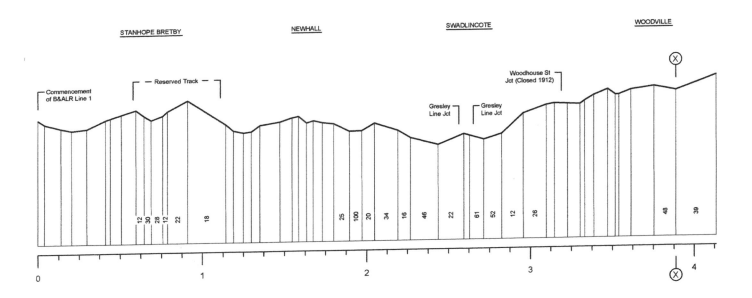

An official MR photograph of Car no.6 bound for Ashby on the section of reserved track between Stanhope Bretby and Sunnyside. The buildings in the left hand background were part of Bretby Colliery. When laid along public roads the B&ALR's lines had to follow the existing gradients, but even on the reserved section the line is more or less following the local contours. Here no.6 is climbing at 1 in 28, hopefully having picked up some momentum from the 1 in 30 descent in the background. This image clearly illustrates the typical roller coaster gradients that the cars were required to traverse during each journey. Midland Railway Study Centre 25242/ The Shelford Archive

Now on home ground, the single line descended towards the first passing loop at Bretby Hollow which was the scene of the runaway horse incident described earlier. Following the opening of the golf course on the north side of the line in 1907, the loop was renamed Burton Golf Links. From here the line climbed towards the next loop at Stanhope Bretby, which began immediately after the bridge over the Midland Railway branch serving Bretby Colliery. At the far end of the loop was the Stanhope Arms public house, then simply a roadside pub but which over the subsequent years has been considerably extended and developed into a popular hotel. 120 yards after passing the pub the line swung to the right leaving the Ashby Road and headed across fields on reserved track towards Sunnyside Loop. At the end of the loop the line crossed the Bretby Road but because the crossing was blind to both road and rail, it was a mandatory requirement for trams to stop before proceeding. After crossing Bretby Road the line continued on a further section of reserved track that ran alongside the footpath to Matsyard Colliery before emerging onto High Street, Newhall.

Here, it would seem an appropriate point to mention the B&ALR signalling system which was installed by Brecknell, Munro & Rogers Ltd of Bristol. Many of the passing loops on the line could not be seen from the preceding one so to prevent cars travelling in opposite directions meeting head-on on a single line section an automatic electrical signalling system was installed. Just before it entered the section, the tram's trolley wheel operated a skid on the overhead line which in turn illuminated one of signal three lights on the loop at the opposite end of the single line section to indicate that the section was occupied. The system was such that two further cars could follow the first one into the section. Each of the additional trams illuminated another of the signal lamps at the opposite end. This did not happen very often, but in the early days at least, chartering several trams to carry parishioners on church outings or children on Sunday School treats to local beauty spots happened regularly in the summer months.

The first single track section equipped with signals was the reserved track between the Stanhope Bretby and Sunnyside Loops. After that, as can be seen on the route diagrams, most of the single line sections were similarly equipped.

Although there is not a tram in sight, this photograph has been included for a variety of reasons It was taken at the Ashby end of the Sunnyside Loop looking towards Newhall and shows the track crossing Bretby Road. The blind nature of the crossing is obvious and it was a mandatory requirement that trams travelling in both directions had to stop before crossing the road. On the right hand side is Pole 81B, one of 566 cast iron poles supplied by James Russell & Sons Ltd., of the Crown Tube Works in Wednesbury. Most were ornate like this, but those out of the public eye, in the Swadlincote depot and on the reserved sections of track were much plainer. The pole also carries a B&A timetable, request stop sign and the array of three lights which indicated whether the single line section ahead was free or occupied.

On the far side of Bretby Road is one of the B&A's two waiting rooms alongside which is the footpath which ran along the south side of Matsyard Colliery. On the far side of the crossing is the short section of reserved track which emerged in High Street, Newhall. Photo: Courtesy of the National Railway Museum DY9901

CARS STOP ON REQUEST

The signalling engineers, Brecknell, Munro and Rogers Ltd are not a particularly well known company. Founded in 1854, they originally produced brass castings, but later began to diversify into several other branches of engineering including the manufacture of tramway (and later trolley bus) equipment. The company, who at their peak had over 1,000 employees, developed the self reversing trolley pole and also supplied pantographs for the MR Morecambe & Heysham line.

The first public house that the B&A encountered after leaving Burton was the Stanhope Arms at Bretby. On leaving the Matsyard Colliery reserved track section into High Street in Newhall, it immediately passed three pubs in a row; the first was another Stanhope Arms, next door was the Angel Inn and next door to that was the Holly Bush Inn. All have long been closed!

▼ Car no.13 poses in High Street Newhall after leaving the Matsyard section during a test run before the line opened for business. This could well be on the first test run between Burton and Ashby on 26th May 1906. Even the two horses on the right seem interested in the proceedings! The target date for opening the system was 31st May 1906 but because of insufficient testing of the diesel generating equipment and to ensure that the motormen and the conductors were adequately trained, the first section of the line, between Burton and Swadlincote, did not open until 13th June 1906. Midland Railway Study Centre/Kidderminster Railway Museum 62277.

The 540 yard long single line section from Sunnyside terminated in the Park Street Loop. From the latter, the track continued along High Street passing three more public houses on the way with the next loop named after a fourth pub, the Hope and Anchor Loop. At some point before reaching this loop High Street had become Union Road. Opposite the Hope & Anchor pub and the loop was Warren Brothers' engineering and boiler works. Doubtless the pub was a popular place with Warren's workmen to slake their thirsts after a long shift and wile away the time whilst waiting for the tram home.

 Soon after leaving the Hope and Anchor Loop the name of the road changed for a second time; Union Road morphing into Newhall Road. The next loop, Midland Road Loop began on Newhall Road before both tracks turned sharp right into Midland Road itself. Before negotiating this bend, Ashby

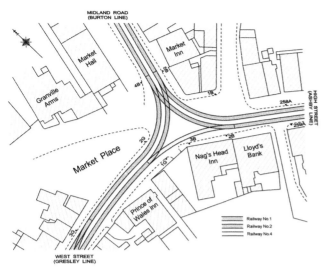

MIDLAND ROAD
(BURTON LINE)

Market
Hall

Granville
Arms

Market Place

Market
Inn

258A

HIGH STREET
(ASHBY LINE)

259A

Nag's Head
Inn

Lloyd's
Bank

Prince of
Wales Inn

Railway No.1
Railway No.2
Railway No.4

WEST STREET
(GRESLEY LINE)

▲ A sketch plan showing the track
layout around Swadlincote Market
Place based on Sheet 11 of the
book of 1:500 plans of the B&ALR
on which the author has indicated
three of the four lines that made
up the Burton & Ashby Light
Railways. The black dots identified
as 258A, 1B and 1G etc., are the
identification numbers of the
poles carrying the overhead wires.

bound cars had to make another compulsory stop by order of the Board of Trade. On leaving the loop, cars continued down Midland Road, crossing the two privately owned railway lines serving the Alliance Colliery. Over the years the mine had had a variety of names but was known by the locals as Shoddy Pit because of the poor working conditions there compared to neighbouring mines The crossing was immediately followed by a new bridge that carried the tramway over the MR's Swadlincote Loop line, just east of the station. The MR agreed to build the bridge so that Swadlincote Urban District Council would withdraw their objection to the tramway crossing the railway via the existing level crossing. The cause of the Council's angst was that the crossing gates were regularly closed for lengthy periods whilst shunting was being carried out. But curiously, even after the bridge was built, the crossing, which was controlled by Swadlincote East signalbox, continued in use until the line closed in the early 1960s!

After regaining the original alignment of Midland Road the single track soon became double as it approached the heart of the B&ALR system in Swadincote Market Place, or The Delph, as it as known to the locals. Just outside the Market Inn, the lines split; one pair veering off to the left which formed the main line to Ashby, the second pair of lines turned to the right. The junction marked the commencement of Railway no.2, the Gresley Line. The short, single line spur between the Prince of Wales and the Nag's Head, which connected the Gresley line with the Ashby line was Railway no.4. The accompanying sketch map of the track layout around The Delph will hopefully make the situation clearer. The Market Inn, the Nag's Head and the Prince of Wales are all now closed. The Granville Arms however lives on albeit much altered and enlarged and renamed the Sir Nigel Gresley. Whilst not altogether inappropriate, the James Toulmin would have perhaps been a better choice for the new name. As it is, the former B&A General Manager is commemorated by Toulmin Drive in Swadlincote.

After rounding the left hand bend in the Delph, the Ashby line continued along High Street. Almost immediately, the single line spur from the Gresley branch trailed into the opposite line outside the Nag's Head Inn. This crossover was technically the end of Railway no.4. Here, Burton bound trams were required by the Board of Trade to stop before proceeding cautiously around the corner into Midland Road.

A few yards later, the line passed yet another Stanhope Arms public house, (the third so far), so this might be an appropriate point to explain the significance of the name. Stanhope, was the family name of the Earls of Chesterfield whose ancestral seat was the nearby Bretby Hall. The Stanhope family had a long and distinguished history of public, military and political service which was commemorated by the proliferation of the name in various ways locally. Bretby Park was a popular destination for local Sunday School Treats, travelling, of course, by tram. Other often visited venues were Brizlincote Park, Ashby Castle and the Bath Grounds in Ashby.

From High Street the double track section continued on into Hill Street, which, as its name suggests provided Ashby bound trams with another stiff climb at 1 in 12 before easing to 1 in 28. Soon after beginning the climb the cars crossed the bridge over the private railway line serving Wragg's Pottery, one of several colliery and pottery lines connected to the Swadlincote loop. As the gradients eased, the double track became single again with the next passing loop being located at the junction of Hill Street and Woodhouse Street where the short short lived line from Gresley to Woodville joined the main line from the right. This was technically Railway no.3, the operation of which was soon found to be uneconomic. The original half

▲ A busy scene in Swadlincote Market Place (known locally as The Delph) with a Burton bound tram from Ashby waiting for any onward passenger from the next arrival from Gresley. This is a fairly early photograph judging by the lack of advertisements on the modesty panels and the original lining style with the three waist panels individually lined. The Market Inn can be seen on the left hand background. The sign on the roof reads "Eadie's Fine Burton Ales" the large red X at each end of the sign was the trade mark of James Eadie and Co. The brewery and its tied estate of over 300 public houses became part of the Bass empire in 1934, Midland Railway Study Centre Kidderminster Railway Museum 62275

Reference has been made in the text to the popularity of chartering the B&ALR cars for church outings and Sunday school treats to local beauty spots, Here we see the children and teachers of the Swadlincote Free Church en route to their trip on 9th June 1908. The character on the left wearing the straw boater with his hands in his pockets is Billy Barton, the Superintendent of the Line, Midland Railway Study Centre/Kidderminster Railway Museum 62271 ▼

Another Swadlincote scene, this time from a hand tinted postcard looking eastwards along High Street as an Ashby bound tram pulls away from The Delph. The set of points in the right hand foreground was the end of the short spur, which was technically Railway no.4. The end of Belmont Street can be seen on the far left.
MRSC 28574

hourly service was progressively reduced culminating in just running on Saturdays only. Even this was not profitable and services were finally withdrawn in November 1912. Following an application by the MR, the Board of Trade issued a closure notice on 23rd May 1913 confirming that the Railway no.3 was officially abandoned. The track was lifted the following year.

Having climbed 100 feet since leaving Swadincote the tram's traction motors had a brief respite through Woodhouse Street loop before the track began rising again through Gables Loop. Just beyond the far end of the loop on the right was Henry Tooth's famous Bretby Art Pottery Works. Their products, which are easily identifiable by the sunburst backstamp, are much sought after today and rarer examples can command high prices. Soon after passing the pottery, a bridge carried the tram tracks over the MR line to Woodville Goods. This was originally the passenger station but was downgraded when a new station on the Swadlincote Loop opened in 1884. Just beyond the bridge was the start of Woodville Toll Gate Loop. Here roads from Burton, Derby, Ashby, Moira and Swadlincote met, the tramway turning right towards Ashby along Woodville High Street.

The original toll house is believed to have been a primitive timber structure resulting in the area being known as Wooden Box. This had long been replaced by a more traditional brick

▼ The final part of the gradient profile of Railway No.1 between Woodville and Ashby. The summit of the line, 569 feet above sea level, was reached at Smisby Old Toll Gate.

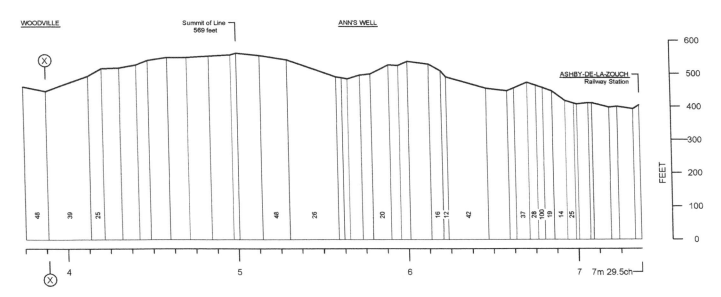

building by the time the tramway was built. In the interim period the settlement had officially adopted the more subtle name of Woodville. As soon as the corner was turned the double track became single again as it passed the New Inn. A little further along the road the line passed yet another pub, the Nelson Inn. In the 1830s the Nelson's publican, Thomas Brunt, in partnership with Samuel Bucknall, a local farmer and maltster, set up a brewery across the road from the Nelson. Known as the Hartshorne Brewery, Brunt, Bucknall & Co were acquired in 1913 by Burton brewers Thomas Salt & Co. Brewing continued on the site until 1927 when Salts became part of Bass and the brewery demolished. However, Brunt & Bucknall's Bottling Stores has survived and at the time of writing, (October 2016) both the Nelson Inn and the New Inn are still open.

Follow on from the Nelson, High Street was lined on both sides by several potteries including Reliance Pottery, Hartshorne Pottery, Excelsior Pottery and Escombe Pottery, the latter being opposite the next B&A loop at the junction of High Street and Station Street where tram passengers could alight for the short walk down Station Street to Woodville station. On returning to single track the B&A tracks passed the massive water tower that supplied Brunt & Bucknall's brewery before crossing the MR's Swadlincote Loop which at this point was some 50 feet below the tram lines as the railway negotiated the 307 yard long Woodville Tunnel.

As the line headed out of Woodville it passed the end of Blackfordby Lane from which emerged the Derbyshire – Leicestershire county boundary which then proceeded to run along the centre line of the track for the next 1600 yards (0.9 miles). Thus, passengers sitting on the north side of the car were in Derbyshire whilst those sitting opposite were in Leicestershire. Assuming the driver was standing centrally on the platform, he would have a foot in both camps! The exceptions to this were the two loops that punctuated the section, Woodville Reservoir Loop and the appropriately named Boundary Loop. Ashby bound passengers would all be in Derbyshire as they traversed the loops; the Burton bound passengers would be in Leicestershire. This unusual geographic phenomenon finally ended as the track passed the Smisby Old Toll Gate, where the boundary veered to the northern side of the roadway, so that the remainder of the journey to Ashby would be exclusively in Leicestershire. Coincidentally, the Old Toll House (which is still extant) marked the summit of the line, 569 feet above sea level. In those days altitudes were measured above the mean level of the sea at Liverpool; today the vertical datum is Newlyn in Cornwall. Since travelling along

Horminglow Street in Burton which was 150 feet above sea level, the B&A cars had climbed over 400 feet. In reality, much of the climbing had been done whilst travelling on the Burton Corporation tracks; the 410 foot contour line had been crossed just before the descent towards the borough boundary began.

Since leaving Woodville the B&A route was through mainly open country, punctuated at intervals by public houses. The first, the Greyhound. is still in business but the Red Lion which gave its name to the first loop after the summit is no more. Pubs were a useful geographic feature to identify loops when there was little else around and the next loop also derived its name from the adjacent hostelry, the Malt Shovel, although in some quarters it was also known as Annwell Loop. Here, the county boundary still lay along the north side of the road so although the loop was in Leicestershire the pub, only a few yards away, was in Derbyshire. Here too Ashby Road became Burton Road. In the winter months, the B&A at this point was susceptible to being blocked by snow drifts, and on more than one occasion B&A trams became stuck in the vicinity and the Malt Shovel provided a warm and comfortable refuge for marooned travellers. The pub is still going strong and after at least two name changes is now known as The Tap House.

Approximately midway between the Malt Shovel Loop and the following one which served the short lived Ashby Ivanhoe Golf Club, the county boundary finally finished following the road and headed off in a north easterly direction. The Ashby Ivanhoe Golf Club had been formed in 1904 and the adjacent loop was named Golf Links Loop (Ashby). The nine hole course was reputed to be quite difficult and closed around 1920 in favour of a new course elsewhere in the town. After that the loop became officially known as Ingles Hill Loop.

Now in the outskirts of Ashby, the next loop, Hill Street Loop was a little way before the junction of Burton Road and Hill Street primarily because the gradient was less steep at this point. After passing the end of Hill Street the line steepened to 1 in 14 as it headed downhill towards the level crossing with the MR Ashby and Breedon line, part of which had originally been the 4'-3" gauge, horse drawn Ticknall Tramway which had opened in stages during the early decades of the 19th century.

Passenger services between Ashby and Derby had begun on 1st January 1874 but the advent of the B&ALR meant that significant alterations were required to the operation of the Burton Road

Crossing. The new works, which included the installation of a new 16 lever frame, were inspected on behalf of the Board of Trade by Major John W. Pringle RE, who subsequently became the Chief Inspecting Officer of Railways in 1916. The inspection was carried out on 7th June 1906 as part of his inspection of the whole B&A and his report (part of which is quoted below) makes interesting reading. For a start it was very clear that the long established standard gauge line would take precedence over the upstart tramway!

"Arrangements have been made in the Burton Road Signal-box to control the working of the cars on the Light Railway as follows:-

Small semaphore signals have been installed in the roadway each side of the level crossing which will indicate by their danger or safety position the closed or open position of the level crossing gates. Trap points on the light railway about 40 feet each side of the crossing are worked from the signal-box and will derail any car passing the above mentioned signals at danger. In addition, when the gates are not in a position for light railway traffic, current is cut off a section of the overhead trolley conductor wires."

A view down Burton Road in Ashby-de-la-Zouch looking towards the level crossing and the town centre. The back of the crossing signalbox can be seen to the left of the poles. A tram is traversing the level crossing. There is no evidence of a "small semaphore signal installed in the roadway," described by Major Pringle in his inspection report, but there does appear to be a light signal on the pole nearest to the camera, (Pole 40A). Midland Railway Study Centre / Kidderminster Railway Museum 62270.

An evocative view of Car. No 11 setting out from Ashby for the 100 minute journey to Burton as it passes the Royal Hotel. The figures in the background mark where the tracks swung to the right from Station Road into Ashby Station forecourt. The scene is still easily recognisable today. Although the trams have long gone, the Royal is still very much in business and even the horse trough (on the right) survives as a flower bed. Photo Courtesy of the National Railway Museum DY9906

In another part of his report the Major expressed concern that if an Ashby bound tram descending the hill failed to stop at the signal for the level crossing and derailed on the trap points, that the traps would not deflect the tram sufficiently to prevent it from hitting the crossing gates. However, having made a note of it, he approved the arrangements.

Fortunately, Major Pringle's concerns were never put to the test.

The reference to small semaphore signals in the roadway is interesting as they also appear on the signalbox diagram so there can be no doubt that this was how the crossing was controlled originally. Exactly what form these signals took is not known, but if the signalbox diagram is a fair representation, they were mounted on conventional signal posts but with smaller arms than the standard MR stop signals. Both the signals were controlled by lever 16 and both sets of trap points were operated by lever 15. The level crossing was one of the compulsory stops specified by the Board of Trade.

How long these signals were used for and the reason for their replacement by electric signals is not known, but it could have been as early as 1908. There is no sign of a semaphore signal in the above photograph, which unfortunately is undated, but there is an electric signal affixed to the pole nearest to the camera.

After carefully negotiating the level crossing, cars heading for the Ashby terminus encountered the final loop of the journey. This was the New Inn Loop which took the line around the sharp right hand bend from Burton Road into Derby Street. It goes without saying that the pub on the corner was named the New Inn! Beyond the end of the loop, the single line zig-zagged from Derby Street across Market Street into Bath Street before curving round in front of the Loudon Memorial onto Station Street. One of the last designs of architect Sir Gilbert Scott (of the Midland Grand Hotel at St. Pancras fame) it bears a strong resemblance to an Eleanor Cross. Today its significance is recognised by a grade 2* listing.

The final major landmark on the B&A journey was the imposing Royal Hotel on Station Road. This splendid Regency structure with a large neo-classical porte cochère, is a reminder that in the early part of the 19th century Ashby had aspirations to become a major spa town. Less than 100 yards beyond the hotel the line turned right into the station forecourt and almost immediately split into two dead end roads which terminated outside the station building. In the spirit of the town's plans to rival the likes of Bath, Cheltenham and Harrogate, the Midland Railway provided an impressive single storey neo-classical building with side pavilions and the entrance flanked by Doric columns in a similar style to the Royal Hotel. Although closed to passengers in 1964 the historical importance of the station has been recognised by English Heritage with a Grade 2* listing.

The various speed limits imposed on B&A trams in Burton have already been quoted so for the sake of completeness, before we return to Swadlincote and look at the Gresley, the speed limits from Boundary Junction to Ashby were as follows. As in Burton, 4 mph was the maximum permitted through all facing points and level crossings. The maximum speed, 12 mph was allowed on Bretby Road from the borough boundary to the Stanhope Arms; along High Street and Union Street in Newhall continuing along Newhall Road in Swadlincote; on High Street in Woodville and on to Annwell (or Ann's Well) and between Inglis Hill (near Ashby Golf Links) and Hill Street in Ashby. Elsewhere the maximum permitted speed was 8 mph. Storer & White in their book, Sixpenny Switchback suggest that the speed limit was 15 mph but your author has been unable to find any confirmation of this. However, whether it was 12 mph or 15 mph, their assertion that it was often exceeded is doubtless true.

Cars 13 (left) and 1 (right) standing on the short double track section outside Ashby Station on 7th June 1906, waiting the arrival of the Board of Trade Inspector, Major John Pringle RE. It can only be assumed that Manager James Toulmin was not a superstitious person judging by his choice of car no.13 not only to carry out many of the trial runs but also be used for the official inspection!

Accompanying Major Pringle on his inspection included several high ranking MR officials; Mr C.H. Gadsby MIEE, the designer and Consulting Engineer of the B&ALR, James Toulmin, Manager of the B&A, representatives of British Westinghouse and Dick, Kerr & Co., and councillors and officials of Ashby and Swadlincote Councils. Although the last cars ran in 1927, the tramlines can be seen in the station forecourt 90 years later! This was because the cost of lifting them exceeded their scrap value! Midland Railway Study Centre / Kidderminster Railway Museum 62281.

SWADLINCOTE TO GRESLEY

The Gresley line, officially Railway No.2, branched off the main line outside the Market Inn on Midland Road, Swadlincote. From the junction, the two tracks veered off to the right, skirting the southern side of the Market Place (aka The Delph) into West Street. In bound trams had a mandatory stop in West Street before continuing through the Market Place and round the corner to join the Burton line outside the Market Inn. Trams approaching from Ashby had a similar mandatory stop. It seems that the Board of Trade were concerned for the safety of pedestrians in the Market Place.

Part way down West Street, the double tracks passed Sharpe's Pottery before swinging round a long left hand bend to begin the 1 in 14 climb up Alexandra Road.

Sharpe's Pottery, founded in the 1820, turned its attention in the 1850s to producing sanitary wares and in 1855 patented the successful rim flush toilet, a principle still in use today. Potteries like Sharpe's spawned a local service industry in the form of crate manufacturers. Toilets, sinks and hand basins were usually packed in crates, surrounded by straw to

▼ The gradient profile of the Gresley Branch which clearly shows the 1 in 14 climb up Alexandra Road in Swadlincote and the 1 in 11 and 1 in 14 descent of Cappy Hill on the approach to the Gresley terminus.

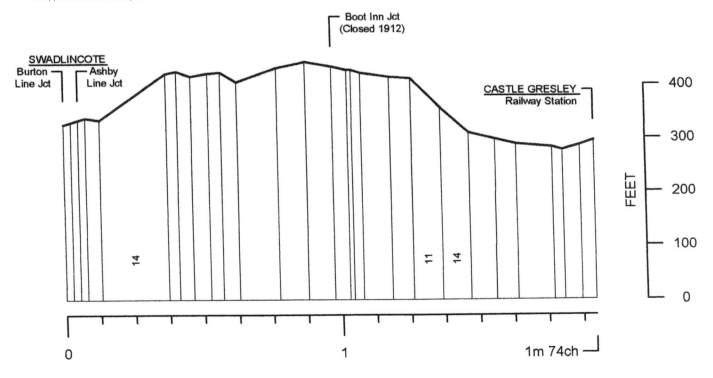

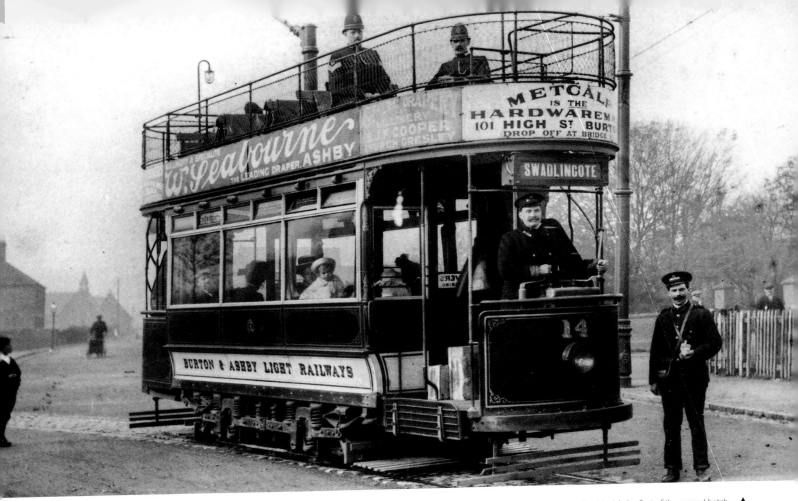

minimise damage whilst in transit. Although Sharpes closed in 1967, part of the site has since been restored and become an interesting museum celebrating the local pottery industry.

The Alexandra Road gradient eased as it neared Hastings Street and the two tracks merged into one which, except for five loops, continued the rest of the way to Gresley. After crossing Hastings Street the single line continued a short distance along Church Avenue before veering left onto Wilmot Road. Towards the end of Wilmot Road the first loop, Common Loop turned through almost ninety degrees before the single line continued by crossing York Road at a very oblique angle and along the western side of Gresley Common on Market Street. Following WW1 this area of the Common was developed by local businessman, Herbert Lea in memory of his son Lieutenant Maurice Lea, who was killed in action in France on 18th August 1916. The Maurice Lea Memorial Park, which opened in 1929 is still a popular and well patronised amenity today.

Car No. 14, the first of the second batch of trams poses near Gresley Common en route to Swadlincote. It is believed that the motorman at the controls is Charles Wells, with conductor Leonard James standing alongside. Note the sergeant and a constable from the Derbyshire Constabulary "on patrol" on the upper deck. After the system closed in 1927, several cars were sold to Tynemouth whilst the remainder were sold locally for domestic and social use as garden sheds etc. No. 14 was one of three sold to a gentleman living in Church Gresley from where over 40 years later it was recovered, fully restored and shipped across the Atlantic to Detroit. One of the first passengers when the car began running in Detroit was the US Presidential Candidate, Ronald Reagan. Happily, No.14 was repatriated to a location in Staffordshire in 2014. Photo: Steve Huson Collection

The next loop, the Boot Inn Loop was where the short lived connection (Railway No.3) from Woodhouse Street Junction on the Ashby Line trailed in to the Gresley Line. Named after the adjacent hostelry, this more or less marked the halfway point in the journey from Swadlincote to Gresley.

The single line then continued along Church Street for a quarter of a mile before encountering the third loop on the Gresley line. Yet again named after the adjacent public house, the Rising Sun, which unlike the Boot Inn at the previous loop, is still open for business today. Immediately after passing the historic parish church of St. George and St. Mary, Gresley bound cars were obliged to come to a stand before negotiating the S bend across St. George's Square into Castle Street. On the south side of the square was the entrance to Church Gresley Colliery which in 1906 employed 700 men. By 1920 the number had increased to over 1,000 and transporting miners to and from the colliery was an important function for the B&A, who ran special early tram services at reduced workman's fares.

Castle Street marked the start of the steep descent at 1 in 11 easing to 1 in 14 and less as the line neared the terminus. This was (and still is) known by the locals as Cappy Hill. Mid way down the hill was the penultimate loop, Mansfield's, which took its name from the nearby sanitary pipe and brick works of H. R. Mansfield. The rails in the final loop, Gresley Station Loop, just prior to the terminus, were 120 feet lower than those in St George's Square. The final few yards to the station were single track.

In case anyone is wondering, the Gresley family, perhaps the most well known member of which is Sir Nigel Gresley, the CME of the LNER, had long been associated with the village. As far back as the 12th century an Augustinian Priory was founded here by William De Gresley and the family remained influential from there on. Sir Nigel Gresley's early years were spent in the nearby village of Netherseal where his father was was the parish priest. He is buried in Netherseal churchyard.

A superb study of Car No.20 at the Gresley Terminus. The motorman is Richard Shipman who joined the B&ALR as a conductor in 1906 and was soon promoted to driver, a position that he held until the end of the line in 1927. Some memorabilia of his career is held by the Midland Railway Study Centre. These include the letter inviting him to an interview with James Toulmin, his uniform, his whistle and driver's handbook. The conductor's name is not known and why the youth with the trombone is included in the photograph is a complete mystery! Midland Railway Study Centre 61993

TECHNICAL SPECIFICATION
OF the B&ALR CARS

Manufacturer	The Brush Electrical Engineering Co Ltd. Loughborough.
Number of Cars	20, ordered in two batches; 1 to 13 and 14 to 20 (1)
Gauge	3' - 6"
Seating Capacity	22 inside, 35 outside, 57 total

The longitudinal inside seating was constructed from pierced birch.
The main upper deck seats were reversible, with additional fixed seating around the stairwells at each end.

Line voltage	550 volts, DC
Truck type	Brush AA
Wheel diameter	32"
Wheelbase	6' - 0"
Overall length	28' - 0"
Height	15' - 5" (2)
Width	6' - 3½"
Motors (2)	Westinghouse Type 80. 25HP
Controllers	Westinghouse Type 20
Livery	Crimson lake with gold lining with off-white tumblehome and modesty

panels.

Warning devices	12" diameter gongs
Lifeguards	Hudson Bowring (3)

The above information has been obtained from Brush General Arrangement Drawing No.11797N This drawing was traced by the Midland Railway Carriage & Wagon Department in December 1919 and given the number 50S S, a copy of which is in the Midland Railway Study Centre – catalogue reference 88-D0611.

Notes
(1) Both batches of trams were almost identical, the main difference being the provision of lockers beneath the stairs in the second order.
(2) Height to the top of handrails around the upper deck
(3) The Hudson Bowring Lifeguard was patent device fitted

to both ends of each car and consisted of two interlinked components. The first part was a hinged fender made from horizontal timber slats which hung vertically just inboard of the front of the tram. The bottom of the lowest slat was approximately 4 inches above rail level. Thus anything larger than 4 inches in height directly in front of the tram would operate the fender. The second part of the lifeguard was a pair of "L" shaped brackets linked by timber slats a little way behind the fender. The horizontal component of the "L" was considerably longer (about 24 inches) than the vertical leg (which was approx 8 inches high). Any obstruction on or between the rails was detected by the fender which immediately caused the "L" shaped brackets to tilt forward and scoop up the obstruction and prevent it from being run over by the tram wheels.

Although it perhaps sounds a little crude, the device proved to be very effective as borne out by the some interesting statistics published by Nottingham City Tramway in 1906. According to the Nottingham Evening Post, during the previous year, the trams had travelled over 2.6 million miles. During that period:

"40 persons had been knocked down or fallen in front of the cars. All were picked up by the lifeguard or pushed clear of the car and escaped with minor cuts and   bruises. 24 cyclists had collided with the cars, one rider and eight machines being picked up by the life guards without sustaining serious injury. Two dogs and two sheep were also picked up by the guards unhurt."

SUCCESS OR FAILURE ?

The Burton & Ashby Light Railways came into being in the zenith of the tramway age which spanned the period between the start of the Edwardian age and the Great War. By the time that Edward VII succeeded his mother to the Throne in 1901, most towns of any note operated at least horse drawn tramways, some, such as Bradford already had electric trams which had started in 1892. Nearer to home, both Leicester and Derby who both operated municipal horse tramways, electrified their lines in 1904. The first electric trams ran in Leicester on 18th May 1904; Derby's first electric trams began a couple of months later on the 27th July. In terms of modernity they were 'pipped to the post' by Burton Corporation whose trams were electrically powered from day one, which was August Bank Holiday Monday (the 3rd) in 1903.

It will be recalled that it was the fear of an eastward extension to the Burton system to serve Swadlincote and the surrounding area that had provided the impetus for the Midland Railway to build and operate the B&ALR. The fact that the MR had had to purchase seven additional cars before opening the Gresley Line indicates that traffic on the Burton to Ashby line exceeded the company's expectations by a considerable amount.

A look at the figures for passenger numbers, receipts and expenditure until the start of the War reveals that whilst there were ups and downs, the overall result was a positive contribution to the MR coffers. Bringing the railways under the control of the government in the guise of the Railway Executive Committee was essentially to co-ordinate and prioritise troop and munitions movements on the main line railway companies. Whilst this had a profound effect on the MR, the repercussions on the B&ALR were, by comparison, minimal.

Certainly, each year up to 1915, the B&A made a positive contribution to the Midland's coffers. The following year, although passenger numbers were not significantly down, operating costs were higher, resulting in a dramatic reduction in profits. In spite of a 50% increase in fares brought in on 1st July 1917, which did not impact on the number of passengers carried, operating costs were disproportionately higher resulting in the B&A's first annual loss.

1918 not only saw the end of the Great War, but also a reversal in the Burton and Ashby's fortunes; an increase in the number of passengers whilst a tight rein on expenditure brought the system back into profit. After the euphoria that followed the Armistice, postwar Britain experienced a period of high inflation. In spite of an 18% increase in passengers during 1919, the tramway's best yet, operating costs rose by 50% which resulted in a considerable loss. The following year saw yet another increase in the number of passengers carried taking the figure to over 3 million for the first, and sadly the last time. Although at the end of 1920 the B&A was still in the red, the loss was considerably less than the previous year, helped to a degree by a fare increase to 75% of the pre war levels on 1st November.

This fare increase was reflected in a downturn in passenger numbers in 1921, but with costs very firmly under control, James Toulmin was able to declare the line's best ever profit of over £4.5k. The following three years were all profitable, but the writing was on already on the wall.

The demands of WW1 had seen many advances in the reliability of internal combustion engines and following the Armistice large numbers of war surplus motor vehicles were sold off at bargain prices. Many were used as lorries, but a number were converted into charabancs and buses. Inevitably, some of these began to operate in competition with railways and tramways; the B&A being no exception. It proved to be a one sided contest. With lower overheads, buses could easily undercut train and tram fares and with greater flexibility with regard to routes, buses provided a cheaper and more attractive travel option which the public were quick to appreciate. A reduction in some fares on 1st January 1923 (the day that the MR and the B&ALR came part of the LMS) reversed the trend a little, but 1925 saw a reduction of well over half a million passengers and an eye watering loss of £11,000.

In an attempt to cut costs, James Toulmin drastically reduced services, and even considered one man operation, but for safety reasons alone, this was unworkable. The B&A's fate was sealed by the loss of over a million passengers during 1926; the General Strike of that year adding to the woes. Clearly, such loses were unsustainable and the LMS applied to the Ministry of Transport for an Abandonment Order for the Burton & Ashby Light Railways. A public enquiry into the abandonment was held in Burton Town Hall on 5th October 1926. The outcome was a forgone conclusion and the last tram ran on 19th February 1927.

To a degree, it was history repeating itself. Almost a century earlier railways had displaced canals and now buses were displacing trams. In the early days the Burton & Ashby provided a cheap and efficient transport service that its owners could not supply on their standard gauge lines. And for most of its life the B&A made a positive, if modest contribution to the Midland's finances. It can be argued that the wartime and post war losses were outside the company's control, so except for the final two years the venture was a success.

With a notable few exceptions, the late 1920s, early 1930s saw the end of most tramways. Tram services were replaced by motor in Burton between 1927 and 1929, whilst in Derby trolley buses took over the tram routes in 1932 – 1934. Leicester bucked the trend by not replacing their trams until the late 1940s.

BURTON & ASHBY LIGHT RAILWAY ANNUAL STATISTICS

Year	Passengers	Receipts	Expenditure [1]	Profit
1906 [2]	977,517	£8,211	£5,734	£2,477
1907	1,845,167	£15,588	£12,672	£2,916
1908	1,745,899	£14,698	£12,457	£2,211
1909	1,599,566	£13,522	£12.395	£1,127
1910	1,637,852	£13,810	£12,029	£1,781
1911	1,619,374	£13,803	£12,443	£1,360
1912	1,641,355	£13,820	£12,663	£1,157
1913	1,904,121	£15,566	£13,039	£2,626
1914 *	1,894,530	£15,544	£13,226	£2,318
1915 *	1,946,701	£15,990	£13,635	£2,355
1916 *	1,884,600	£15,460	£15,059	£401
1917 *[3]	1,967,581	£18,108	£18,253	-£145
1918 *	2,256,899	£22,454	£20,386	£2,068
1919 *	2,664,956	£26,450	£31,993	-£5,543
1920 *[4]	3,010,285	£32,151	£33,018	-£867
1921 *	2,332,604	£34,853	£30,269	£4,584
1922	1,935,684	£28,304	£26,413	£1,891
1923 [5]	1,944,778	£26,586	£25,071	£1,515
1924	2,028,544	£27,049	£25,311	£1,738
1925	1,447,021	£16,883	£27,997	-£11,094
1926	330,686	£3,439	£11,241	-£7,802
1927 [6]	- No data available -			

Notes

(1) Includes an allowance for depreciation. Between 1907 to 1921 this amounted to just under £4,000 per annum. In 1922 the amount was increased to £7,000 per annum.
(2) System opened in stages between June and October 1906
(3) Fares increased by 50% on 1st July 1917
(4) Fares increased to 75% of pre-war level on 1st November 1920
(5) Some intermediate fares were reduced on 1st January 1923
(6) System closed on 18th February 1927
 * Under Government Control

BIBLIOGRAPHY

Allwood, John	The Great Exhibitions	Studio Vista, London	1970
Anderson, P.H	Forgotten Railways – The East Midlands	David & Charles	1973
Barnes, E.G.	The Rise of the Midland Railway 1844-74	George Allan and Unwin	1966
Biddle, Gordon	Britain's Historic Railway Buildings	Oxford University Press	2003
Billson, Peter	Derby and the Midland Railway	Breedon Books	1896
Bown, Mark	The B&ALR on Old Picture Postcards	Reflections of a Bygone Age	1991
Campbell, Christy	Band of Brigands	Harper Press	2007
Carter, Oliver	British Railway Hotels 1838-1983	Silver Link	1990
Clark, Ronald H.	Scenes from the Midland and Great Northern Railway	Moorland Publishing	1978
Davis, John R.	The Great Exhibition	Sutton Publishing Ltd.	1999
Ellis, C. Hamilton	The Midland Railway	Ian Allan	1955
Freeman, Michael	Railways and the Victorian Imagination	Yale University Press	1999
Frost, Barbara	Memories of the Midland [Manchester]	Stockport Printing Co	1992
(Guise, Barry & (Brook, Pam	The Midland Hotel. Morecambe's White Hope	Palatine Books	2007
Gilliver, Keith	Return to the Sixpenny Switchback (2016)	Ashby-de-la-Zouch Museum	2016
Huxley, Ron	Rise and Fall of the Severn Bridge Railway	Amberley	1984
Jewell, Rod	Memory Lane, Belper, Ambergate	Breedon Books	1998
Julian, Philippe,	The Triumph of Art Nouveau – Paris Exhibition 1900.	Phaidon Press	1974
Kay, Peter	Midland Railway Distance Diagrams (Reprints):	Vol. 2 Peter Kay	1997
		Vol. 4 Peter Kay	1997
Marriott, W.	Forty Years of a Norfolk Railway	M&GNJRS Publications	1999
Mountford, Colin E.	The Private Railways of County Durham	Industrial Railway Society	2004
Rapier, Richard	Remunerative Railways for New Countries	RareBooksClub.com	2012
		(Reprint from 1878)	
Radford, J.B.	Derby Works and Midland Locomotives	Ian Allan	1971
Redfern John	The Burton & Ashby Light Railways	Magic Attic Archives	2010
Sheeran, George	Railway Buildings of West Yorkshire 1812 – 1920	Ryburn	1994
Simmons, Jack	The Railways of Britain	Routledge and Kegan Paul	1961
Tuplin, W.A.	Midland Steam	David and Charles	1973
Vaughan, John	Rails to Newquay	Oakwood Press	2007
(White, Peter & (Storer, Joe	The Sixpenny Switchback [B&ALR]	J. M. Pearson	1983
Williams, F.S.	Midland Railway – Its Rise and Progress (5th Edition)	David & Charles	1968